INTRODUCT

This book is the first of a three part trilogy based on my experience as a bush pilot flying for Susi Air in Indonesia. For 4 years I've flown Cessna Grand Caravans in one of the most challenging environments for aviation in the world. This book features the good stories, the bad stories, and the down right unbelievable stories.

I must confess, I've spent a very long time deciding whether or not to publish this book. Here's the thing...I'm now a Boeing 737 Captain for a major European airline, and unsurprisingly, I value my career very much. So publishing a book about these bush flying adventures (and occasional mishaps), isn't necessarily going to impress my current employers...or future employers for that matter. You could perhaps describe publishing this book as "career suicide".

This somewhat undesirable situation of losing one's career, might just explain why I'm the first Susi Air pilot to publish a book like this. Yes, the sensible thing to do would be to keep my mouth shut. Just stay under the radar and avoid any adverse consequences to the career that I have worked so hard to get. But how could I keep the greatest adventure of my life to myself? I needed to write this book. This isn't just my story. This is the story of every pilot who was fucking nuts enough to come fly for Susi Air.

Needless to say, the real identities of both myself and my colleagues at Susi Air will remain anonymous in this book. I have no doubt that some Susi Air pilots, both past and present, will know exactly who I really am. However to any of those pilots reading this book, I do ask that you keep my real identity private, much in the same way that I have kept your real identities private in this book.

All of the stories in this book are real. Only the names have been changed.

PAPA KILO – DAN RICHWORTH © ALL RIGHTS RESERVED

CHAPTERS

PROLOGUE..4
CHAPTER 1 – The End and the Beginning...6
CHAPTER 2 – A Brief Guide to Indonesia..11
CHAPTER 3 – The Interview...18
CHAPTER 4 – A Brief Guide to Susi Air..32
CHAPTER 5 – McVisa and Fries...42
CHAPTER 6 – Ground School..48
CHAPTER 7 – Monkey Island..54
CHAPTER 8 – Meeting Susi..59
CHAPTER 9 – Epidemic...66
CHAPTER 10 – First Flight...69
CHAPTER 11 – Graduation...83
CHAPTER 12 – A Brief Guide to Sumatra..89
CHAPTER 13 – Arriving in Medan...92
CHAPTER 14 – Line Training..101
CHAPTER 15 – First Tour...111
CHAPTER 16 – Susi Air on Holiday..118
CHAPTER 17 – A Brief Guide to Java..126
CHAPTER 18 – The Singapore Air Show..128
CHAPTER 19 – Arriving in Jakarta..137
CHAPTER 20 – Microburst...145
CHAPTER 21 – Training Associate...150
CHAPTER 22 – A Brief Guide to Papua...156
CHAPTER 23 – Arriving in Biak...161
CHAPTER 24 – The Mulia Shooting..167
CHAPTER 25 – Manokwari...168
CHAPTER 26 – The Highlands..175
CHAPTER 27 – Wamena..185
CHAPTER 28 – Storm of the Century...190
CHAPTER 29 – A Brief Guide to Kalimantan......................................200
CHAPTER 30 – Arriving in Balikpapan..203
CHAPTER 31 – The Longest Flight of My Life....................................208
CHAPTER 32 – The Grey Area...213

PAPA KILO – DAN RICHWORTH © ALL RIGHTS RESERVED

CHAPTER 33 – A Brief Guide to Timor……..………………………………....219
CHAPTER 34 – Arriving in Kupang…………………………………………..222
CHAPTER 35 – Saturday Night……………..…………………………….…..225
CHAPTER 36 – Upgrade Assessment………………………………………...232
CHAPTER 37 – A Nicer Side to Ahmed………….………………...…..……..238

PROLOGUE

So here I am, sitting in the right seat of a Cessna Grand Caravan, as a First Officer. Myself and my Captain are flying 12 passengers to Jakarta, and we're getting ready for our descent. However we have a few problems.

There is, what could best be described, as a "super cell", in front of us. A thunderstorm of 50 miles in diameter, stretching up to 60,000 feet in height, has engulfed not only our destination airport, Halim, but also all of the other airports in the region of Jakarta! Bandung, our enroute alternate, is covered in a separate thunderstorm. The weather had already deteriorated at our point of departure, Cilicap, and neighbouring Nusawiru.

In fact, we honestly don't know of any airport in the whole of Java which isn't submerged underneath severe weather! We try to get weather updates from Air Traffic Control, however the frequency is saturated with calls from other desperate pilots. We hear the crew of a Lion Air Boeing 737 scream "Mayday Mayday!", whilst declaring a fuel emergency, following a go around.

Myself and my Captain discuss our options.

OPTION 1: FLY BACK TO CILICAP / NUSAWIRU

This seems like a tempting solution at first. However as far as we know, we may well have the same problem there in regards to the weather. The only difference being is that we would have 350 lbs less fuel in our tanks, and no instrument approach for guidance in the bad weather.

OPTION 2: LAND OFF FIELD

In very exceptional circumstances, landing in a random field away from an airport is also an option. We could conduct a "precautionary landing" over the various fields below us to inspect for threats such as rough ground and electricity pylons, before landing. However it is apparent that the only fields below us are small rice padis. There would be a serious chance of flipping the aircraft over during landing.

OPTION 3: FLY STRAIGHT THROUGH THE CENTRE OF THE STORM

The weather is horrendous in Halim, however at least we have an ILS (Instrument Landing System). This ILS will provide guidance for us towards the runway, which is important given that we won't be able to see a single fucking thing outside! The obvious downsides of flying straight through the centre of a super cell, includes severe turbulence leading to LOC (Loss Of Control), hail stones, lightning strikes, microbursts, torrential rain and low visibility.

I'll let you know what option we picked, further on in the story. However first, let me tell you about how I got into this situation in the first place. It all started a few years earlier, after I had completed my training to become a Commercial Pilot...

CHAPTER 1

THE END AND THE BEGINNING

It was July 2008, and life was great! After years of saving up and studying for my Commercial Pilots Licence and Instructor Rating, I had finally landed my first pilot job; a full time Flight Instructor position at a flying school in Florida. Given that I'm from England, where low paid Flight Instructors spend more time on the ground than in the air due to the not-so-great British weather, this was a pretty good gig.

I was now getting paid good money to train students for their Private Pilots Licence, whilst enjoying the sunshine and easy life of Florida. I was flying a lot too, usually maxing out at 100 flying hours a month (the maximum legal limit for a pilot). During the day myself and my students would be soaring above the Floridian coastline, practising various aerial manoeuvres and navigation exercises. In the evening we would all go out for dinner and beers. The social aspect was similar to that of going to uni. The only difference was that I was earning money, not paying money. I was more than happy to continue working at that flying school for a year or two whilst I waited for my first airline gig. More than happy.

Yep, life was great indeed. So you can perhaps understand my disappointment when later that year, Lehman Brothers and a whole bunch of other corporate banks which nobody had even heard of up until that date, went bankrupt. The following domino effect would lead to the largest global financial crisis of the 21st Century. This was of course a bit of a downer for the subprime mortgage customers which Lehman Brothers and the like were indirectly ripping off; many of whom would end up getting their homes repossessed. But it also created a few issues for anyone looking for a loan, including the 90% or so of student pilots who couldn't otherwise finance the £50,000 plus training fees.

Above Left: Myself crouching next to a PA28 at my flying school in Florida.

Above Right: The cockpit of a PA28, one of the single engine aircraft at my flying school.

Needless to say, given my particular profession, I was now slightly fucked. In December 08, myself and my colleagues had our pay cut, just before Christmas. In January 09, we had our hours cut. And in February? Well let's just say, that was the final nail in the coffin. I had zero students. I checked my colleagues rosters; similar story. Asides from the occasional "trial flight" (a one off flying lesson which is usually the customer's unwanted Christmas present), all of our rosters were empty. Myself and another instructor, Byron, talked about our futures over a beer one evening. Byron was a US citizen who'd just passed the pilot selection with the US Navy. Byron was going to spend his future landing F18s on aircraft carriers. Byron was going to be just fine. However I was a UK citizen with no A Levels, let alone a degree. Regardless of my flying experience, the RAF weren't going to touch someone like me with a bargepole. To make matters worse, airlines in both the USA and Europe were sinking faster than a fat guy on the Titanic. Airlines were laying off pilots, not recruiting them.

Reluctantly, I packed my bags and returned to England. I needed to move back in with my parents whilst I looked for a new job outside of aviation. At 24 years of age, this was definitely a massive set back. Back home the only job that I could find was for a part time barman. Given that I had previously worked as a doorman before my first gig as a pilot, earning twice the hourly wage of a barman, it was a double slap in the face. But since my days of "working the door", I hadn't been to the gym in nearly a year. I'd lost nearly 15 kg of muscle mass from becoming a vegetarian (it was a bad idea and a long story). Even if I wasn't as weak as a kitten on chemotherapy, my "SIA" licence to operate as a doorman had also expired and I simply didn't have the money to renew it. But the barman job was still a job. And besides, at least behind the bar I didn't need to worry so much about getting my head kicked in.

I would spend the next 2 soul destroying years of my life working random jobs outside of aviation. Eventually I found a weekend job as a Flight Instructor at my local airport. The pay for the weekend instructing wasn't great, however on weekdays I had a job selling fruit and vegetables door to door. OK, it wasn't exactly the most glamorous of jobs, however with my 2 wages combined I could still save a small amount of money each month. If I was going to get back into commercial aviation I would need to save around £3000 just so I could renew my Instrument Rating; a qualification which allows pilots to navigate by sole reference to their instruments. (In layman's terms, an Instrument Rating is a qualification to fly through clouds). Without a current Instrument Rating I wouldn't even be able to apply to an airline, let alone get a job.

But even in 2011, over 2 years since the beginning of the global recession, airline jobs were still hard to come by. Every week I would search various pilot forums and recruitment websites, hoping to find that major break. One day in October 2011, I found a potential opportunity on a well known pilot's forum. Susi Air, a small airline in Indonesia, were recruiting foreign pilots on their Cessna 208B "Grand Caravan" fleet. I sent my resume and cover letter to Susi Air's recruitment email. To my surprise, they emailed me back just a few days later, asking me to attend an interview at their training base in Java. And it appeared that they were in a hurry to recruit; the interview date was for early the following month. It was just as well I'd saved up some money; now I had just 2 weeks to renew my Instrument Rating and buy a return ticket to Jakarta!

Frankly, I wasn't quite sure what to expect from this job. Asides from the time and place, Susi Air hadn't given me much information about the interview, let alone their operation. I hadn't even heard of Susi Air until I saw the job advertised, and at the time I knew very little about Indonesia. At first my plan was to simply go to the interview, and if I passed, stay for a year or two whilst I waited for an opportunity to fly a larger aircraft back home in Europe. But as it would turn out, this mystery interview would be the beginning of a 4 year adventure of a lifetime. I was about to explore an archipelago of 17,000 islands, each one encompassing natural beauty, history and at times, civil unrest. I would meet people from many different cultures and witness mountains which peaked higher then we could fly, thunderstorms so large that they breached the stratosphere, political and religious uprisings, and the (very occasional) volcanic eruption.

Above: Casually flying past a volcano in Sumatra when it suddenly erupts without warning. Photo taken by an anonymous friend.

CHAPTER 2

A BRIEF GUIDE TO INDONESIA

Before I go any further with my story, now would probably be a good time to give you, the reader, a crash course on Indonesian history, culture, religion and geography. Without this basic information, the rest of the book is going to make about as much sense as an inflatable dartboard.

Indonesia is an archipelago of some 17,000 islands, with the largest islands comprising of Sumatra, Java, Kalimantan (also known as Borneo), Sulawesi, Timor and Papua. Indonesia is both technically and legally one united country, however in reality it is more like a federation of different countries, with each region encompassing it's own culture, history, religion and language.

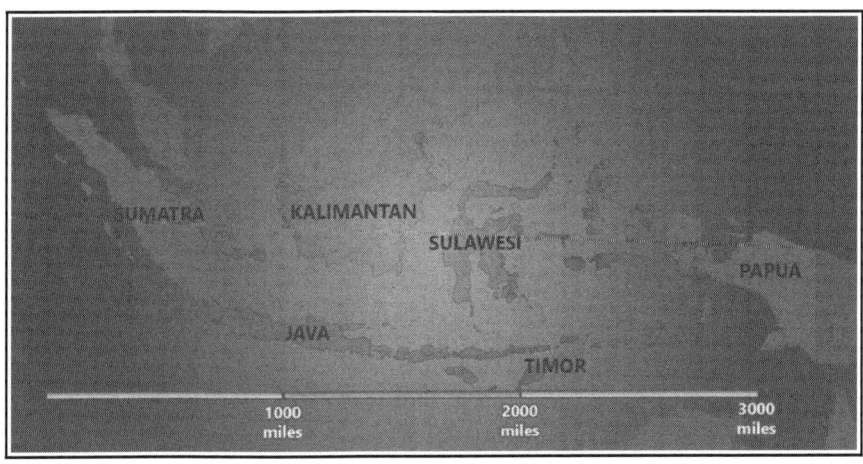

HISTORY

The Indonesian archipelago is thought to have been first inhabited by humans approximately 1.5 million years ago, however the first traces of civilisation dates back around 1300 years ago from the Srivijayan people of Sumatra, who were predominantly Buddhist and Hindu. The Srivijayan empire would later go on to kick start many other civilisations in Java and other Indonesian islands. Around 500 years later, in the 13th Century, Arab and Indian migrants would eventually dominate Northern Sumatra, bringing with them Islam. This Islamic influence would gradually spread towards the East to Java.

Europeans first traded, and later colonised, parts of Indonesia from the 16th Century onwards. Eventually all 17,000 islands of the archipelago would fall under Dutch rule. The Dutch would have a large influence on not only technology and civilisation in Indonesia, but also the language. There are around 600 or so native languages which either exist or did exist in Indonesia, with each one completely different to the other. This naturally created problems in regards to important things such as trade, as nobody could bloody understand each other. The Dutch standardised the Indonesian language with Bahasa Indonesia, the official language of Indonesia today. Bahasa Indonesia, or Bahasa for short, is a mixture of Malay, Javanese and Dutch. Although Bahasa tends to be the first language of Indonesians living in the more urbanised parts of Indonesia, for the more rural areas it is spoken as the second language, after their native language.

In 1942 the Japanese invaded the Indonesian archipelago, freeing Indonesians from Dutch rule, only to replace that rule with a much harsher dictatorship. However many Indonesian nationalists used this invasion as an opportunity to gain independence, such as the famous Indonesian Nationalist leader, Sukarno. Sukarno, gambling that the Japanese would eventually lose the war with the Allies, waited patiently for an opportunity. By the end of WW2, with neither the Dutch nor Japanese to worry about, Sukarno's nationalist movement would seize control and declare independence in Indonesia. The Netherlands attempted to recolonise Indonesia following their independence, using both military and diplomatic means, however to no avail. In 1949 the Dutch Government finally conceded and formally recognised Indonesia as a sovereign nation.

Above: Indonesia's first President, Sukarno, on the left, with his first Vice President, Mohammed Hatta, on the right.

Sukarno, Indonesia's first President, would implement a policy known as "Guided Democracy". As this oxymoron would suggest, Sukarno's politics weren't particularly democratic. Some people were a bit unhappy with this new dictatorship and wanted their own independence. Namely the people of West Papua. Sukarno and his allies weren't going to let this happen. The following decades would be paved in armed uprisings, land grabs and even genocides. Indonesia would gradually evolve into a partial democracy, however even to this day, the military still have a great deal of power over democratically elected officials, and corruption in all branches of the Government is rife.

It's worth noting that Indonesia's neighbour, Singapore, gained their independence from the British Empire at around the same time. Singapore, unlike Indonesia, is one tiny island with next to no natural resources. It would later emerge to become a superpower of the East. Singapore, (although like Indonesia also has a questionable human rights record), has a high GDP per capita. It is clean and virtually crime and corruption free. The key to Singapore's success was that unlike Indonesia, their independence was gained peacefully through a transition period. They kept a great deal of the legislative and political framework of their predecessors, together with all of the technology, commerce and infrastructure. Due to the way in which Indonesia gained their independence, for the most part, they needed to start again from scratch.

CULTURE AND RELIGION

It is important to note that although Indonesia is a predominately Muslim country, the majority of it's provinces are secular with a small minority of Buddhists, Hindus and Christians. With the exception of the Aceh province in Northern Sumatra, (which is under Shariah law and has public caning for such trivial offences as wearing immodest clothing), Indonesia at a federal level is not an Islamic theocracy. It is nothing like Saudi Arabia or Iran...at least not yet. Most Muslims in Indonesia are very moderate. Some Muslims simply attend their local mosque every once and a while in order to keep up appearances with their local community, shortly before nipping down to their local bar and getting drunk in the evening on the local moonshine, commonly known as "Arak".

But the lack of religious enthusiasm from some Indonesians doesn't take away the fact that there is a mosque on pretty much every street. And unlike most mosques we see in the Western world, they do indeed announce the "call to prayer", at full blast, from large megaphones located on each tower...5 times a day...starting at 4:30 in the morning. It wouldn't necessarily be so bad if all the mosques within ear shot were synchronised to start at the exact same time and with the exact same song. It also wouldn't necessarily be so bad if those singing through the microphone could actually hold a tune. However sadly neither is the case. Needless to say, it's not always easy to get a good night's sleep in most parts in Indonesia.

GEOGRAPHY

Indonesia has a population of just over 260 million people, with almost half of that population living in the island of Java. Java is by many standards severely overpopulated, with a population density of around 2500 people per square mile, which is similar to that of Bangladesh. Although Indonesia as a nation is fairly wealthy, and a member of the G20, the divide between rich and poor is massive. Poverty is rampant on most islands.

The ugliness of this poverty is in stark contrast to the beauty of Indonesia's natural landscape. Indonesia boasts hundreds of thousands of square miles of rainforest which covers much of the mountainous terrain. The coastline as well is remarkable, with white sandy beaches, colourful coral reefs, palm trees and turquoise blue water. Unfortunately pollution, deforestation and overfishing have destroyed a great deal of this nature. Large chunks of rainforest are routinely set on fire to make way for palm oil plantations and beaches in the more populated areas are covered in litter. The larger cities like Jakarta are immersed under thick layers of smog from all the gridlocked traffic, and if you go swimming at your local beach, don't be too surprised to see plastic bags floating in the water, with the very occasional used nappy. (It's hard to tell those things apart, so it's best just keep your distance).

However there are still plenty of regions of Indonesia which are for the most part, unspoilt by humans. World heritage sites such as the Komodo Islands (around 200 miles east of Bali) and Raja Ampat (a group of islands off the coast of Papua), being two such examples. Although the natural destruction of large parts of Indonesia has indeed been devastating, it is always reversible. It's just a question of *when* the damage will be reversed. I hope sooner rather than later...but I'm not going to hold my breath.

Above: Most of the coral reefs in Komodo Islands are still free from pollution and damage. This is a screenshot from a video I made in 2014.

Above: Manta Rays often migrate around the Komodo Islands. I needed to hold my breath for a long time to take this photo!

Indonesia is also sitting on top of a gold mine...quite literally. The Grasberg mine in Papua is by far the largest gold mine in the World, and also the second largest copper mine in the World. Indonesia has a great deal of wealth from precious metals, coal and oil, however this natural wealth doesn't tend to be spent on important Government services such as education and healthcare, both of which are poorly funded. If Indonesia could combine their natural wealth with a "Singaporean style" Government, it truly would be a world superpower with an outstanding quality of life for it's citizens.

The Indonesian archipelago and surrounding islands are located on what's known as the "Ring of Fire". In other words, there are volcanoes everywhere. Although many of these volcanoes are for the most part, dormant, there are still quite a few active volcanoes; 127 to be precise, with some of those volcanoes erupting on a regular basis. Between 2010 and 2018 alone, 798 people have been killed by 3 separate volcanic eruptions in Indonesia.

Every once and a while there will be a mega eruption somewhere in Indonesia. In the 1800s, 2 such mega eruptions from Mounts Krakatoa and Tambora killed over 107,000 people globally. Approximately 75,000 years ago, Mount Toba in Sumatra erupted so violently that the volcanic ash cloud plunged the entire planet into darkness for several years and wiped out an estimated 98% of humanity globally. Humans came very close to becoming extinct because of this one volcano. What's left over from Toba today is an island the size of Singapore, laying in the middle of one of the world's largest, and deepest, fresh water lakes. Today, it's pleasant scenery and serenity actually makes it a very nice place to visit for a holiday. It's dormant now, however it's not extinct. It will erupt again...it's simply that nobody knows when.

CHAPTER 3

THE INTERVIEW

I was now sitting on a 21 hour flight to Jakarta, with two brief stopovers in Abu Dhabi and Singapore. I spent the last 2 weeks preparing for my mystery interview with Susi Air; I renewed my Instrument Rating, studied my notes from flight training and booked my hotel in Jakarta. I also quit my job in order to get time off for the interview and spent what little savings I had on my IR renewal and trip to Indonesia. I was now officially broke. If I didn't get this job with Susi Air, I wouldn't have had anything left for me when I got back to England.

Failing this interview simply wasn't an option for me. Fortunately however, I had an ace up my sleeve. Shortly before my trip to Jakarta, I found another candidate who was also coming for an interview with Susi Air at the same time as me. His name was Vladik, a Hungarian pilot who also happened to be a genius. We found each other on an online pilots forum and we arranged to meet up in Jakarta shortly before the interview...and this brings me to the first lesson of this book.

LESSON 1: YOU CAN NEVER PREPARE TOO MUCH FOR A JOB INTERVIEW

Prior to my interview, I had studied a lot. Not just the basics of aviation, such as principles of flight and air law, but more specifically, studying the Cessna Grand Caravan. I downloaded the Caravan's AFM, or "Airplane Flight Manual", and carefully studied the specifications, limitations and diagrams of the 536 page document. I had prepared a lot for the interview...or at least so I had thought. That was until I met up with Vladik in Jakarta. Vladik, unsatisfied with just studying the Caravan's AFM, had also decided to study all of the aircraft's maintenance manuals. These are documents specifically designed for engineers, not pilots.

Vladik was a geek, and I mean that in the nicest possible way. He was a couple of years younger than me and was also a Flight Instructor who had worked in Florida. After meeting him in Jakarta it was soon apparent that he knew a lot more than I did about the Caravan. And for me, that was a serious wake up call. If the other candidates were up to the same standard as Vladik, I would be going home empty handed. I knew I had a good knowledge of aviation, but this guy really was a whole new level.

However fortunately for me, Vladik wasn't only incredibly smart and knowledgable, he was also a really nice guy. He gave me all of his study notes and taught me a few things about the Caravan which I didn't previously know. I thought this was a particularly kind gesture given that we were potentially competing for the same job. To this very day, I still have the highest regards for him. If anyone deserved to succeed in life through their intellect, work ethic and kindness to others, it was Vladik.

The following day Susi Air would fly myself, Vladik and the other interview candidates from Jakarta to Pangandaran, a coastal town in the South of Java. Pangandaran was the home of Susi Air's owner, Susi Pudjiastuti, and also the training base for all of their pilots and engineers. It was there that we would have the interview and assessments. We arrived at Halim Airport, a busy regional airport in the South of Jakarta, at 9am to ensure that we had plenty of time to check in prior to the 10:30am scheduled flight. Whilst waiting in the departure lounge we would meet two other interview candidates; a Spanish guy called Alejandro and a Canadian guy called Naseem.

The first thing that would strike me from this first meeting is that myself, Vladik and Alejandro were all smartly dressed, wearing pilot shirts and black trousers. Naseem on the other hand was wearing shorts and t-shirt. This seemed a tad bizarre, given that we were flying to Pangandaran for a job interview. Yes, it was hot as hell. And yes, perhaps wearing a suit and tie would have been a bit inappropriate for that particular latitude of the

World. But shorts and t-shirt? Really? However what Naseem lacked in dress sense (and also common sense), he made up for in good humour. The guy couldn't stop smiling...or talking. He was the kind of guy who you'd just love to drink a beer with. Just the one beer though, as after that he would probably get a bit annoying.

Above: Halim Airport, situated in South Jakarta.

At around 10.15am our small, single engine Caravan landed in Halim and taxied to the terminal. The fact that the wingspan was just a third that of the other aircraft parked up on the apron, didn't take away the fact that our little Caravan had a whole parking stand to itself, a parking stand big enough for a Boeing 737. We were summoned to the gate, along with 8 other fare paying passengers, where we preceded to board the 14 seater aircraft. Myself and the other interviewees naturally rushed ahead of the other passengers so that we could sit up front and view the cockpit. We weren't disappointed with our seats. The Captain and First Officer turned around and introduced themselves. They were only too eager to show us what they were doing.

After the First Officer completed her final walk around of the aircraft, the Captain started the engine. Although the Caravan has a propeller, that propeller is powered by a jet engine as opposed to a piston engine. It is known as a turboprop aircraft. And to low houred pilots like us, there was nothing sweeter than the sound of a jet engine spooling up. After the Captain completed the engine start, he gave the hand signal for the ground crew to disconnect the ground power. About 1 minute later we began our taxi to the holding point of the 3 km long runway. Naturally, being in a small Caravan, we didn't need to taxi all the way to the end of the runway. We instead taxied to the closest holding point, approximately half way down the runway.

It didn't take too long for Air Traffic Control, or ATC for short, to clear us for take off. After lining up, the First Officer, who was the pilot flying, slowly advanced the power lever halfway until the propeller speed stabilised to 1900 RPM, before advancing the power lever further to approximately 1800 foot-pounds of torque. We accelerated quickly down the runway, lifting off in just 15 seconds. Even though we started the take off roll halfway down the runway, we still had enough tarmac in front of us to land again after lift off. The Caravan is known as a STOL aircraft (Short Take Off and Landing), meaning that it is perfectly engineered to transport heavy payloads to and from short landing strips.

The weather was hazy, which was normal for Jakarta due to the smog and humidity. We could see many buildings below us, however we had virtually no forward visibility. Passing 5000 feet, the visibility began to improve. We could now see Jakarta in a way in which people simply couldn't see from the ground; a city surrounded by mountains and rainforest. We reached our cruising altitude of 11,500 feet, and that's when the fun began. Despite being morning, the cumulus clouds in front of us had already began to grow upwards due to the blistering equatorial heat. The weather radar on board showed large patches of magenta, indicating high levels of water vapour and turbulence inside the clouds. The clouds had already peaked above our cruise altitude and were still growing vertically.

We couldn't climb above the weather due to our aircraft being unpressurised, and we couldn't fly under the cloud due to the terrain. That of course left just one option; to navigate around the weather. Myself and the other interviewees watched as the pilots made various turns from left to right to avoid the worst of the weather. This avoision technique is known in the industry as "cloud surfing". The aim is to avoid flying into the cloud whilst deviating from track as little as possible in order to save fuel. It's a technique which is actually quite fun to practice, and takes a while to master. It also gives the passengers a more interesting ride than simply flying straight and level. Some passengers enjoyed this technique anyway. Not so much the nervous flyers.

About 45 minutes into the flight, we began our descent into "Nusawiru" Airport, a small tarmacked airstrip approximately 10 miles away from Pangandaran. The descent would be high speed, accelerating from around 130 knots in the cruise, to 165 knots in the descent. Ahead of us we could see a ridge of smaller mountains separating us from the South coast of Java. We passed approximately 1000 feet over the top and around one mile either side of these mountains, during our descent. Our pilots at the time were flying visually, however it was clear to see that there wouldn't have been much margin for error had we deviated off track whilst flying inside cloud. Flying in Indonesia, especially in smaller aircraft, is very unforgiving. There have been plenty of good pilots, and their passengers, who have paid the ultimate price for misjudging the height and position of the terrain, especially when flying in poor visibility.

Above: Final approach to runway 07 in Nusawiru. Nusawiru Airport is surrounded by rainforest and hills to the West, and the sea to the East.

After clearing the terrain, we turned to the left onto a long final approach for runway 07 in Nusawiru; a medium sized, 900 meter landing strip. The touchdown from the First Officer was relatively smooth, although the tarmac on the runway was far from it. Both the runway surface, and that of the apron, was bumpy and distorted from the extreme heat and precipitation, which was normal for Indonesia. We were marshalled onto a relatively small parking area. Susi Air only shared Nusawiru Airport with a small flying school, so there was plenty of space for our Caravan to park.

Shortly after the engine had shutdown, the ground crew opened up the rear passenger door and we disembarked. We headed to the terminal; a small, single story building, where we picked up our luggage. Two Susi Air minibuses were waiting for us outside. It would be a 45 minute drive from hell to get to the headquarters in Pangandaran. The narrow road was covered in potholes the size of craters. However that wouldn't stop our driver from weaving around these potholes, (and the oncoming traffic), at between 80-90 kph (about 50-60 mph). Needless to say, we were all very happy to arrive at our destination.

The Susi Air headquarters covered several hectares of land. On the West side of the compound were the office buildings, on the East side the pilots hotel, and on the North side Susi's personal mansion, surrounded by a large lake resembling something like a moat around a castle. We were greeted at the Susi Air compound by Taufik, an Indonesian working for Susi Air's HR department. Taufik helped us check into the hotel and gave us our rosters for the rest of the day. We were to each share a bedroom with another interviewee (separate beds of course). In my case, I was sharing with Naseem.

Above: Photos of the Susi Air compound in Pangandaran.

Myself and Naseem had a similar roster; after lunch we would spend the rest of the day taking the online exams, whilst the following day we would have the simulator assessment and interview. The online exams started with the "Compass Test"; a gruelling 3 hour long exam, testing everything from maths, spacial awareness, personality and reaction times. The Compass Test wasn't necessarily that difficult, however due to the length of time involved it was wise to use the toilet before you started. After a 15 minute break, we then continued with the other two shorter exams. One technical exam for the Caravan and one exam on Air Law. Both exams were fairly straight forward, multiple choice exams. We weren't given the results for any of these exams straight away, however I was fairly confident that I had passed them all.

Later that evening, after dinner, Naseem asked me if I wanted to go out for a beer in town. I was reluctant at first. Naseem was quick to point out that neither one of us had any assessments rostered until after lunch the following day. He also pointed out that we hadn't yet had a chance to explore Pangandaran. He was kind of right. We'd been inside the Susi Air compound ever since we arrived, and yeah, we definitely needed to explore. I agreed to go out for a beer...just one beer.

There weren't any taxis or buses in Pangandaran; if you wanted to go somewhere, you either walked, took your own transport or waved down a "becuk". A becuk is an Indonesian version of a rickshaw, with the driver peddling a bike which pushes the passenger compartment in front. Becuks are designed to carry 2 passengers, however not in our case. You see, Naseem wasn't just larger than life, he was just large. At 6 foot in height and 220 lbs in weight (100 kgs), I certainly wasn't going to fit in with him. We took two separate becuks. I felt kind of bad for Naseem's driver. He looked like he was around 80 years old and about to collapse from a heart attack.

Above: Becuks and motorbikes are the primary method of transport in Pangandaran and many other small towns in Indonesia.

We went to a bar on the beach front called "Bamboo Bar". Bamboo Bar would be the first of many bars by that name in Pangandaran. Unfortunately the original Bamboo Bar which we were drinking in would be mysteriously destroyed in an "accidental" fire later that month, shortly before several competitors would open their own "Bamboo Bars" across the road. That's just how competition works sometimes in Indonesia.

Not knowing anything about Indonesian beer, we ordered two "Bintangs". Bintang, which is Bahasa for "star", was the most popular beer in Indonesia. It also tasted like fermented pipe cleaner. Disappointed with our first choice, myself and Naseem then ordered two "Ankers" from the bartender. Anker was the second most popular beer in Indonesia. Unlike Bintang, it was actually drinkable, at least in my opinion. That's not to say it was a particularly good beer, but it was the next best option to nothing. Naseem would spend the following hour teaching me the Canadian national anthem. Not wanting to get particularly pissed before our important assessments the following day, I decided to leave Bamboo Bar after about an hour. Naseem reluctantly followed me, shortly before downing a final shot of "Arak" for good luck, which was given to him on the house by the bartender. That would be the last time that I would see the original Bamboo Bar.

Myself and Naseem woke up the following morning with a mild hangover. I had only drunk two bottles of beer the night before, but there was something very toxic in that Indonesian beer. Heads spinning, we walked downstairs for breakfast. Waiting for me downstairs was Taufik. He informed me that the roster for the day had changed and that I was now due to be in the simulator in just one hour. Naseem however still had his original roster. Naseem had several hours to get rid of his hangover and prepare for his simulator assessment. He casually walked into the dining room and sat down for breakfast without a care in the World.

After a couple of slices of plain toast and 2 extra strong cups of coffee, I proceeded to the simulator room. I was to fly a simulator of a PA28, an aircraft that fortunately I was all to familiar with. The assessment was by sole reference to instruments, i.e. nothing to see outside the window. Nothing particularly tricky, just some holds, radial incepts and an ILS (Instrument Landing System) approach. My examiner seemed like a nice enough guy. He introduced himself and asked me some questions about myself and my previous flying experience, shortly before giving me a quick brief regarding the simulator assessment. There weren't going to be any emergencies or failures, he just wanted to see that I had a basic level of instrument flying competency and that I had good spacial and situational awareness.

Despite a slight headache from the night before, my assessment went fairly smoothly. The examiner changed the direction of the wind a few times to see if I would notice and make the necessary heading corrections, but otherwise the assessment was straight forward. Approaching the Minimum Altitude on the ILS (and of course not being able to see anything outside), I executed a go around. The examiner then paused the simulator and informed me that I had passed, before complementing me on my altitude and track keeping. I thanked him and left the simulator room with a confident smile on my face. That was one less assessment to worry about.

A few hour later, as I was studying for the final interview in our room, Naseem came in looking a tad pissed off. It turned out that he had completely balls up his simulator assessment. And when I say that he completely balls it up, I mean that despite having all of his navigation equipment fully functional, he managed to get lost. Not just deviate off track, but actually get completely lost. Don't ask me how, but it happened. Despite this, the examiner, with permission from the Training Manager of Susi Air, informed Naseem that he would be given one more chance at the simulator assessment. He would have just one more hour to prepare for his second, and final, simulator assessment.

Not wanting to see him upset, I offered to help him prepare for his simulator assessment. Vladik had helped me previously with my interview preparation. Reciprocating his kind actions with another interview candidate was the least I could do. I sat down with Naseem at a table in the dining room downstairs with a pen and a few sheets of paper. It was soon apparent that this guy didn't even know how to join a holding pattern (a very basic task for a pilot), let alone stay in that hold without deviating off track. I drew him some diagrams of hold entries. It all seemed new to him. Alejandro, the other interviewee, came to our table and also helped explain some of the basics to Naseem.

I had my final interview at the same time as Naseem's simulator assessment. Not wanting to distract myself from my own priorities, I left Naseem in the capable hands of Alejandro and walked to the Training Manager's office, where the final interview would be held. After a 10 minute wait outside, I was invited into the office by "Mr Cheung", the Training Manager, and Irvin, the HR Manager. There were two things that I would later learn from the other pilots in Susi Air regarding Mr Cheung. Firstly Cheung was actually his first name, not his last, and secondly, nobody else prefixed his name with "Mr". It appears that he just wanted the new guys to call him that for some bizarre reason, despite the rest of the company being on a first name basis (with the exception of Susi herself).

Cheung was a former Singaporean Air Force pilot, or at least so he would claim. He had a very good theoretical knowledge of aviation, however his practical knowledge, or lack there of, would cause many pilots in Susi Air to question his previous flying experience. Irvin was an Indonesian national who had been working for the owners of Susi Air, Susi Pudjiastuti and Christian Von Strombeck, since the very beginning in 2004. Irvin was, for the most part, Susi's right hand man, or a spy within the ranks, you could say. He wasn't necessarily the best man for the position of HR Manager, however he was trusted a great deal by Susi. Most Susi Air employees, quite rightly, distanced themselves from Irvin.

Irvin would initiate the interview with a few personal questions about my background, which lasted about 5 minutes, whilst Cheung looked through the results of my online and simulator assessments. Cheung informed me that I had performed well on all the assessments. He then initiated the "technical" part of the interview. He asked me a few random questions on aviation knowledge, including one question where I needed to correctly identify 4 different types of flap systems which he had drawn on the white board, and explain the advantages and disadvantages of each. He then showed me an "approach plate" of a nearby airport. An approach plate is an official document with all the necessary diagrams and information regarding a given instrument approach procedure. The only problem was that this particular approach plate didn't appear to be an official document. It was a (very) amateur home made approach procedure with a low resolution Susi Air logo copied and pasted in the top corner.

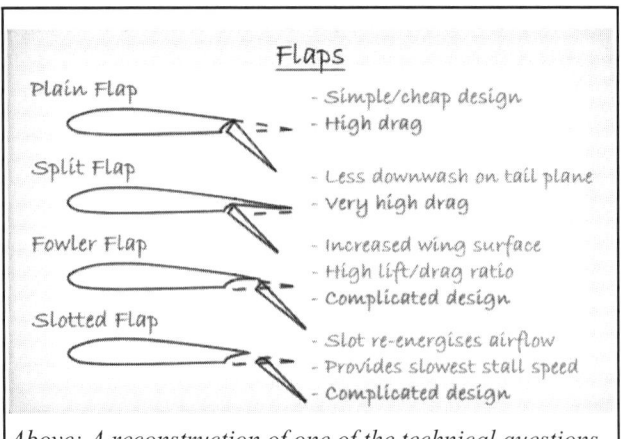

Above: A reconstruction of one of the technical questions in my interview. Various different flap systems (high lift devices which extend from the back of the wing).

Cheung asked me what was wrong with the approach plate. This appeared to be a trick question. Not wanting to state the obvious regarding this amateur attempt at passing off an official document, I closely inspected each part of the page. I didn't want to just blurt out that some idiot in the Training Department had designed their own home made approach without the necessary legal and safety process. Maybe he expected us to fly these home made approaches? Who knew.

I noted that there was no published Minimum Sector Altitude, or MSA, for this approach, and bought it to Cheung's attention. He smiled and replied "Yes...and?". I looked again at the approach plate. Was it a trick question? I bought to Cheung's attention that there was no validity date on the approach plate. He smiled again and replied "Yes...aaand?". This appeared to be a test of honesty more than anything else. I just came right out and said it. "Errr...this isn't a proper, safe or legal approach plate". Cheung grinned, he appeared to be delighted with my final answer.

Cheung asked me a few more questions relating to the Caravan, from basic limitations to the affect of the slipstream from the propeller on the tail fin.

Cheung then made me an offer which I simply couldn't refuse. Cheung told me that he would offer me a job right there and then...but on one condition. He wanted me to join the Training Department as an Instructor just 6 months after I would get my upgrade to Captain. This was amazing, I thought! I was expecting to wait at least a couple of weeks after the interview before I would even be offered a job. And his job offer also included an early promotion?! Sure, he was probably desperate for new instructors as very few of the other pilots seemed to want to work for the guy. But nonetheless, this was an excellent opportunity.

Needless to say, I agreed and shook his hand. I now had my first commercial flying job!

CHAPTER 4

A BRIEF GUIDE TO SUSI AIR

Susi Air was founded in 2004 by German pilot Christian Von Strombeck and his Indonesian wife, Susi Pudjiastuti. Susi was the owner of a fisheries business in Pangandaran, which specialised in lobsters. She originally took out a loan to buy two Cessna Grand Caravans for the purpose of transporting lobsters and other seafood from Pangandaran to Jakarta, where it would then be flown by larger aircraft to various destinations around Asia. This would mean that her stock could be sold for significantly more money than if it was sold locally.

Susi's husband, Christian, who was a foreign national, was unable own his own company in Indonesia. He would build the airline using Susi's name. Christian Von Strombeck was by all intensive purposes the founder of Susi Air. For the most part, Susi managed the lobsters whilst Christian managed the air transport. However asides from the cargo, Susi would also contribute to the air transportation in a very important way. By using her Indonesian nationality for the legal paperwork, and also by accessing financial backing through her friends in BRI, Indonesia's state owned bank, Susi would play a vital role in Susi Air's creation.

Shortly after the first two aircraft were purchased, the Boxing Day tsunami hit Banda Aceh and the surrounding regions in North Sumatra. Christian assisted the rescue efforts by using their two Caravans to transport aid to the affected areas. It was this relief effort, which was initially intended as a charitable gesture from Christian, which would lead to the rapid expansion of Susi Air. The Indonesian Government offered to pay Susi Pudjiastuti, who was technically the owner of Susi Air, money to operate regular flights to and from Banda Aceh to assist with the longer term aid efforts. With this new capital, the husband and wife team purchased another Caravan, specifically for the purpose of serving Aceh.

Christian and Susi would continue to buy more Caravans and expand to other regions of Indonesia. By the end of 2008, just 4 years after the company was founded, Susi Air would operate 10 Caravans. By the time I joined Susi Air in the end of 2011, Susi Air had approximately 50 aircraft, including 2 helicopters, 6 Pilatus Porters, 3 Piaggio Avantis and more Caravans than I can remember. Susi Air may have operated small aircraft, but it certainly wasn't a small company.

Above: A very rare photo of the Susi Air Caravan, Porter and Avanti flying in close formation. The difference in speed range between the Avanti and Porter made this formation flight especially challenging for the pilots.

CESSNA GRAND CARAVAN

- Maximum Take Off Weight: 9,062 lbs (with payload extender kit).

- Maximum Speed: 175 knots.
- Maximum Cruise Altitude: 25,000 feet (although rarely operates above 12,000 feet due to being unpressurised).
- Powerplant: PT6A turbine engine with 675 Shaft Horse Power.
- Unit cost: $2,600,000 USD.

Above: Cessna Grand Caravan taxiing to the apron after landing.

The Cessna Grand Caravan fleet is by far the largest in Susi Air, with over 30 aircraft (the exact number varies year to year). Although this aircraft is certified to fly with just one pilot, Susi Air always operates this aircraft with two pilots. As the Caravans in Susi Air are fitted with more than 8 passenger seats, they require a second pilot for legal reasons. The Caravan is operated in all main bases in the Susi Air network, and is primarily used to fly passengers on scheduled flights, with the occasional VIP charter and cargo flights. New pilots joining Susi Air can expect to fly as a First Officer (or FO) on this aircraft for anywhere between 1-2 years before they get their upgrade to Captain, depending on availability.

PILATUS PORTER

- Maximum Take Off Weight: 6173 lbs.
- Maximum Speed: 125 knots.
- Maximum Cruise Altitude: 25,000 feet (although rarely operates above 12,000 feet due to being unpressurised).
- Powerplant: PT6A turbine engine with 550 Shaft Horse Power.
- Unit cost: $1,900,000 USD.

Above: Pilatus Porter turning on to final approach in Malinau, Kalimantan.

The Pilatus Porter is used for survey flights and also transportation of cargo and passengers to very short mountain strips. Due to it's low stall speed, the Porter can service air strips which would otherwise be too short for a

Caravan. Unlike the Caravan, Porters have a slow cruise speed, limited range and very limited payload. For this reason, Porters are usually only used for transport when the air strip is less than 500 meters in length, as the Caravan would otherwise be more commercially viable. Unlike Caravans, Porters are flown by one single pilot. There are two ways to become a Porter pilot in Susi Air; either you need previous experience flying the Porter for another company, or you can start off on the Caravan for a year or two and pay for your own tail wheel endorsement. Most Susi Air Porter pilots have taken the latter route.

PIAGGIO AVANTI

- Maximum Take Off Weight: 12,100 lbs.
- Maximum Speed: 400 knots.
- Maximum Cruise Altitude: 41,000 feet.
- Powerplant: 2 x PT6A turbine engines with 850 Shaft Horse Power each.
- Unit cost: $7,400,000 USD.

Above: Piaggio Avanti on display at the Singapore Air Show.

The Piaggio Avanti is the fastest turboprop aircraft in the World, rivalling many small private jets in regards to speed and range. In Susi Air, the 3 Avantis are operated with two pilots and are used for VIP flights and medical evacuations. Although this very unique aircraft is a joy to fly, it is also an absolute pain in the arse to maintain. Due to it's streamlined design, there are no hatches to the avionics bay, hydraulics or engine. Routine maintenance requires large pieces of the fuselage skin to be painstakingly removed, screw by screw. Although there is certainly an appeal for a pilot to want to fly this beautiful aircraft, the roster isn't particularly inspiring. Due to the ad hoc nature of VIP charters and medical evacuations, Avanti pilots can expect to be on near permanent standby, and only fly 100-150 hours a year. It's more like a retirement job; Avanti pilots are generally those Susi Air pilots who have been with the company so long that they have grown tired of bush flying in the middle of no where and now just want to live a relatively normal life in Jakarta.

BASES

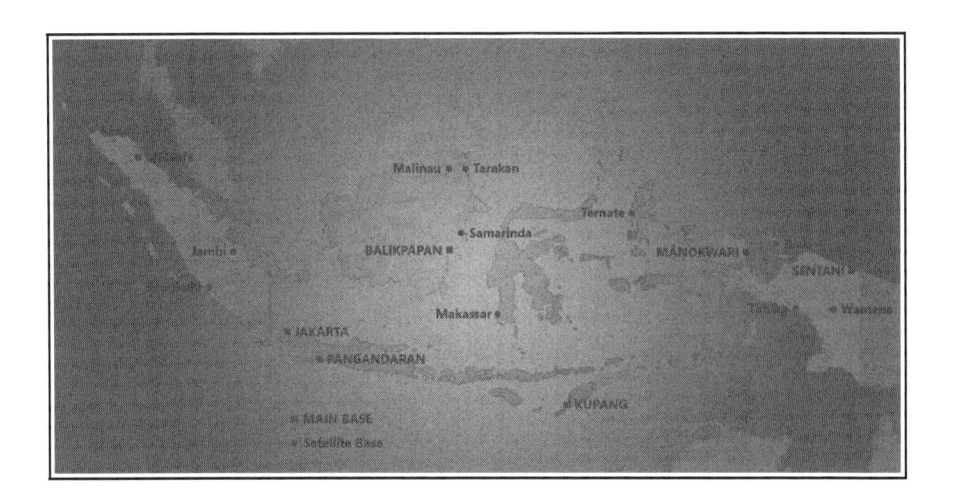

Susi Air has, at some time or another, operated from every major island in the Indonesian archipelago. Susi Air has 7 main bases in the network, with several more satellite and temporary bases. The main bases include:

- Medan – A large city in Northern Sumatra with several satellite bases, including Banda Aceh. Northern Sumatra has the second highest level of thunderstorm activity in the World, second only to Central Africa.

- Jakarta Halim – Home to both Caravans and the entire fleet of Avantis. Jakarta based Caravan pilots operate both scheduled and VIP flights, and are often sent to other regions of Indonesia to assist with temporary contracts.

- Pangandaran – The training base. Sometimes also used as a satellite base for Jakarta.

- Balikpapan – A city in South Kalimantan with several satellite bases. The satellite bases in Northern Kalimantan often service "low risk" mountain strips.

- Kupang – The capital city of West Timor. Thunderstorm activity in this region is fairly low compared to the rest of Indonesia, however very strong winds make this base equally as challenging. Some flights enter the airspace of East Timor, which is now an independent country with a very frictional relationship with Indonesia.

- Manokwari – Also known as the "Papua Lowlands". The terrain here is mostly low level, however the landing strips are still very short, which presents many challenges. This base is often a stepping stone for both Captains and First Officers, before they progress to the Highlands. Biak, an island nearby Manokwari, is used as a satellite base.

- Sentani – Also known as the "Papua Highlands". Widely regarded as the most challenging of the Susi Air bases. This base has several remote satellite bases, each servicing "high risk" mountain strips. These mountain strips are very short and usually steeply sloped up the side of the mountain. They often have "committal points" for take off and landing, which prevents the Captain from executing a Go Around or Rejected Take Off past a certain point. Due to the risk involved in this operation, Papua Captains usually require specialist training for each mountain strip that they fly to, with the exception of highly experienced "Grade 3" Mountain Captains, who are allowed to "self check" themselves into new strips.

LIFE OF A SUSI AIR PILOT

In many ways, Susi Air pilots really are living the dream! The typical roster is 6 weeks on, 2 weeks off, or in the case of Medan, Jakarta and Kupang, 3 weeks on, 1 week off. On top of these days off is an addition 28 days of annual leave. Accommodation, transport and meals are all provided by Susi Air, and the salary is tax free. As you can probably imagine, the combination of time off and disposable income means that Susi Air pilots enjoy some amazing holidays. I mean seriously amazing.

However with the good things come the bad. The quality of the company accommodation and food varies greatly. Sometimes the accommodation and food is actually quite good, however usually pilots will be sharing a dirty, rundown house with their colleagues in the middle of nowhere. You can also expect regular power cuts and running water isn't always guaranteed. If the food provided is inedible, that's tough luck. If you're based in a city like Jakarta or Medan, you can always go to the supermarket or eat out, but if you're in a remote base, you either eat what you're given or you starve. This, combined with the threat of contracting serious illnesses such as Dengue Fever and Malaria, can sometimes put off pilots from staying in Susi Air for much longer than a year or two.

SAFETY

At the time of publishing this book, Susi Air has had 3 fatal accidents. Two of these accidents involved Caravans in CFITs (Controlled Flight Into Terrain), both of which occurred shortly before I joined Susi Air. The last fatal accident involved a Pilatus Porter, and occurred a few months after I joined Susi Air.

After some careful consideration, I have decided not to go into these accidents in any further detail in this book. This is for 3 fundamental reasons:

1. I didn't know any of the pilots in these accidents, and even if I did, I am not an expert on air accident investigation.

2. Unlike large airliners, the aircraft involved in these accidents were not equipped with Flight Data Recorders or Cockpit Voice Recorders. With that in mind, the causes of these accidents involve some speculation.

3. Given that I intend to profit from this book, personally, I feel it would be inappropriate to go into further detail regarding these tragedies.

What I will say however, is that all of the pilots involved in those accidents were good aviators, and more importantly, good people. At the time of those accidents there were certainly flaws in the training for pilots at Susi Air, partly due to the rapid expansion of the operation. This made flying in what was already a very hazardous environment, even more risky. However these training flaws were of no fault of the pilots involved.

It is important to remember that flying low altitude aircraft around high terrain and thunderstorms, especially into small airstrips in the mountains, is inherently dangerous. However many of these risks can indeed be, at the very least, mitigated through well thought out SOPs (Standard Operating Procedures), as well as good training.

Above: This photo was taken from a Mountain Flying training course in Tarakan, Kalimantan.

CHAPTER 5

McVISA AND FRIES

Just over a month following my interview I received the joining instructions from Susi Air. My first stop would be Singapore, where I would need to apply for my Indonesian "business visa". I would need this visa to operate as a pilot in Indonesia. I read the instructions from Susi Air very carefully. I was to meet their agent, Mr Nahib, in a McDonald's in the centre of Singapore, where he would process my documents for the visa application in exchange for me paying him 200 Singapore Dollars in cash (approximately £100). A fast food restaurant was perhaps a tad unconventional as a meeting point for a visa application. Given the nature of what we were doing, I would have expected to meet Mr Nahib in his office or in the Indonesian Embassy. However it would later emerge that Mr Nahib, assuming that was his real name, had no office. He worked out of his briefcase. He had no fixed abode. It all seemed a bit dodgy.

Following a 13 hour direct flight from Heathrow the night before, I arrived at the McDonald's meeting point at 9:30am, 30 minutes before I was due to meet Mr Nahib. This was of course the perfect time to order a bacon and egg mcmuffin, or at least it would have been if Singapore wasn't a predominantly Muslim country. I needed to make do with a "facon" and egg mcmuffin instead. (First world problems, I know). After finishing my breakfast, I took a stroll around the indoor and outdoor seating areas to see if there was any sign of Mr Nahib. The McDonald's restaurant was fairly quiet at the time. I noticed four people sitting down at a table with various printed documents. We made eye contact with each other; it was apparent that they were also there waiting for Mr Nahib.

I went over to say hi. It turned out they were also pilots who were joining Susi Air. In fact, we were all going to be on the same training course; Amit from the USA, Maria from Portugal, Gavin from Scotland and Ron from New Zealand. A few minutes later I had an unexpected surprise; someone who I already knew, Mo, an English guy who did his flight training at the same flying school that I previously instructed at, also approached the table. He was also going to be on the same training course. The World of aviation can sometimes be very small.

We had been waiting at the table for about 15 minutes when we noticed a suspicious looking man wearing wide lens sunglasses and a sun hat sitting in the corner of the outdoor seating area. He had a brief case on the table and kept looking over his shoulder to see if anyone was watching him. "Yep, that must be Mr Nahib", joked Amit. We laughed and walked over to him. Sure enough, that was indeed Mr Nahib. Mr Nahib gave us the visa application forms to fill out. We completed these forms on the table adjacent to him. He then asked for our passports and the cash.

He informed us that he would need to take our passports with him, and that he would meet us back at the same McDonald's at 3pm in the afternoon. We weren't allowed to go with him to the Indonesian Embassy for some bizarre reason. Needless to say, I felt a bit uncomfortable giving a random stranger in McDonald's my cash and passport and just letting him walk away, especially in a foreign country 7000 miles away from home. I think we all felt a bit uncomfortable. This seemed wrong on so many levels. But we all needed a job. As wrong as it was, now really wasn't the time for us to be rocking the boat with Susi Air. We just did what we were told.

The six of us now had 4 hours to kill. Naturally, having just arrived in a new country with a completely different culture, history and geography to what we were all accustomed with in the Western World, we decided to go down the nearest pub. Sightseeing was for tourists. We ordered a round of small, yet over priced beers from the bar, and started to get to know each other. Ron, like myself, also had some previous experience as a Flight

Instructor, whilst the other's were fresh out of flight school. That said, none of us had flown passengers commercially before, yet alone flown an aircraft the size of a Caravan, so we were all pretty much in the same boat. Ron and Mo were definitely the most lively of our group, whilst Gavin and Maria were a bit more reserved, although still sociable.

A few hours later, after a late lunch, we strolled back to the McDonald's to meet Mr Nahib. Sure enough, he arrived at 3pm with our passports and visas. We already had our flights booked to Jakarta for the same night. I was on the same flight as Amit and Maria; Singapore Airlines, departing at 7.30pm. It was the perfect time for us. The others needed to wait until 9pm for their flight.

We were picked up from Jakarta "Sukarno-Hatta" Airport at 10pm by a minibus driver from Susi Air. We were to spend that night in Jakarta so that we could have our Indonesian aviation medical exams the following day. The driver took Amit, Maria and myself to a cheap hotel in "Blok M", the red light district of Jakarta. The other guys were going to be staying in company accommodation when they arrived. I had a quick shower and went straight to bed after checking in to the hotel. We were all pretty tired from the jet-lag.

We were picked up the following morning at 7am for the medical exam. Mo and Ron where hanging from the night before. It turned out they had spent most of the night exploring and drinking in Blok M. Fair play to them. I don't think I would have had the guts to do that the night before my medical exam, especially before I started a new job. After we arrived at the aviation medical centre, the driver gave us each an envelope with instructions and cash. We approached the reception desk where we were given application forms to fill out. We returned our completed applications to the reception desk and were each given a piece of paper with a list of different medical items to be checked and signed off.

I started off by going upstairs for the hearing test. There was a short wait, followed by a quick test, followed by a sign off from the nurse. The process seemed straight forward enough. Next was the eye test, same again, straight forward. Next on the list was the dental exam. Teeth seemed like a bizarre thing to be checking for an aviation medical. (It certainly wasn't checked for aviation medicals in the USA and Europe). I went over to the dentistry room; a large open room with 6 separate dentistry chairs. One of the dentists invited me to come over to her work station. She asked me to sit down and rinse my mouth out with a cup of water. And this brings me to the next lesson of this book.

LESSON 2: ALWAYS TAKE A BOTTLE OF WATER WITH YOU TO AN INDONESIAN AVIATION MEDICAL EXAM

The plastic cup that she offered me appeared to have never been washed, to the extent that mould was now beginning to grown around the rim. It was also evident that the saliva of the previous pilots was quite obviously floating on the top of the water. To make matters slightly worse, I'm actually quite OCD about cleanliness. Trying to contain my absolute disgust at this blatant lack of hygiene, I politely smiled at her and said "no thank you". However she was very insistent that I rinse my mouth with the cup of spit filled water. Again, I politely refused. She just wasn't going to take no for an answer and I needed her to sign me off for the dental exam.

Well, it may have been gross as fuck, but at least I was up to date on my Hepatitis A vaccination before I flew to Indonesia. I tightly closed my mouth and pretended to take a sip of the bacteria invested water. I could feel the warm, sticky, second hand saliva softly brush up against my top lip. I cringed. I put the cup down, thoroughly wiped my mouth and pretended to spit in the sink next to my chair. This appeared to be good enough for the dentist to proceed with the exam. I looked around the room at the other pilots. It was apparent that the smart ones had bought their own bottled water with them for the dental exam. I would always remember to do the same thing for future medical exams.

Following my dental exam I walked to the toilets to wash around my mouth...needless to say, there wasn't any soap. I continued with the rest of the items to be checked for my medical; ECG (heart monitoring), chest x-ray, blood test, urine test and the final doctors exam. In Indonesia, it's not unheard of for the blood and urine specimens to get swapped with other pilots. As mentioned in the second chapter of this book, Indonesian officials can sometimes be a tad corrupt. Some pilots of some airlines might slip the examiners some cash in return for not testing positive for various recreational drugs. For this reason aviation medical exams in Indonesia can be a bit like playing Russian Roulette. You may have never taken any illegal drugs in your life and still fail the drugs test, if you happen to be one of the unlucky ones who were mismatched with a pilot who was positive for drugs.

After all the medical items were signed off, we handed the forms back to reception. We were told to come back after lunch for the results and medical certificate. The six of us went next door to a food court for lunch. It was here that I would first try the national delicacy of Indonesia, "nasi goreng". Nasi goreng is basically rice which has been fried with egg, a bucket full of palm oil and sugar. It's one of the few Indonesian dishes which actually tastes good, but it's also about as healthy as a brain tumour.

After we finished our lunch we returned to the medical centre to wait for our medical certificates. After about one hour's wait, all six of us had been issued with our Indonesian medicals. The Susi Air driver drove us from the medical centre to Halim Airport, where we waited for our 4pm flight to Nusawiru. It was at the Halim airport where we bumped into the pilots from the previous "Initial" First Officer course at Susi Air, one of whom was Vladik. After being offered the same deal as myself by Cheung at the interview, Vladik asked to jump onto the next available Initial course, which happened to start just a few days after the interview. Vladik and five other pilots had just completed their final flight exam at Halim airport. Now they were each waiting to be sent to their first base.

We wished each other luck and headed through security to the boarding gate. Following the one hour flight to Nusawiru, and 45 minute drive to Pangandaran, we arrived at the Susi Air compound just as the sun had begun to set. We walked into the dining room for dinner, where we met Miranda, Francois and Ricardo, the three remaining pilots who were also going to be on our Initial training course. There would be 9 "Initials" in total, including myself.

It took a while for our bedrooms to be allocated to us. After dinner we sat down in the lobby of the Susi Air hotel with all of our suitcases. The preceding 3 days had involved a lot of travelling for us. We were tired, we were jet-lagged. We just wanted to sleep. The 9 of us were now the only ones left in the lobby and most of the lights had already been switched off. I rested my head on the table I was sitting at. I remember waking up about one hour later to see that the others were also sleeping. Eventually a receptionist came over to us to give us our room keys. I was to share a room with Gavin. Slightly disorientated, we made our way to our rooms. We needed as much rest as we could get. Our first day of training would start the very next morning.

CHAPTER 6

GROUND SCHOOL

I woke up bright and early on Monday, for our first day of ground school...to the sound of the loudspeakers from the mosque next door. I opened the curtains onto our balcony. It was still pitch black outside. It was 4:30am and this would be the first of 5 calls to prayer which would be announced on that day (and every other day of the week for that matter). It would have been 9:30pm back in the UK, and I had no chance of getting back to sleep. Apparently oblivious to the noise, Gavin lay motionless in his bed in what could have best be described as a vegetative state. He wasn't going to wake up anytime soon. I dressed into my pilots uniform and headed downstairs for an early breakfast.

The flight crew for the Jakarta flight were sitting in the downstairs lobby, waiting for the minibus to the airport. They were the same crew who had flown us from Jakarta the day before. I made myself a coffee in the dining room and joined them at their table in the lobby. It turned out that the Captain of the flight, a New Zealander called Matt, was also a Flight Instructor for the Susi Air training department. He gave me some basic info regarding the itinerary for the ground school, which was nice to know given that nobody had actually told us what to prepare for yet. Day 1 would be fairly straight forward; an introduction to the company, Indonesian language and customs, staying safe in Pangandaran etc. The more challenging subjects, like technical training and procedures, would start the day after. The ground school would take approximately 3 weeks in total, with a further 4 days of flight training at the end.

The minibus for the airport arrived outside of the lobby to collect Matt and his FO. I thanked him for the heads up and walked back into the dining room for breakfast. The self service breakfast buffet consisted of a choice between 2 boxes of various sugar coated cereal (both of which were crawling with ants), or a plate of stale bread which had been left over from the day before, with a choice of peanut putter or jam. I decided to pick the latter option. Also awakened early by the noise of the loudspeakers, Mo and Francois came downstairs for breakfast. They didn't seem too thrilled about the food either. Our first day of ground school would start at 8am. We still had 3 hours left to kill. About 30 minutes later Miranda and Maria joined us. Gradually the others rocked up to the dining room, one by one.

At around 7:45am we made our way across to the other side of the Susi Air compound to the office building. It was on the top floor of this office building that the classrooms were located. On each desk was a sheet of folded paper with our name and a stack of various different training manuals. We were greeted by Mitch, a Canadian pilot in his late 40s who was the Chief Ground Instructor at Susi Air. Unbeknown to us at the time, despite his high ranking teaching position, Mitch was actually still an FO in Susi Air. He had a background in engineering and knew the Caravan better than any Captain in the company. Mitch had been with Susi Air for over 3 years, and through no fault of his own, had been passed over for command time and time again, for "operational reasons". The irony was, he was the guy in charge of training the Captains! Basically Susi Air couldn't afford to lose him as the boss of the ground school. He simply did his job too well.

Mitch began the lesson with the usual introductions you'd expect from a training course or group interview. We all took it in turns to state our names, where we were from and our previous flying experience. At this point we already knew most of this info about each other, but I think it was mainly for Mitch's benefit and also to break the ice. He continued the lesson with some basic information about Susi Air; such as the history, the management team and the different bases. He then went on to explain the geography and demographics of Indonesia, and certain regions where we could potentially expect trouble, such as in Papua (where they want their independence from Indonesia), and the Aceh province in Sumatra (a semi autonomous province which falls under Shariah law). Or as Mitch put quite eloquently, "Aceh is the Saudi Arabia of Asia".

Mitch explained to us that Indonesia was somewhat of a ethno-nationalist-protectionist country. Outsiders like ourselves, commonly referred to as "bules" by Indonesians, were generally treated with respect. (The term bule basically implied anyone who was not of South East Asian origin). However as bules, we would also be looked upon with a certain amount of suspicion, as both ethnically and culturally, we would be seen as very different to them. Many Indonesians might have a "them and us" type attitude. Mitch advised us to be careful in regards to who we had relationships with, especially in the more remote parts of Indonesia.

Mitch ended his lesson with some words of advice about staying safe in Pangandaran. "Be careful swimming at the beach, as the rip tides will take you straight out to the ocean". "Don't drink Arak, it could make you go blind". "Be careful walking back to the Susi Air compound late at night, as there isn't any street lighting". Mitch's latter warning brings me to the next lesson in this book.

LESSON 3: NEVER GO OUT IN INDONESIA AT NIGHT TIME WITHOUT A TORCH

The previous year, Susi Air had managed to "lose" one of their new First Officers whilst he was taking his Initial course. He didn't turn up for ground school one morning, and after failing to locate him anywhere in the Susi Air compound, the instructors decided to set up a search party to look for him in various locations in Pangandaran. They later found him (fortunately still alive, but with a broken leg) in a massive 3 metre deep ditch about half a kilometre from the Susi Air compound. It turned out that he'd been out drinking the night before and decided to walk back to the Susi Air hotel by himself in the pitch black. Unfortunately for him, the side walk abruptly ended at the edge off this ditch. He was following a path which quite literally led him right off the fucking edge. No fences, no signs, no street lights. That's Indonesia for you.

Above: A massive chunk of the side walk on the main road to Pangandaran beach is missing. You probably wouldn't want to walk down this road in the dark.

Later that day we had our first Bahasa Indonesia lesson, taught by a native Indonesian speaking language teacher. Irvin came to our classroom shortly afterwards with our employment contracts. Up until that point we hadn't even seen a draft of this contract. Irvin didn't give us much time to read the terms either; he was quite insistent that we sign the contract immediately. Not wanting to rock the boat on our first day of ground school, we each signed our souls away to the devil himself. Finally, Mitch gave us a timetable of the lessons for the next 2 weeks. As previously mentioned by

Matt, the technical training would start the following day on Tuesday. We would then continue with this training until Saturday, when we would be given our first written exam. If our exams went ok, we would then have the Sunday off.

The following day our ground school instructor was a Captain named Bart, a 6 foot 5 Dutch guy with a very dry, dark sense of humour. He'd flown Caravan's for many years, including in Africa with another company. This guy knew exactly what he was talking about. Bart would be teaching us the Standard Operating Procedures, or SOPs, for the Caravan. The Standard Operating Procedures are basically the rules which a company gives to pilots flying their aircraft, based on the type of aircraft and the operation. In the case of the Susi Air Grand Caravan, the SOPs were a document of around 142 pages. It covered everything from the preflight preparation, starting the engine, taking off, landing etc. This lesson would take the better part of a day to cover, however Bart was very good at keeping the lesson interesting and entertaining.

Right from the start I had a lot of respect and admiration for Bart. I think most of us did. Not only was he very humble and light hearted when it came to teaching us, he also had zero tolerance for people in authority giving him any shit. Namely Mr Cheung. As the Training Manager, Cheung was effectively the boss of Bart and every other instructor in the Training Department. However that wouldn't stop Bart from taking Cheung down a few pegs in front of our entire class. Bart knew that Cheung knew nothing about the Caravan, or bush flying in general for that matter. Whereas the other instructors were perhaps a bit more submissive to authority, Bart would always have a difficult relationship with the management, especially with managers who he deemed to be incompetent.

For the rest of the week, Bart and Mitch would take it in turn to teach us about the various different systems of the Caravan. The electrical system, the fuel system, the engine, the avionics, the aircraft limitations and a whole lot more. Each day we would start at 8am, take a short break for lunch, finish at around 5pm and then continue studying after dinner. On Saturday we had our first exam on memory items and limitations. Memory items are basically items of a checklist which you need to be able to recall from memory in the event of an emergency. If you have an emergency like an engine failure after take off for example, you simply haven't got time to pull out a checklist. You just need to remember what to do. The limitations exam coved a wide range of topics from maximum and minimum airspeeds, engine limitations, weight limitations and a whole lot more. We needed to score a minimum of 100% on both exams, and quite rightly so. However we didn't disappoint our instructors. All 9 of us passed both exams, first time.

On Saturday night we went out to celebrate the results of our first exams. We had the following day off and we all needed a break from studying. All of the Initials, instructors and managers headed to the new Bamboo Bar situated on Pangandaran beach. Across the road were the charred remains of the old Bamboo Bar which had "mysteriously" burnt down a few weeks earlier. (I never did find out what happened to the owner of that bar). Over at the new Bamboo bar however, we had a pretty good turnout of people; probably about 20 or so Susi Air employees in total. It was a good chance for us to get to know the instructors and managers at Susi Air.

After a few beers, myself and the other Initials began to contemplate what we were going to do for our day off on Sunday. An American pilot called Tod, who was the Chief Flight Instructor for Susi Air, offered to take us to the nature reserve next to Pangandaran. This nature reserve was commonly referred to as "Monkey Island". Monkey Island was located on the peninsula branching off from the East of Pangandaran beach. As the name suggested, it was infested with monkeys. As we would find out the next day, some of those monkeys would be friendly, however the other ones would be little shits.

CHAPTER 7

MONKEY ISLAND

I woke up on Sunday morning hungover and dehydrated. During the night the air conditioning had broken down and the sun was shining through the very thin, almost transparent, curtains. Our bedroom was like a sauna, only with dozens of mosquitoes and other flying insects buzzing around. Gavin was still asleep. I downed a small bottle of water from my bedside table and went to take a much needed shower. Myself, the other Initials and Tod had arranged to meet in "Relax Cafe" at 11am. Relax was owned and run by a Swiss lady, and was one of the few places in Pangandaran where you could buy a half decent meal.

Myself and the other Initials had rented 3 scooters between all of us. Yep, there were 9 of us in total, not including Tod, who had his own bike. However in Indonesia it wasn't uncommon to see a family of 5 riding one single scooter. Having 3 bules ride on a scooter would have been just fine. Tod offered to take Mo on his bike. The rest of us needed to decide between ourselves if we wanted to either drive, hang precariously off the back of the scooter or get intimately sandwiched inbetween 2 other guys. We mutually decided that Maria and Miranda would get the middle seats. We rode our bikes to the end of Pangandaran beach and parked next to the exit of the nature reserve. We then took 2 small taxi boats from Pangandaran beach across to White beach, located to the East of Monkey Island.

White beach really was quite stunning. As the name suggested, the sand was bright white in colour. The sea was a translucent turquoise and giant palm trees towered over the beach. There were a few other tourists there, however for the most part we had the entire beach just to ourselves. It was exactly what you would expect to see in a tropical paradise. The boats dropped us off about 10 metres from shore. From there, we needed to paddle knee deep to get to land, whilst carefully avoiding getting our phones and backpacks wet. The taxi boats left us there on the beach and returned back to Pangandaran. From that point onwards, the only way out was through the forest.

Above: Flying past Monkey Island, a peninsula located on the coast of Pangandaran. We hired a boat from Pangandaran beach to White Beach, then travelled over land through the nature reserve, eventually returning back to Pangandaran.

We left our belongings on the beach and went for a swim in the warm, shallow water. We didn't go too far out...and it was just as well. From the sea we could see a troop of monkeys gather around our belongings on the beach. One cheeky monkey looked at me swimming in the water, then looked at my backpack, before looking back at me again. He appeared to be calculating as to whether I would be close enough to catch him if he stole my backpack. We swam back to shore and the monkeys began to back off our belongings. About 5 or 6 of them continued to watch us from a distance. They seemed to be very intelligent and curious.

Tod took some fruit out of his backpack and offered it to the Monkeys. They cautiously approached him and gently took the fruit from his hand. They seemed surprisingly polite and friendly! About 10 metres from us we could see a mother monkey carry her baby in one arm as she walked with her remaining three limbs across the sand. We all simultaneously made the sound "Aaaaw!", in perfect unison. It was actually really cute. I wish I had time to take a photo. We sat down on the beach for a further 15 minutes or so, enjoying the nature around us. It was then time for us to start our journey through the forest.

Tod took the lead and showed us the correct path to take. Monkey Island may have looked small from the air, however it was actually pretty damn big. Underneath the thick vegetation and multiple paths, it would be very easy to get lost if you didn't know where you were going. There seemed to be something very prehistoric about the tropical vegetation which we were walking though. I started humming the theme tune to Jurassic Park. 10 seconds later we were all humming the same tune whilst laughing. I was almost waiting for a flock of Velociraptors to jump out of the undergrowth and start disembowelling us.

About 20 minutes into our journey we came to a small clearing in the middle of the rainforest. I sat down on a fallen tree trunk and drank some water. It was then that I realised that we weren't alone. Up in the trees surrounding the clearing that we were resting in, a troop of maybe 20 or so monkeys had surrounded us. I looked at Tod. He appeared to be slightly concerned. "Yeah, we should probably head on now guys", he told us. We promptly followed Tod out of the clearing, only to be stopped by what could be best described as the monkey "chief", who jumped out of a nearby tree to block our escape. We were now completely surrounded.

I could perhaps best compare this situation to walking through a dodgy council estate and being surrounded by a group of wannabe gangsters. This was all about territory. We walked onto their turf without their permission, and now they wanted blood. There were 10 of us in total, and to be fair, the monkeys were only about two feet tall. But they also had razor sharp teeth and quite possibly, rabies. Now would have been a very good time for us to make peace with the overly aggressive little dip shits.

The monkey chief walked up to the tallest person he could find in order to impose his dominance, which in this case, happened to be Gavin. Gavin, although quite skinny, was about 6 foot 2. In many ways it was actually quite amusing to see the monkey chief midget square up to the tall, lanky Scotsman. The monkey chief swaggered up to Gavin with his chest puffed out and his arms raised to his sides, as if to say, "Come on then ya fuckin' wanker!".

You could have cut the tension with a knife. Now would have probably been a good time to try to diffuse the rapidly escalating situation. However Gavin instead thought it would be a good idea to try to feed the monkey chief a leaf which he had found on the ground. To this day I still don't quite understand what Gavin was trying to achieve by this. The monkey chief took one look at the leaf in Gavin's hand, then took one look at Gavin. In utter disgust at the lack of respect, the monkey chief slapped the leaf out of Gavin's hand, then proceeded to let out a mighty screech, which the other monkeys repeated endlessly. They were not happy.

Tod shouted at us to "Get the fuck out of here", before legging it out of the nearest pathway. We quickly ran after Tod. And this brings me to the next lesson of the book.

LESSON 4: ALWAYS TAKE AN UMBRELLA WHEN VISITING MONKEY ISLAND

As we were running out of Monkey Island, it began to rain large brown drops of a gooey substance. I saw this substance hit the people in front of me and it appeared to stick to their hair and clothes. It smelled a lot too…like shit. I looked behind me. There were at least 10 monkeys swinging from tree to tree, each taking it in turns to hurl their own excrement at us. I tightly shut my mouth and lowered my head, sprinting as fast as I could after the people in front of me.

We made it to the exit of the nature reserve in record time, into a nearby souvenir market. I looked around at the others. Like myself, everyone else was panting. Some were also laughing, whilst others looked a bit traumatised. I quickly checked my hair and clothes. Fortunately the monkeys had missed me. The locals at the souvenir market stalls were also laughing. They'd no doubt seen this happen to countless other tourists. We looked around at each other. It appeared that one of us was missing…Mo. Mo was the smallest person in our group. Ron joked that the monkeys had probably mistaken him for a baby monkey and adopted him into their troop.

We wouldn't see Mo again until later that evening, when he walked through the lobby of the Susi Air hotel, absolutely caked in monkey shit. He didn't speak to us for the rest of that evening.

CHAPTER 8

MEETING SUSI

The following week we continued with the technical ground training for the Caravan. There was a lot to learn, especially in regards to the avionics (the various computer systems onboard). On Saturday afternoon we were to have our first practical lesson; ditching. The ditching lesson was basically survival training in the event that we needed to land on water. Given that we were flying single engine aircraft in the World's largest archipelago, this was pretty important to learn. Later after dinner that same day, we were to all meet Christian and Susi for the first time in their private mansion, located at the back of the Susi Air complex.

For the ditching course myself and the other Initials would train alongside the pilots on the "Upgrade" course, (the FOs who were upgrading to become Captains). Mitch was to be our instructor for the ditching, whilst the venue was to be the hotel swimming pool. What made this particular lesson mildly amusing was the fact that the Susi Air hotel wasn't exclusively for pilots. Paying customers would also stay at this hotel, and they seemed somewhat disappointed to see 15 pilots and a fucking life raft floating in the middle of the swimming pool which they had just paid for.

Mitch began the lesson with some basic warm up exercises, followed with a simulated aircraft evacuation on water where we would need to help injured passengers onto the life raft. In order to maintain realism, we all wore shirts and trousers in the swimming pool for added weight and drag. Later the lesson would become a bit more challenging. Mitch taught us some techniques which would help us hold our breath underwater for long time periods. Using these techniques, we would each take it in turns to time one another holding our breath underwater. We then repeated the same exercise, however this time, inverted. Mitch instructed us to float on our backs and rest our legs on the edge of the swimming pool. When we were ready, we were to lay back against the side of the swimming pool so that we would be submerged upside down.

Above: Ditching (survival) training in swimming pool of Susi Air hotel.

The first thing that I noticed from being inverted underwater, was that the water would instantly flood through my nose and fill up my sinuses. It was very uncomfortable. It wasn't even remotely similar to being underwater the right way up. On the first attempt, I gave up after just a few seconds. Most of the others did the same. However on the second attempt, after I knew what to expect, I managed to remain inverted underwater for a good minute or so. So why did Mitch want us to practice this inverted exercise? Well even if we were to land on water the right way up (which may not always work out), there would still be a chance that the waves could flip the aircraft over onto it's back, even if the aircraft had successfully landed on the surface of the water. The only thing that could make being submerged upside down under the water even worse, would be to panic due to lack of familiarity. If you panic underwater, especially when strapped into a seat inside of an aircraft with closed doors, the chances are that you will run out of oxygen before you have a chance to get out. The same would apply to the passengers, who we would also need to save. Mitch had planned this lesson very well indeed.

We ended the lesson with a short debrief from Mitch, then headed back to our rooms to get showered and changed for our first meeting with Christian and Susi at 6pm that evening. We were to wear our uniforms for the occasion. Mitch and the other instructors escorted us from the hotel lobby to Christian and Susi's private mansion, located on the other side of the complex, about 3 minutes walk away. The mansion in question had some resemblances to a castle. Surrounding the mansion was a large moat, with a narrow pathway leading up to the dining area of the mansion, which was located underneath Christian and Susi's private living quarters.

Guarding the pathway to this castle like mansion were Susi's two "pet" geese. Mitch warned us that these geese would sometimes attack Christian and Susi's guests without warning. It appeared that Susi simply bought these geese for her own personal amusement. Like dogs, these geese would sense any hostility from their owner towards other people, and would behave accordingly. If Susi liked you, then chances were, the Geese would back off. However if you were in Susi's bad books, or you showed any fear around the geese, then you could expect to be charged at and bitten by the two very large and aggressive birds. She would basically set the geese upon any dissenting employees in her company. After both hearing the stories, and seeing the geese for myself, my first impression of Susi was that of a low grade James Bond villain. I mean if you already have a moat around your multi million dollar mansion and you want to scare the living shit out of your employees, at least upgrade your geese for some piranhas instead.

We continued to walk up to the dining area of the mansion. Sure enough, Susi's two geese were waiting for us outside of the entrance of the dining area. Like doormen at a nightclub, Susi's geese carefully eyed up each and everyone of us. With their silent approval, we promptly walked into the dining area and each found a seat at one of the 5 dining tables inside. I was sharing a small table with Gavin, Ricardo and a Spanish Upgrade called Jose. The largest dining table appeared to be reserved for the instructors and managers.

Christian and Susi's personal waiting staff approached our tables with pots of vegetable soup, lobster tails and rice. Jose, who had already been with the company for over a year, advised us not to eat the lobster tails. Apparently these were from the lobsters which had died amongst the live lobster catches. Susi's personal staff were instructed to fish out the dead lobsters floating at the top of the tank with a net and then recycle them in the employee food.

I looked around the dining area. No sign yet of Christian and Susi. Everyone else had already started eating. I served up a small bit of rice and poured some vegetable soup over the top. There was next to no protein in the meal, but to be fair, it wasn't much different to the other meals that Susi Air had provided us so far. If you wanted a nutritious meal, you would need to eat out. Apart from the food though, it was actually quite nice to be in a social environment with the experienced Susi Air pilots. Jose, who had previously been an FO in the Papua highlands, gave us all some much needed information on what flying on the line was like. The whole dining area was somewhat lively with the sound of 25 or so people socialising with one another.

About half an hour later however, the dining area went quiet. I looked behind me. Susi walked into the dining area, followed by Christian and a small entourage of personal assistants. Everyone stood up. Susi walked past all of the tables without making eye contact with anyone, and proceeded directly to the sofa next to the bar. Two of her assistants rushed over to her with a bottle of gin, one single glass and an ashtray. Susi lit a cigarette whilst one of her assistants nervously poured her a drink. We were all still standing up awkwardly, facing Susi, waiting for some kind of acknowledgement from her. I looked at Jose. He shrugged his shoulders and sat back down. We did the same. Christian approached the table with the instructors and managers to say hi, then proceeded to each of the other tables to introduce himself to the new pilots. Susi continued to sit on the sofa smoking her cigarette.

Christian approached our table and shook our hands. The first thing that I noticed was that he was a big guy. He was almost the same height as Bart, at around 6 foot 3, however unlike Bart, he was actually quite wide also. If it wasn't for the fact that he was such a nice guy, his appearance would have been somewhat intimidating. But he was actually quite friendly and seemed genuinely interested in getting to know us. Unlike Susi however, who was still sitting on the sofa and now appeared to be having an argument with her assistant regarding the strength of her gin and tonic. Christian and Susi appeared to be quite a contrast.

The waiting staff approached us with a tray holding several glasses of wine. Wine is actually incredibly difficult to buy in most places in Indonesia. Despite being a predominantly Muslim country, even beer was easy to find in most places, at least in Pangandaran. Even spirits could be bought in some places. But wine really was a rare treat in Indonesia. A very expensive treat at that, assuming that you could actually find it on the menu.

About 15 minutes later, Christian sat down on the sofa next to Susi. We were instructed to each grab a chair and make a circle next to the couple. Now was the beginning of the formal meet and greet. Starting at the beginning of the circle, Susi asked us each to stand up, state our names, our previous flying experience and where we would see ourselves in 5 years time. Naturally, we all lied and said that we would still be flying with Susi Air in 5 years. Christian appeared to have a great sense of humour. "So you have no plans to join the airlines and fly bigger planes?", he asked Mo. Mo, being very diplomatic, was very insistent that he wanted to fly with Susi Air for the rest of his life. Christian was in stitches of laughter, as were everyone else. If you're going to tell a lie, at least make the lie believable.

The next up for the introduction was an Upgrade who was a bit on the large side. Susi, being blunt as hell, made a reference to the poor guy's size; "I don't want to hear about you offloading any cargo to make up for your extra 30 kg of weight!". The room went silent with shock. The Upgrade nervously laughed; "Err, no, that won't happen Ibu Susi". Christian looked down at the ground as Susi spoke. He appeared to be absolutely disgusted with her. Slightly embarrassed, the Upgrade sat back down. Next it was my turn to speak.

I sheepishly stood up and introduced myself. I told them that I was previously working as a Flight Instructor, and before that, had worked odd jobs here and there to save up for my flight training. "How long did it take you to save up for your flight training?", asked Christian. "About four years in total", I replied. Satisfied with my answers, Christian and Susi looked at the person next to me, and I sat back down. Back then I was actually quite shy around large audiences, so it was quite a relief for them to move on to the next person. Susi, by this stage slightly drunk, ended the meeting with a short speech, explaining how she didn't like pilots who complained. "If you don't like it here, then just leave!", she shouted. Susi's awkward rant seemed somewhat inappropriate given that no pilot in that room appeared to have any complaints. Christian once again looked down at the ground. He really seemed quite ashamed of his rude, and somewhat drunk, wife.

This meeting was getting a bit awkward. Mr Cheung saved the day by politely asked for us all to be excused. Before Susi had a chance to reply, we quickly scurried out of the dining area, only to be confronted by Susi's two pet geese who were waiting for us outside. They seemed pissed off. We promptly rushed past them as they shrieked and flapped their wings at us. We were pissing ourselves laughing, it all seemed so surreal. Although we could all see the funny side of the awkward meeting, I don't think there was a single pilot there who still wanted to be inside the Susi Air complex at that particular moment in time…I suspect Christian included.

We all hurried to our rooms to get changed from our uniforms into shorts and t-shirts, so that we could go out for drinks in Pangandaran. The beginning of the evening may have been a complete disaster, but it was Saturday night, and we had the following day off!

Bamboo Bar, here we come!

CHAPTER 9

EPIDEMIC

I know what you're thinking. So far you've read about my life before Susi Air, my interview, the ground training and also about Mo getting covered in monkey shit. But when exactly am I going to get to the stories about flying? I know that the bush flying was the whole purpose of the book, but please just bear with me for one more chapter. There is just one more short story that I need to share about life in Pangandaran.

Ever since myself and the other Initials had arrived in Indonesia, we had all felt a bit sick from time to time. That's to be expected when adjusting to a new climate, a new cuisine and also to a new standard of hygiene. But what started as occasional, mild sickness, would become far more serious. Approximately 10 days after we had arrived in Pangandaran for the training, one of the management consultants that Christian and Susi had hired to assist with the company's expansion, fell ill. I mean very ill. He was a New Zealander in his late 60's and had been working and living in the Susi Air complex for a few months.

One day he collapsed at work and was evacuated by air to Singapore in order to receive life saving treatment. He was in a critical condition and almost died. At the time of his medical evacuation, nobody knew what was wrong with him. It was possibly malaria, dengue fever or perhaps even a heart attack. Either way, there was no hospital in Pangandaran, and even the "hospitals" in Jakarta were so questionable that I needed to write the very word in apostrophes. He was flown from the beach strip in Pangandaran to Halim airport by Caravan, then by Avanti to Singapore. He would spend the following week in intensive care, whilst a team of doctors struggled to diagnose his condition.

A few days after the management consultant's collapse, on the same night following the pilot's meeting with Christian and Susi, I was woken up by Ron, who burst into our room in a state of panic. "Come quickly! Mo's sick!", he shouted. Dazed, myself and Gavin got out of bed and followed Ron downstairs to the lobby along with the other Initials. Mo was slumped over a table, completely motionless. Ron checked his pulse and shook his arm to wake him up, whilst Maria and Ricardo shouted in his ear. Mo slowly moved his head but he couldn't focus his eyes. His speech was slurred and incomprehensible. Cheung, who was sleeping in the bedroom next to the lobby, came outside to see what all the commotion was about.

Cheung arranged for one of the drivers to take Mo to the nearby medical centre. This medical centre was not a hospital. It didn't even have a doctor on duty. However it did have saline in stock, along with a much needed IV line. Air evacuations were not possible from Pangandaran at night time, due to the lack of reliable runway lighting on both the beach strip and Nusawiru airport. Regardless of how serious Mo's situation was, he was going to be stuck in Pangandaran until sunrise. It wasn't like the UK where you could simply dial 999 in an emergency.

The following morning, Mo stabilised and his consciousness improved. He was still very ill, however his situation wasn't quite bad enough to warrant a medical evacuation to Singapore, (which would have cost the company upwards of 8,000 USD). However as Mo's health gradually improved throughout the day, another two pilots, this time on the Upgrade course, would fall seriously ill. They too needed to be taken to the local medical centre. I too was ill, as were most of the pilots living in the Susi Air complex, however we weren't quite as bad as the others who needed medical assistance.

So what was going on? Why were so many people living in the Susi Air complex becoming so ill? A team of managers inspected the kitchen in the Susi Air complex for problems with hygiene. The dining area in the pilot's hotel was also closed off as a precaution. We would need to eat in Christian and Susi's private dining area for the next couple of days. However regardless of how hard the managers tried to investigate the cause of the

Pandemic, there simply weren't any obvious problems with food hygiene. However the following week I would find out the real reason for the epidemic from one of the engineering consultants, Ray, over a beer one night at Bamboo Bar. Which brings me to the next lesson of this book.

LESSON 5: NEVER DRINK FROM ANY CUPS IN THE SUSI AIR COMPLEX UNLESS YOU HAVE WASHED THEM YOURSELF

No seriously, if you ever happen to end up in the Susi Air complex in Pangandaran, whether as a pilot or as a guest in the hotel, then never drink from the cups unless you wash them thoroughly yourself. If you could see the photos and video that Ray showed me, you'll understand why. Located on each floor of the office building were facilities for making tea and coffee. The cups always appeared to be stained on both the inside and the outside, from what we all assumed was from the tea of the previous users. Yes, it was a bit gross to drink from a cup with brown marks all over it, however it turned out that those brown marks weren't from the teabags.

Ray, concerned with hygiene, had filmed the housekeepers (known as "cicis" in Indonesia), clean the toilets in the office building. He filmed from a distance as they first mopped the floor in the toilets, then used the same mop to clean the inside of the toilet bowl! I mean literally, they used the same mop to wipe the skid marks from the inside of the toilet bowl. But it got much, much worse. I must admit, after I watched this video, I almost threw up. In the video, after cleaning the floor and the toilet bowl, they then rinsed the mop in a bucket of soapy water. They then used the same bucket of (now brown) water to clean the fucking cups and glasses!

That's right. All that time we were getting ill, we had quite literally been drinking each other's shit. After Ray discretely showed the video and photos to the senior management, everybody's health gradually began to improve. Partly because the cicis were advised to clean the cups separately to everything else, and partly because after word had spread over the real cause of the illness, nobody dared to drink from those shit-stained cups again.

CHAPTER 10

FIRST FLIGHT

There is always one fundamental problem with starting a new job in December; the Christmas holidays. Yep, bah humbug. Christmas isn't all fun and games. Usually the Initial course takes less than 4 weeks including flight training, (assuming that the Training Department actually have enough instructors), however that wasn't going to be the case for us. We'd completed all of the ground training a few days before Christmas, including a 1 hour long verbal assessment on company SOPs and aircraft systems with Mitch. However as Christmas day approached, all of the instructors began to leave the Training Department in Pangandaran so that they could cover the other Susi Air pilots on the line, who had holidays booked for the festive season.

The Flight Instructors, Bart, Matt and Tod, worked tirelessly to finish the flight training for the Upgrades before the holidays. However the rest of us would need to wait until after Christmas before we would have our first lesson in the Caravan. Myself and the other Initials were now all alone in Pangandaran with the only member of training staff being Mr Cheung. Cheung, despite being in charge of the instructors, wasn't even qualified to fly the Caravan, let alone train us. Not wanting to see his Initials sitting around doing nothing, Cheung put us all to work with part time administrative duties to keep us occupied. We were bored as hell. We just wanted to fly.

We spent Christmas day at Bamboo Bar along with a couple of the Upgrades who were still waiting to be allocated their first base as Captain. One of the Upgrades suggested that we play "Scooter Jousting" the following day, to kill time. As the name suggests, Scooter Jousting is a modern day innovation of the popular medieval sport. Safe in the knowledge that there would be no inbound flights that day, the plan was to drive two scooters from opposite ends of the 700 meter long beach strip, whilst each driver would hold a broom under their left arm. Upon closing in on their opponent travelling in the opposite direction, they would then need to shove the other rider off their bike with the soft end of the brush (not the stick at the end, that would have been pretty dumb). They would of course also need to ensure that the stick end of the brush wasn't pointing at themselves either, in order to avoid possible impalement. Naturally helmets, visors, padding and a few bottles of Bintang were needed in order to take part in this game. I decided not to try it myself. However even to this day I am still intrigued by the idea.

(Disclaimer: please don't try anything that dumb yourself).

Above: Approaching Runway 09 on the beach strip in Pangandaran. Used for both aircraft and drunk people on motorbikes.

A few days after Christmas, Bart returned to Pangandaran so that we could begin our flight training. Given that there were 9 of us in total and we had just one instructor, we would be divided into groups of three. Each person in the group would take it in turns to have a one hour long flying lesson with Bart, whilst the other two in the group would sit in the back of the aircraft watching. We would then alternate. Myself, Francois and Miranda were going to be in the same group. We were picked up the following morning at 6am from the lobby of the hotel and taken to Nusawiru Airport by minibus.

Above: Nusawiru Airport in the early morning.

After arriving at Nusawiru, Bart escorted us out to the apron where the training aircraft was parked. We began the lesson with the pre-flight inspection of the aircraft. As we walked around the aircraft, Bart pointed out the various things to check, from worn tyres, broken antennas and chipped propeller blades. He showed us how to open up the cowling (the hatch on the nose of the aircraft), so that we could inspect the engine. After inserting the "tail stand" (the support stick for the tail of the aircraft which prevents the aircraft from tipping backwards during passenger boarding), Bart showed us how to open and close the rear passenger door. The pre-flight inspection took us about 30 minutes in total. On the line however, this inspection would take an experienced pilot around 5 minutes.

With the pre flight inspection complete, it was now time for the flight training. Francois was going to be the first to fly, followed by Miranda, then myself. Miranda and I would have the luxury of learning from Francois' mistakes, before we would take the controls of the Caravan ourselves. Myself and Miranda sat down in the back of the aircraft whilst Bart showed Francois how to perform the "final walk around" (the final check performed by the FO, which included closing the passenger doors and removing the tail stand). Myself and Miranda plugged our headsets into the observer ports and sat down on the second row from the front. We couldn't sit any further forward due to the weight and balance of the aircraft, as the rear passenger seats were empty. We then sat back and watched Francois' first flight in the Caravan. Which brings me to the next lesson of this book.

LESSON 6: NEVER UNDERESTIMATE THE BENEFITS OF A "BACK SEAT" FLYING LESSON

Back in my days as a Flight Instructor, I always use to encourage my students to sit in the back seats of each other's flying lessons, whenever they had the chance. Why? For two reasons. Firstly, when you learn to fly for the first time, or in our case, learn to fly a new type of aircraft, your mind is going to be over loaded with information...not to mention stress. As a result of this, it is only natural that a passenger observing from the back seat is going to have far greater "Situational Awareness", or SA, than the student pilot sitting up front. As observers in the back, we could see things that Francois simply wouldn't have been able to see, as his workload would have been so high. Secondly, it's a free lesson. Susi Air may have been paying for our training, however that still didn't take away the fact that we would only get 4 one hour flying lessons each. By sitting in the back seats on each other's lessons, those 4 flying lessons would effectively now become 12 flying lessons.

Above: The controls of a G1000 "Glass Cockpit" Caravan. 3 large computer screens have replaced the analogue instruments found in older aircraft.

Bart, sitting in the left hand seat, started the engine whilst Francois, sitting on the right, monitored the instruments. Myself and Miranda smiled as we heard the sound of the jet engine spool up. Bart went through the call outs for the engine start; "Timer started, starter energised, prop rotating, oil pressure rising, NG rising...stable". Bart then moved the Fuel Condition Lever, or FCL, to the low idle position, thus allowing fuel to be injected into the engine. A couple of seconds later, we heard a woof as the fuel ignited in the combustion chamber of the engine, causing the turbines to accelerate and the engine to howl a high pitched tone. Bart continued the call outs; "Light off! Fuel flow rising, NG rising, ITT rising...stable".

After Bart started the engine, it was now Francois' turn to work. As the First Officer, it was his job to set up the weather radar and enter the "Bluesky" flight plan after the Captain completed the engine start. Bluesky was a system which Susi Air used to track all movements of their aircraft. It also allowed the flight crew to make and receive phone calls and text messages from the air, and also to alert the Operations Control Centre in the event of an emergency, using the "Quick Position" button. The QP button was especially important when flying in the more remote regions of Indonesia, where radio communication with Air Traffic Control wasn't always guaranteed. With help from Bart, Francois programmed the Bluesky device on the right side of the instrument panel with important information such as the destination, expected flight time and most importantly of all, the total POB (People On Board). In the event of an accident, rescuers would need to know exactly how many people they needed to save.

After completing the Before Taxi checklist, it was time for a brake check. Both Bart and Francois took it in turns to taxi forward slightly and apply the brakes, located on the top of each rudder pedal. The Caravan is for the most part a very reliable aircraft...with the exception of the brakes. There is sometimes a tendency for air bubbles to build up in the brake lines, which makes the brake pedals "spongy" and unresponsive. This is even worse with the FO's brake pedals, as the crossbar which connects with the Captain's brake pedals can become bent over time. On this occasion, both Bart and Francois had successful brake checks, with the aircraft coming to a complete stop for both sets of brake pedals. However this wasn't going to stop Bart from teaching us all a very important lesson. "Now let's say we had a brake failure right now, how are you going to stop the aircraft?", he asked Francois. Francois immediately moved the power lever to back to maximum reverse, causing the propeller blades to point backwards and the engine power to increase. We came to a stop, and Francois moved the power lever back to idle. Bart grinned at Francois, "very good", he said.

Francois continued to taxi to the holding point of the runway whilst checking his instruments during the turns. Nusawiru airport didn't have any Air Traffic Control. Instead they had a radio operator who would advise aircraft of any other traffic in the vicinity. Bart advised the radio operator that we were approaching the holding point and intended to backtrack runway 07. The radio operator replied with "OK Cap! Runway clear!". However the runway wasn't clear at all. People were crossing on motorbikes, using a path which cut directly across the runway. A plained clothed security guard stood on top of his truck next to the runway crossing. He signalled to the next motorbike rider to stop. We continued the backtrack down runway 07, whilst Bart and Francois completed the Taxi and Line Up checklists. Reaching the end of the runway, Francois turned the aircraft around 180 degrees with assistance from Bart.

The first take off was to be a "max performance" take off. A max performance take off meant that we needed to hold the brakes as we set the take off power, so that the aircraft would be stationary. Once we would release the brakes, the aircraft would then accelerate faster than had the power been set as the aircraft was already rolling. This take off technique also had the advantage of making it easier for students like us to set the correct power, as we wouldn't need to look out of the window at the same time that we needed to look at the engine instruments. If you applied the power too quickly, you would create a "prop surge", where the propeller would momentarily exceed the 1900 RPM limit. Carefully following the instructions of Bart, Francois slowly advanced the power lever whilst they both held the brakes. The prop momentarily surged, but nothing too extreme. As per the SOPs, Francois, who was the Pilot Flying (PF) asked Bart, who was the Pilot Monitoring (PM), to "Set take off power". Bart then set 1800 foot pounds of torque on the power lever, then confirmed that the "Engine Ts and Ps in the green". Francois then called for "Brake release!" and we began to accelerate down the runway.

Francois began to slowly lift off the tarmac at around 60 knots, before pitching up to approximately 8 degrees. Bart advised Francois to climb straight ahead to 5000 feet, so that we could practice some aircraft handling exercises overhead Pangandaran Bay. The first part of the lesson would consist of 30 degree bank turns, 45 degree bank turns, slow flight and stall recovery (recovering from loss of lift due to a very low speed). After these exercises were completed to his satisfaction, Bart then instructed Francois to fly back to Nusawiru so that he could practice "touch and goes". A touch and go is a landing which is immediately followed by a take off on the same runway. It is a technique which is used primarily for student pilots who need to practice multiple take offs and landings, as it saves time taxiing back to the end of the runway after each landing. Both myself and Miranda watched Francois' lesson very carefully from the passenger seats so that we could perform to a high standard when we would be flying ourselves. To be fair though, asides from his first landing which was a bit too "assertive", Francois actually performed pretty damn well. Francois' third landing was a "full stop" landing. As the term suggests, a full stop landing means that the aircraft will vacate the runway and taxi back to the apron.

After shutting down the engine, Miranda swapped with Francois. It was now her turn. I continued to sit in the same passenger seat as Bart went through the same lesson with her again, starting from the final walk around. During Miranda's flying lesson, Francois told me about his experience flying the Caravan. He warned me that one of the things which caught him out was the prop "disking". When you bring the power lever to idle, especially at high speeds, the Caravan's propeller will create a large amount of drag as opposed to thrust. This is especially important to know when coming in to land, as unlike the light aircraft that we were accustomed to flying, we would need to apply power right up until the flare. With a disking prop, the Caravan glides like a brick. Miranda finished her lesson with two touch and goes and a full stop landing. Like Francois, aside from her first landing (which is usually far from perfect when flying a new aircraft), she performed well for her first lesson. At the end of Miranda's lesson, Bart instructed her to taxi back to the apron and shutdown the engine.

Now it was my turn to fly. Seeing both Francois and Miranda perform so well during their lessons gave me a lot of pressure not to fuck up. I was both nervous and excited. Fortunately Bart wasn't just a good instructor, he also had a cracking sense of humour. This helped put me at ease. I walked up the ladder into the cockpit, plugged in my headset and adjusted my seat with the assistance of Bart. The first thing that I noticed was just how high up we were. We may have been flying a small plane, but it was a big small plane. There was a ladder to reach the cockpit for a reason; the floor of the cockpit was over a metre off of the ground! I stepped back out of the aircraft so that Bart could show me how to perform the final walk around. After closing the passenger door, I removed the tail stand of the aircraft and placed it in the cargo pod located underneath the aircraft. After a short brief on the itinerary of the lesson, I stepped back up into the right side of the cockpit. My heart was racing with adrenaline.

After the engine start, Bart instructed me how to set up the weather radar and the Bluesky flight plan. After completing the Before Taxi checklist, we were ready to go. I checked my brakes, then Bart checked his. I continued taxiing slowly to the runway, controlling my speed with "beta" (a position on the power lever which points the propeller blades backwards for drag). Unintentionally, my taxi speed began to increase. Bart yelled "Brake failure!", at the top of his lungs. Startled, I immediately applied maximum reverse to stop the aircraft, before moving the power lever back to the idle position. Bart laughed, "Don't worry, I'm just testing you", he said, "But never taxi too fast in this aircraft, the brakes are pretty crappy". We continued our taxi to the beginning of runway 07 and completed the Taxi and Line Up checklists.

After lining up, Bart gave me some final words of advice for the take off. "Make sure that you hold the control column semi aft as you roll down the runway, otherwise you could get a prop strike", he said. The runway was rough and there was a real danger that the propeller tips could strike the tarmac. By holding the control column back partially towards myself, the weight would be taken off of the nose wheel. Bart assisted me hold the brakes of the aircraft whilst I carefully advanced the power lever forward. After seeing Francois and Miranda's lessons, I managed to avoid surging the prop myself. I then asked Bart to "set take off power". There was a lot of power in that engine. I felt the brakes slipping and the airframe vibrate as full power was applied to the 675 shaft horse power engine. Bart confirmed that the "Engine Ts and Ps were in the green", and I called "Brake release!" We accelerated down the runway. Due to the position I was holding the control column, the nose wheel began to lift off of the ground at around 40 knots, a speed far to low to take off. "Just let the nose wheel hover above the tarmac, the aircraft will lift off when it wants", Bart said. Sure enough, after a few small bounces on the bumpy tarmac, the main wheels lifted up off of the ground at around 60 knots and I smoothly pitched for 8 degrees nose up.

"How does it feel to fly a Caravan?", asked Bart. "This is amazing!", I replied. I couldn't wipe the grin off of my face. At 400 feet I lowered the nose slightly so that we could accelerate and retract the flaps. Bart then asked me to perform a "Vx" climb. Vx, in the world of aviation, means the speed for the best angle of climb. Pitching up to attain this low speed of 72 knots, when combined with maximum power, would provide the highest obstacle clearance. It also meant that we were shooting up into the sky like a rocket. I gradually levelled the aircraft off approaching 5000 feet and allowed the speed to accelerate to 130 knots, before setting cruise power. We continued with some turning exercises with 30 and 45 degrees of bank. I noticed that a lot of rudder input was needed whenever I rolled the aircraft. As the wings of the Caravan were particularly long, the aircraft suffered from "aileron drag". This basically meant that you needed to stamp down on the rudders every time that you wanted to roll the aircraft. After practising the turns, we moved on to slow flight and stall recovery.

The first stall was fairly benign. In the "clean" configuration (flaps up), Bart reduced the power to about 350 foot pounds of torque, a setting which would neither produce a significant amount of thrust nor drag. It was my task to maintain the altitude as the air speed gradually decreased, up until the point that the wings would stall due to lack of lift. The stall warning activated at around 65 knots, and at about 60 knots, the nose dropped a few degrees, which indicated an actual stall. I executed the stall recovery technique by pitching down and gradually increasing the power. "That was easy", Bart said, "But now let's try with flaps extended". We tried the same exercise again, only extending the flaps as the air speed decreased. This time the aircraft stalled at about 45 knots, however it was far from benign. With the flaps extended, the centre of lift becomes more centralised and the aircraft becomes laterally unstable. Both the nose and the right wing violently pitched down, and I needed to immediately push the control column forward to prevent us from entering a spin. Bart grinned and remarked, "That was fun!". He didn't appear to be easily phased.

Above: A "wing drop" associated with a stall with flaps extended to the full position. This photo was taken from the back of a Caravan during training.

We returned back to Nusawiru to practice some touch and goes. During the descent, Bart asked me to intentionally bring the power lever all the way back to idle so that the prop would disk. Each time I disked the propeller, we would be flung forward into our shoulder harnesses from the sudden deceleration. "Make sure you don't do that on final approach", he advised. I descended down to the circuit altitude of 1000 feet and joined on a left downwind leg for runway 07, with an air speed of 110 knots and flaps 10. Bart advised the Nusawiru radio operator of our position, whilst closely inspecting the runway for any vehicles, people or animals. Turning on to the final approach, I asked Bart to select flaps full and to complete the Finals checklist. The approach was looking good. I wasn't too high or too low, and my speed was around 75 knots, which was ideal for our weight. I thought about Francois and Miranda's first landings. They chopped the power too soon and landed hard. Learning from their mistakes, I decided to keep the power in for a bit longer. At around 10 feet above the ground, I gradually raised the nose of the aircraft for the flare, whilst stepping on the rudders to maintain the centreline of the runway. I then (very) gradually reduced the power. The aircraft touched down relatively softly and in the right position on the runway. "Very good!", Bart remarked. He then set the power and we took off again.

We continued with another circuit around Nusawiru, followed by another touch and go. The second landing, although wasn't perfect, was relatively smooth and in the correct touchdown point of the runway. Bart appeared to be impressed so far. At the end of the lesson we would need to land on the beach strip, next to Pangandaran, so that Bart could have his lunch break before training another 3 students in the afternoon. After the second landing, whilst we were on the downwind leg, Bart made me an offer; "If this landing is also good, I'll let you land on the beach strip". Wow! For me, this was an honour. The beach strip was more shorter, narrower and rougher than Nusawiru. It was also far less forgiving of mistakes. Despite this, Bart appeared to trust me enough to land there. The third touch and go at Nusawiru was successful. After taking off again, Bart instructed me to climb to 2000 feet in the direction of the beach strip, which was just 5 minutes flight away.

After a very short brief from Bart, I descended down to 800 feet on a (very) close downwind leg for Runway 27, so that he could closely inspect the beach strip. Unlike Nusawiru airport, the beach strip had very little security. Pretty much anyone, or anything, could loiter on the beach strip without being challenged. As the name suggested, it was located on a public beach. Bart appeared to be happy with the inspection, and I broke off to the right so that I would have a longer base leg and final approach. On final approach, I asked Bart once again for flaps full and to complete the Finals checklist. However half way through the checklist, he paused, then squinted outside. I briefly looked at him, then looked forward to see what he was looking at. In the distance, I could see 3 motorbikes being driven side by side from the far end of the beach strip towards us. They appeared to be having a drag race! At this point, we were just 300 feet above the surface. I grasped the power lever firmly, anticipating a go around. I looked closely at the 3 bikers. They could clearly see that our aircraft was coming in to land, however they made no attempt to vacate the runway. They appeared to be deliberately playing chicken with us!

"Oh for fucks sake!" Bart yelled, "My controls!". "You have control!", I replied, as I let go of the control column and power lever. At this point, we were now just 100 feet above the surface and the bikers were approximately half way down the runway. Well I guessed Bart was going to be executing a go around now, I thought. Was he fuck! Bart, having needed to go around more than enough times in the past due to inconsiderate bikers playing chicken with him on the runway, decided that he wasn't going to put up with their shit any more. He increased the power slightly, however not quite enough to climb away. Instead he levelled off 10 feet above the beach strip, buzzing right over the heads of the motorbike riders! We were so low that I could see the expression of shear terror on each of their faces, as they closed their eyes and flinched, no doubt expecting our aircraft to hit them. They were anticipating that we would go around much sooner, however unfortunately for them, they challenged the wrong pilot to a game of chicken. As mentioned earlier in this book, Bart had a very low tolerance for other people's bullshit.

Once clear of the bikers, Bart asked me to set "go around power", before pitching up to establish a climb. I looked back at Miranda and Francois, they appeared to be as surprised as me. Myself and Bart looked at each other; we both laughed. That may not have been a particularly legit thing for Bart to do, but to be fair, they shouldn't have been on the runway anyway. They probably weren't going to be drag racing on the beach strip again anytime soon. Bart levelled off at 800 feet and broke off to the left.

Rather than go all the way back around for Runway 27, he turned around so that the aircraft was aligned with the opposing Runway 09. The wind was relatively calm, so we could have landed in either direction. He then handed the control back to me so that I could land, on what was now a clear landing strip, free from any trespassers. We landed without incident. Bart gave us all a short debrief on the minibus back to the hotel.

Even to this day, that was quite possibly the most interesting flying lesson that I have ever had.

CHAPTER 11

GRADUATION

Following our first flying lesson in the Caravan, we would each have a further 3 training flights. The third flying lesson was particularly fun for all of us, as it involved practising non normal manoeuvres such as emergency descents and engine failures. The emergency descent involved disking the propeller so that it would act as a brake, whilst pitching 20 degrees nose down to 170 knots with flaps 10 (just 5 knots below the maximum speed). We would then plummet out of the sky from 5000 feet down to 1000 feet in the space of about 45 seconds, all the while pinching our noses to equalise from the extreme pressure change. The objective of this manoeuvre was to land in the quickest possible time in the case of an uncontrollable fire onboard the aircraft.

Once levelled off at 1000 feet, we would then climb back up to 5000 feet for the engine failure training. Whilst flying over Pangandaran Bay at 5000 feet, Bart would shout "Engine Failure" at us, whilst moving the power lever all the way back to idle so that the propeller would disk. We would then need to promptly shout out the memory items for an engine failure; "Air speed 95 knots! Idle power, propeller feather, FCL cut off!". After shouting the correct memory items, Bart would then set a zero thrust / drag setting on the power lever, (about 350 foot pounds of torque), to simulate an engine failure with a feathered (zero drag) propeller. If you didn't shout out the correct memory items, Bart would continue to disk the prop so that you would plummet down to earth at about 2000 feet a minute. It sounds harsh, but that's exactly what would have happened in real life with an engine failure. Fortunately neither myself nor my group forgot their memory items. Other pilots, yes. But they wouldn't forget their memory items again after that learning experience.

With the memory items completed and a zero thrust / drag power set, we would then need to glide the aircraft to land on the beach strip. To assist us with our judgement, we would nominate "key points" for certain altitudes. The turn onto final approach would be a fixed point at 500 feet and the turn onto base leg would be a fixed point at 1000 feet. If we were too low over our key point, we would turn in and cut the corner. If we were too high, we would turn out to increase our track miles. Fortunately I had about 600 hours experience as a Flight Instructor on single engine aircraft, prior to joining Susi Air. I used to practice simulated engine failures with my students all of the time. These were commonly known as "Practice Forced Landings" or PFLs.

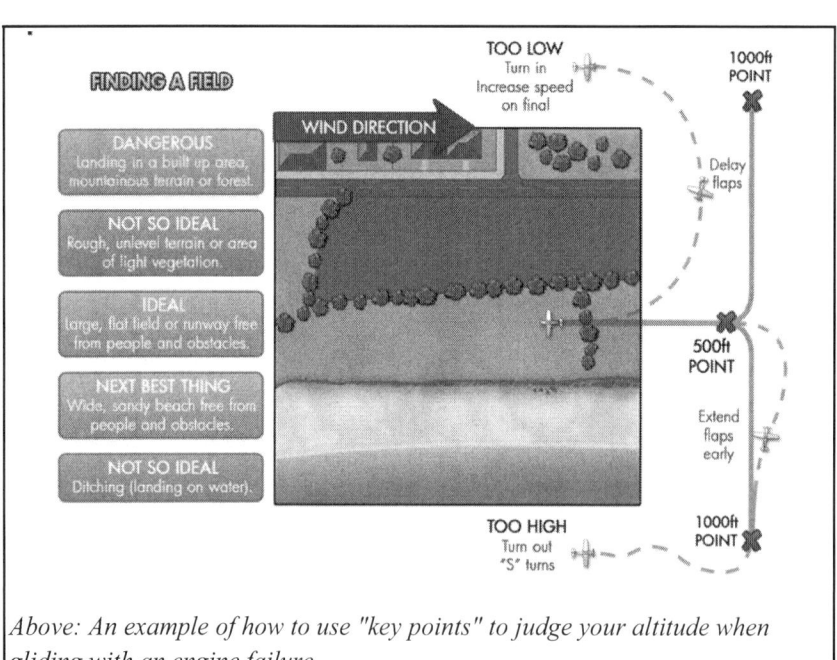

Above: An example of how to use "key points" to judge your altitude when gliding with an engine failure.

We would spend New Years Eve in Pangandaran whilst we waited for our final flying lesson. Pangandaran was just a small town at the time, however that didn't stop thousands of people from the surrounding areas to rock up on the beach to celebrate. Myself and the others spent the evening in Bamboo Bar celebrating the New Year and also celebrating (almost) finishing our training. We took our beers onto the beach to join the locals in their celebrations. It was so crowded that we could barely move. A lot of people on the beach had fireworks. It wouldn't have been so bad if they had aimed these fireworks directly up into the air. Unfortunately many of the fireworks were launched horizontally. After seeing a few people get hit with the stray rockets, and one poor sod getting set on fire by accident, we decided it would be best to go back to Bamboo Bar for cover. Don't get me wrong, I'm all for having a laugh, but I have my limits.

A couple of days later, for our fourth and final flights, we were to fly from Nusawiru to Cilicap, an airport about 15 minutes flying time to the East. This time we would be flying with a different Flight Instructor, Matt, who was now back from Medan after covering another pilot who was on holiday. The point of this flight was to simulate a normal line flight from A to B with passengers and also to practice an instrument approach into Cilicap. The only problem was that there wasn't actually any authorised instrument approach in Cilicap. Remember me telling you about that dodgy home made approach plate that I was given at the interview? Well take a crazy guess which airport that was for.

Starting with myself, then Miranda and then Francois, we each took it in turns to fly from Nusawiru to Cilicap, where we would conduct an instrument approach followed by a go around, then return back to Nusawiru for touch and goes. The final approach path of the instrument approach was offset to the runway by about 15 degrees, the descent angle was unusually steep, and the obstacle clearance was questionable. Fortunately we were visual for the entire approach. It would have taken some balls fly that approach in bad visibility, not to mention some serious stupidity. We each completed our final lesson to a high standard. After Francois, who was the last to fly, landed back in Nusawiru, we had a quick debrief from Matt. And just like that, we had finished our training.

The following day, all 9 of us were flown back to Jakarta whilst we waited for our "DGCA" flight exam. The DGCA, or Directorate General for Civil Aviation, was the Indonesian authority for flight crew licensing. They were responsible for issuing our Indonesian Commercial Pilot Licences. The DGCA required us all to undergo a flight exam with their inspector. Whilst waiting for our exam, most of us would be staying in the company accommodation in Senjaya, located in an up market neighbourhood in the centre of Jakarta. Unlike most of the accommodation in Susi Air, the houses in Senjaya were actually quite nice. All of the rooms were spacious and clean. Unfortunately as there wasn't room for all of us, Mo and Gavin needed to stay in Patria Apartments, located about 15 minutes drive away. Unlike Senjaya, Patria could best be described as being a shithole. The rooms were tiny, the mattresses were stained and all of the apartments reeked of BO and tobacco.

We had the DGCA flight exam booked for a couple of days after we arrived in Jakarta. Matt and another FO flew a Caravan from Nusawiru to Halim for our flight exam. We met him in the Susi Air VIP lounge at Halim airport where he proceeded to brief us on our flight exam. "Don't worry guys, this is just a formality", he told us. "You're each going to make a touch and go at Halim, then swap around with the next Initial on the downwind leg. The inspector is going to sit in the back. He'll be asleep for most of the exam". We laughed when he said that, as we all assumed that he was joking. Matt looked at me sternly; "I'm not joking", he said. Our DGCA inspector, Captain Hasri, arrived at Halim airport in style, on an Air Asia A320. Apparently he was was conducting a check on the A320 crew. He was quite a nice, friendly guy. He gave us all a quick briefing, basically confirming everything that Matt had just said, of course with the exception of him being asleep for the flight.

We all walked out to the apron where our Caravan was parked. Ricardo was the first up in the cockpit. The remaining 8 of us boarded the aircraft through the rear passenger door with Captain Hasri. After Ricardo completed the final walk around, Matt started the engine. Shortly after take off, Captain Hasri asked Ricardo to swap with the next FO. Apparently he wasn't interested in seeing if Ricardo could actually safely land the plane. Mid flight, whilst on the downwind leg, Ricardo moved his seat back and unstrapped his belt and harness. He then precariously shuffled from his seat into the passenger compartment. Maria, who was sitting in the first passenger row, then got up and carefully manoeuvred herself on to the FO's seat. After getting strapped in, Matt gave her control so that she could perform a touch and go on the runway. Following Maria's (relatively) smooth touch and go, after levelling off at 1000 feet circuit altitude, Matt then took the controls back whilst she swapped with Mo.

As Matt had already briefed, Captain Hasri was now fast asleep. This was somewhat unfortunate as Mo's landing was hard enough to knock your teeth out. I looked over at Captain Hasri; he briefly woke up after the violent thud onto the tarmac, snorted a couple of times, then drifted back to sleep a few moments later as we began to take off again. We continued this game of musical chairs for just under an hour, under the (not) so watchful eye of our DGCA inspector, until all 9 of us had performed either a take off, a landing, or both. After taxiing back to the apron, Matt shutdown the engine and woke up Captain Hasri. We then headed back to the Susi Air VIP lounge where Captain Hasri signed our paperwork. All we needed to do now was wait for the DGCA to issue our licences and for Susi Air to assign our first bases.

We all spent the next couple of days in the Jakarta company accommodation relaxing. During the day we ordered takeaways and watched TV, then in the evening we headed out to the bars and nightclubs of Jakarta. We were expecting to be assigned with our bases soon. We were previously advised by Cheung that new FOs who were fresh out of training would usually be split between the two largest bases; Medan in Sumatra and Balikpapan in Kalimantan. Balikpapan had a reputation for being the party base in the Susi Air network, as when the pilots weren't flying they were always going out and having fun. They also had an amazing roster, with 6 weeks on and 2 weeks off! With all of that time off and a disposable income, pilot's in Balikpapan enjoyed some incredible holidays around Asia. Medan's roster on the other hand wasn't quite so generous, with just 3 weeks on and 1 week off. Medan is also located in Northern Sumatra, which has the most severe weather of any other place is Asia. In fact, it actually has the second highest level of thunderstorm activity in the entire World, shortly after Central Africa. There really wasn't much comparison between these two bases. Balikpapan was where everyone wanted to go.

Take a crazy guess which base I was going to be assigned? Yep. Along with Francois, Miranda and Ricardo, I was going to spend my first 3 weeks as a First Officer in Medan, navigating around some of the most severe weather that I would ever see in my entire aviation career!

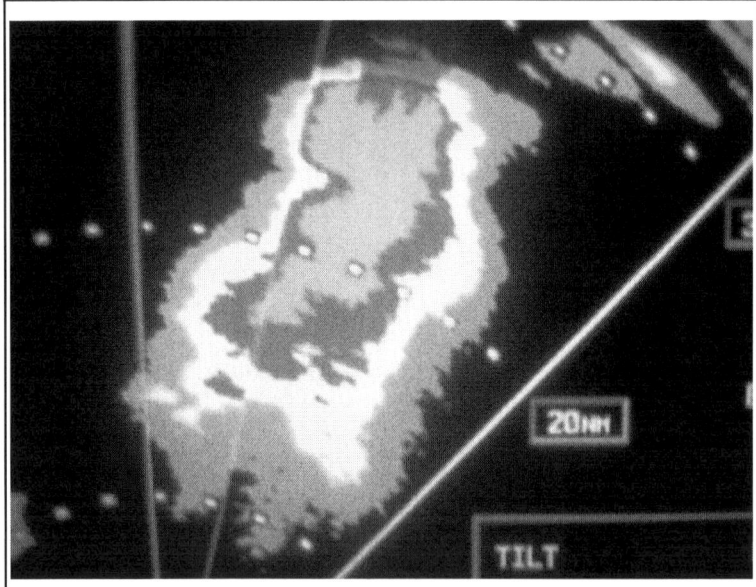

Above: A typical day flying in Northern Sumatra. This is from the Caravan's weather radar. The size, steep gradient and appearance of magenta (purple), indicates that this is a particularly violent storm.

CHAPTER 12

A BRIEF GUIDE TO SUMATRA

Sumatra is the largest island in the Indonesian archipelago, covering a total of 480,000 square kilometres. Unlike Java, (which has less than half of the land mass of Sumatra), Sumatra isn't densely populated. It is home to approximately 55 million people, compared to Java's population of 260 million. Like most regions of Indonesia, Sumatra is blanketed underneath a thick layer of rainforest. Unfortunately like most regions of Indonesia, this rainforest is being destroyed at an alarming rate to make way for palm oil plantations and the like. Since the beginning of the 1980's, almost half of Sumatra's plant and animal species have become extinct, with many more species such as Orangutans, Sumatran Tigers, Elephants and Rhinos becoming critically endangered.

Sumatra, like Java, is covered with volcanoes, with the largest and deadliest being Lake Toba. Volcanic ash and eruptions are always a hazard when flying in Sumatra. The weather is also horrendous, with the North of the island around the Malacca Straight having the second most severe thunderstorm activity on the entire planet. Earthquakes and tsunamis are also a major threat in Sumatra. The Boxing Day tsunami of 2004 killed approximately 170,000 Indonesians living on the North coast of Sumatra, most of whom were in Banda Aceh.

The city of Medan was the main base of Susi Air for Sumatra. Medan is a reasonably clean, modern and vibrant city, at least by Indonesian standards. This was where the Sumatra based pilots lived, and for the most part, worked. However every once and a while, these pilots would be sent on "tour" for a few nights in the satellite bases in Banda Aceh, Jambi and

Bengkulu. These satellite bases were used to fulfil specific, temporary contracts for Susi Air.

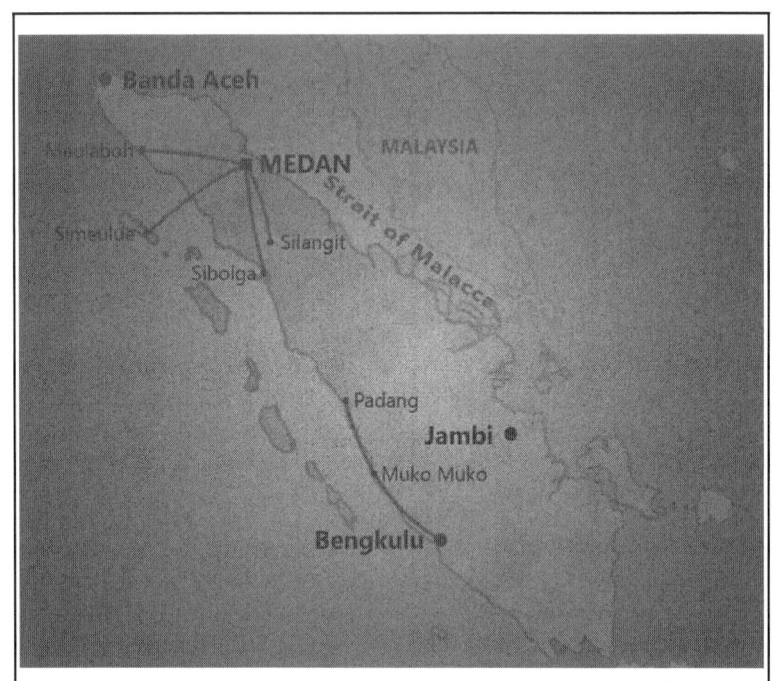

Above: The Sumatra base (Medan), satellite bases (Banda Aceh, Jambi and Bengkulu) and destinations that I flew to, during my 4 weeks in Sumatra.

A large minority of the population in Medan (around 35%) is Christian, many of whom are from Chinese decent. As a result of this particular demographic, there are many shops in Medan which import food and drinks from outside of Indonesia. Unlike most cities in Indonesia, Medan also boasts many bars and upmarket restaurants. The quality of life in Medan is actually quite good. This modern, secular city is in stark contrast to the rest of Sumatra, which is predominantly conservative Muslim.

Jambi and Bengkulu are both small to medium sized cities, where the vast majority of the residents are from a conservative Muslim background. Naturally, there are no bars or shops which serve alcohol in either of these cities, and entertainment of any kind tends to be quite limited. There aren't many things to see or do in these cities, so life can sometimes be a bit tedious when you're not flying. However at least the people are still pleasant, friendly and appear to be welcoming of non Muslims.

The Aceh province, surrounding the city of Banda Aceh, is a semi autonomous region of Indonesia. It was granted this special status by the Indonesian Government following a failed uprising in 1958. Unlike the rest of Indonesia, Aceh is indeed an Islamic theocracy which implements most forms of Shariah law, including public caning for dressing immodestly (and no, tourists are not immune from these archaic laws). The authorities in Aceh have previously claimed that the public caning is solely for humiliation, and is not intended to cause excruciating pain to the unlucky victim. (Not that it would be ok either way).

Aceh hasn't quite got to the stage yet where they publicly execute people for religious offences, like they do in Saudi Arabia and Iran. However unfortunately they appear to be heading in that direction. Many Imans in the province preach that the tsunami was a direct result of Allah's rage, as Aceh wasn't quite "Islamic enough". They have exploited the fear from this tragedy in order to further their own agenda...removing the civil rights from the citizens of Aceh.

I'm actually quite glad that the main Susi Air base in Sumatra was located in Medan.

CHAPTER 13

ARRIVING IN MEDAN

Prior to being based in Medan, Miranda, Ricardo, Francois and myself would need to leave the country. One of the requirements of the 12 month "Business Visa" which we each held, is that we weren't allowed to remain in Indonesia for any longer than 2 months at any one time. Leaving the country for just the one day was absolutely fine, however the Indonesian authorities wanted us to leave and come back on a regular basis. I assume it was to make it easier for them to kick us out of the country in the event that we ever pissed them off. The whole thing seemed a bit daft, but ultimately it was their country and their rules. As we would be based in Medan, the Susi Air ticketing department booked each of us tickets to Kuala Lumpur in Malaysia for our "visa run". From there it would be just a short flight across the Malacca Straight to Medan.

Kuala Lumpur was a 90 minute flight from Jakarta. We arrived in KL at around 9am and spent the rest of morning exploring the modern and vibrant city. We visited the Petronas Towers; the tallest twin towers in the World. At just under half a kilometre in height, these towers really were quite amazing to view, especially from directly below. Not only were the sheer scale of these towers mesmerising, but the architecture was also aesthetically pleasing. They weren't simply large slabs of glass and concrete which you'd find in most cities. A great deal of thought had been put into designing these structures so that they would appear to be both modern, yet have a traditional Malaysian style of architecture.

Above: A photo of the Petronas Towers which I took from about 100 metres from the main entrance. Due to the sheer scale of these buildings, it was only possible to photograph the top half.

Nearby the Petronas Towers was a food court where we went for lunch. Strangely enough, there didn't appear to be any Malaysian cuisine anywhere in this food court, or any type of Asian cuisine for that matter. We instead made do with an "Italian" takeaway. I ordered a vegetarian pizza. The staff served me a soggy microwaved pizza with frozen peas and carrots on the top. This bizarre pizza topping hadn't quite defrosted yet. The others found this amusing, however lost their sense of humour when the spaghetti bolognaise which they each ordered, turned out to be overcooked pasta with what appeared to be tomato ketchup over the top. Despite being a relatively affluent and modern country, it turned out that the food in Malaysia was almost as bad as the food in Indonesia. Almost. We ate what we could of our lunch, then headed back to the airport for our connecting flight to Medan.

The flight from KL to Medan was bumpy as hell. The crew of our A320 made multiple turns in the cruise to avoid the worst of the weather. It was the late afternoon, and the Malacca Straight dividing Malaysia and Sumatra was littered with thunderstorms large enough to penetrate the stratosphere. I must admit, this actually made me a tad nervous. Normally, as a passenger on an airliner, I really couldn't care less about turbulence or bad weather. But the problem was, in just a couple of days time, I was going to be flying in this very same region in a small aircraft, just a fraction of the size of this Airbus. If we were getting violently thrown about in a 70 tonne airliner, I would have hated to imagine flying a Caravan in the same weather.

The Base Manager of Sumatra was Rik, a Dutch pilot who had been flying Caravans for Susi Air for about 4 years. Rik had previously sent us an email welcoming us to the base. In this email, Rik confirmed that our transport and accommodation had already been arranged. He also included a link to the schedule and an intranet site which he created for new pilots with information about the base. He was very organised. Base Managers in Susi Air were senior pilots who were responsible for scheduling and keeping the other pilots in check. I have to say, Rik was one of the best Base Managers that I would meet throughout my time in Susi Air.

After landing in Medan "Polonia" airport, we taxied to the apron. I could see 2 Susi Air Cessna Grand Caravans parked close to our stand. This was pretty damn exciting! Very soon we would be flying real passengers from this very same airport. After collecting our checked luggage from the conveyor belt, we made our way outside of the arrivals hall to meet our driver. There wasn't any space for us in the company accommodation, so instead Rik had arranged for us all to stay in a 4 star hotel in the centre of Medan. This guy was amazing!

We checked into the hotel and spent the rest of the evening chilling by the pool. It was there that we would meet a French Susi Air FO who was also staying in the same hotel. It turned out that Susi Air had recently "lost" one of the houses that they had used for pilot accommodation. When I say that they "lost" the house, I mean that Susi apparently decided not to pay the rent. As a result, all the pilots in that house were kicked out by the owner, and Rik needed to make arrangements for them to stay in a hotel instead. The French FO seemed quite happy though. He had been staying in that 4 star hotel for over a week before we arrived, and was currently running up a massive room service bill. Steak, beers, desserts. You name it, he ordered it. He was a pretty easy going guy. He always had a smile on his face and really just couldn't give a fuck if he got into trouble. He was an absolute legend.

Although we had completed our Initial course in Pangandaran, our training would continue in Medan. We would first need to spend a day doing "observation flights", where we would sit in the front passenger seat of a scheduled flight and watch the pilots perform their duties. Once this was complete, we would then be rostered for our "line training", where we would fly with an experienced Captain for our first 10 days of flying. During these 10 days, the Captain would tick boxes on our line training forms in order to confirm that we had completed various different procedures to an acceptable standard. However the term "experienced" Captain, was a fairly loose term. Our line training forms stated that it could be anyone with more than 100 hours flight time as a Caravan Captain. In other words, brand new First Officers like us, could potentially be flying with brand new Captains! This was a tad concerning.

I was rostered for my observation flight the following day. The Sumatra District Manager (not to be confused with Base Manager), Fitri, had previously sent me a text, confirming that my driver would pick me up from my hotel at 5:30am and take me to Polonia airport. I woke up the following day at 4:30am and dressed into my pilots uniform. I looked at myself in the mirror, wearing the pilot shirt which I had carefully ironed the night before. I slid on my 3 bar epaulettes on to each of my shoulders. My dream had finally come true; I was finally going to be a commercial pilot! Today I would just be an observer, but very soon I would be flying those passengers myself.

It may have been early in the morning, but I was full of energy and excitement. I made my way downstairs to the restaurant for breakfast.

However with the excitement, I also felt a sense of nervousness. I may have just been an observer, however it was still my first day on the job. What if I didn't make a good impression on the other pilots? What if I said something dumb? What if I got lost at the airport, trying to find the crew room? Looking back, these were all pretty daft things to be worrying about. However as a result of this anxiety, I couldn't eat anything for breakfast. I simply had too much adrenaline inside of me. Or was it the extra strong Sumatran coffee which I'd just drank? All that I knew was that I was eager to get to the airport.

I waited outside for the driver. It was still pitch black outside. I waited...and waited...and waited. It was now 5:45am, and still no driver. The flight itself was a 7am departure, and the hotel was only 15 minutes drive from the airport. I second guessed myself. Maybe I was in the wrong meeting point? I double checked the text from Fitri; it specifically stated the hotel lobby at 5:30am. This was odd. I was standing outside of the only entrance to this hotel. I walked inside and searched the lobby for anyone appearing to be a Susi Air driver. However the lobby was completely empty. I went over to the reception desk and asked if the driver had arrived. However they hadn't seen anyone. I went back outside. It was now nearly 6am, and still no sign of the driver. My flight departed in one hour. I was getting worried.

I phoned Fitri to ask her about the driver, however there was no answer. Crap! This was my first day on the job and I was going to miss my flight! I rushed back to the reception and asked them to book me a taxi. They confirmed that it would arrive in 10 minutes. I continued to phone Fitri multiple times, however still no answer. She must have still been asleep. The taxi driver arrived at 6:15am and took me straight to the airport. I went through security to the departure lounge. It was from there that I would need to ask a member of staff to let me out through the doors leading to the aircraft apron. From there I could then walk to the Susi Air crew room, a small portable cabin located next to the main terminal building. Back in those days, Susi Air pilots didn't carry aircrew IDs. I was actually a bit concerned that I wouldn't be allowed out onto the apron because of this. However the boarding agent that I spoke to appeared to be happy enough to open the door for me, leading airside. Back then, due to their hierarchical culture, pretty much anyone could wear a uniform in Indonesia and go pretty much anywhere they wanted, without being challenged.

I checked the time on my phone, it was now 6:55am! I rushed towards where the crew room was located. As I ran, I heard the distant humming of a Pratt & Whitney PT6 turboprop. From behind the portable cabin that Susi Air were using as a crew room, I saw a Caravan taxiing towards the runway. There were 4 Caravans based in Medan, maybe that wasn't my plane? I continued to run to the portable cabin, so that I could check the apron from behind. There was nothing to see. All of the Caravan's had now departed.

Two of the Susi Air ground crew were sitting inside of the portable cabin, staring at me from out the door. One of them stood up and came outside to speak to me. "That your plane!", he shouted with a grin on his face, pointing to the Caravan, which was by now, backtracking down the runway. The other ground crewman came outside to get in on the joke. He was laughing hysterically. "Cap! Cap!", he shouted, less than a meter away from my face, "That your plane!". And this brings me to the next lesson of this book.

LESSON 7: MAKE SURE THAT YOU HAVE A GOOD SENSE OF HUMOUR WHEN VISITING INDONESIA

I looked blankly at the Caravan, which was now rolling down the runway. My soul was crushed. I'd missed my first day at work. Was I going to get into trouble? This definitely wasn't how I'd hoped to begin my career as a commercial pilot; missing my own flight! The first ground crewman stood next to me, looking in the same direction of the departing aircraft. "Look, look! That your plane!", he shouted, pointing at the Caravan, which was now completely airborne. Not appreciating my joyless reaction, he tugged gently on my shirt to get my attention. "That your plane, Cap!", he repeated. "Err...yeah, I kind of guessed that", I muttered. The other ground crewman looked at me, by this stage pissing himself laughing. They both found this situation hilarious. However as irritating as it may have been given the circumstance, their laughter was somewhat contagious. They continued to taunt me until I finally broke; I burst out laughing too. Fuck it, I thought. What's done is done.

Eventually I managed to get through to Fitri to explain the situation. She assured me that I wouldn't get into any trouble as a result. She advised me to wait at the airport for the pilots to return back. I was rostered to observe 4 sectors for that day, however I would still be able to observe the last 2 sectors. The pilots were rostered to return to Polonia at 9.15am, then depart on the last 2 sectors at 10am. I returned back to the terminal whilst I waited for the pilots. Inside the terminal I found a VIP lounge, where for 50,000 Rupiahs (about £3), I could wait inside a relatively comfortable, air conditioned area, with free food and drinks. By this stage the adrenaline had worn off, and tiredness was kicking in. I found an unoccupied arm chair in the lounge, sat down, and rested my eyes for a while.

At 9am, two pilots entered the VIP lounge and headed straight for the buffet. I looked at them from my table. They had no tie and no ID. They must have been Susi Air pilots! The Captain, a fairly short, skinny chap with a bald head, made eye contact with me. With his mouth half full of food, he shouted "You must be Dan!", from across the lounge. He must have been the Captain who I was supposed to be observing. I went over to shake his hand and apologise for missing the first 2 sectors. "No problem!", he replied with a smile on his face, "My name's Ned by the way". Ned was a Danish Captain who'd been flying for Susi Air for around 3 years. He seemed like a pretty happy go lucky guy. He was accompanied by his Finnish FO, Alex. As I chatted with them, it turned out that one of the drivers in the base would often turn up late, if not at all. So Ned was actually quite sympathetic of my situation.

At 9:30am we headed back to the portable cabin where the aircraft was parked. The next stop would be Silangit, an airport located to the South of Lake Toba. This was one of the shorter flights of Susi Air in Sumatra, scheduled at just 40 minutes each way. I sat down in the first row and plugged my headset into the auxiliary jack. I watched Ned and Alex carefully as they each completed their pre flight duties. Ned completed and signed the ATC flight plan, whilst Alex completed the weight and balance form. After the boarding and final walk around was complete, Ned started the engine. He then loaded the route into the GPS, whilst Alex set up the weather radar and Bluesky flight plan.

Alex was going to fly to Silangit, then Ned was going to fly back to Medan Polonia. As Ned was the Pilot Monitoring for that flight, it was up to him to make the passenger briefing...in Indonesian. This was something which we never practised during training! I listened carefully as Ned read out the Indonesian passenger briefing from memory, taking approximately 20 seconds to complete the 120 word announcement, with flawless pronunciation. Christ! This guy was like an Indonesian auctioneer! How was I supposed to say that? I knew that I would need to start practising the passenger briefings as soon as I got back to the hotel.

After take off, Ned and Alex had a few Cumulonimbus clouds to avoid. A Cumulonimbus cloud, abbreviated in aviation to CB, is a large, mushroom shaped cloud with a high level of water content. A CB is usually the beginning of a thunderstorm, and creates a very large amount of turbulence in the surrounding areas. Ned and Alex made some deviations to their heading in order to avoid the worst of the CBs. Once clear of the weather, we proceeded directly to Silangit.

We crossed over the top of Lake Toba, the largest lake in Indonesia. A lake which is in fact, far larger than Singapore, an entire country! Due to the haze and the sheer size of this large mass of water, I couldn't see from one side of the lake to the other. However I could clearly see the island located in the centre of this lake; a large, inhabited land mass called Samosir. Ned looked back at me and pointed to down. "Have you ever been there?!", he shouted over the noise of the propeller. "Not yet!", I replied. Ned advised me that is was a good place to visit for a holiday. The water was pristine and the temperature was cooler and less humid than the rest of Indonesia, due to the high elevation.

With the sightseeing over, Alex began his descent into Silangit. Ned once again made a flawless passenger briefing in Indonesian. (I really needed to practice those briefings). Silangit was a medium sized airport. The runway was large enough to land a medium sized jet, however it was mainly used by small turboprop aircraft like ours. Alex made a text book landing at Silangit and taxied to the apron. The passengers disembarked and the next passengers arrived. It was a fairly quick turnaround of 15 minutes. Now it was Ned's turn to fly us back.

The flight back was for the most part uneventful…until we approached Medan. The CBs which we had seen on our outbound flight had now grown up into very large thunderstorms, one of which was now directly over Polonia airport. After consulting with ATC, Ned proceeded to orbit in his current location. He looked back at me and pointed at the fuel quantity indicator. "Make sure you tanker fuel over here, even on the short flights!", he advised. He was quite right. The weather in Indonesia changes very quickly, especially in Northern Sumatra. Ned had approximately 750lbs of fuel left in his tanks. That worked out at an extra 1 hour of fuel before we reached our 400lb reserve. Ned continued orbiting for about 20 minutes whilst the storm passed over Polonia. He then asked Alex to request a "direct to final" approach to the runway, from ATC. 15 minutes later, we were safely on the ground, albeit a bit late.

After securing the aircraft for the next flight crew, I thanked Ned and Alex for their time, and shook their hands. I'd learned a lot that day:

1. The importance of taking extra fuel.

2. The importance of having a good sense of humour.

3. And the importance of saving the phone number of a reliable taxi firm in case the driver didn't bother turning up!

CHAPTER 14

LINE TRAINING

This was the moment that I had been waiting for ever since I knew that I wanted to be a pilot; my first commercial flight with passengers! I had been rostered as an FO for my first flight just two days after my observation flights. The Captain who I would be flying with would be the boss of Sumatra himself, Rik. He was going to be in charge of my first day of line training. My remaining 9 days of line training would be rostered with various other Captains.

Unlike my previous observation flights, my flights with Rik would be afternoon flights. This had it's advantages, in the sense that I could now wake up at a more reasonable time in the morning. However the downside of flying in the afternoon is that the weather tends to be fucking horrendous, especially in Northern Sumatra. Rik had rostered us both to fly a 4 sector day together. From Medan Polonia, we would first fly to Silangit, then back again to Polonia. We would then stop for about an hour to have lunch, before then completing another return flight to and from Meulaboh, a large town located on the West coast of the Aceh province.

Fortunately on this particular occasion, the driver actually turned up for my first flight. After arriving at the airport, I proceeded through security and made my way to the portable cabin that Susi Air were using as a crew room. It was there that I would meet Rik for the first time in person. Rik had been sorting out paperwork in the cabin before our flight. He may have been a pilot flying nearly 100 hours a month, however as a manager he also needed to organise the office. Regardless of how busy he must have been, he was only to happy to drop what he was doing when I arrived. He came outside to introduce himself and shake my hand. He was a really friendly and humble guy. That was somewhat of a relief, as I was actually dreading to fly with the boss for my first ever scheduled flight!

About 10 minutes later, our aircraft taxied to the apron after completing the morning schedule. I followed Rik as he walked over to greet the last crew flying the aircraft. They were sat inside the cockpit completing the last of the paperwork for the flight. We briefly introduced ourselves and then swapped seats. The fuel truck arrived and Rik gave them the fuel figures. I plugged in my headset and began the pre flight inspection with Rik. As we were completing the external inspection, Rik quizzed me on various items to make sure that I knew what I was checking. He paid particular attention to the engine compartment. "What does it mean if you see blue dye on the bottom of the engine cowling?", he asked. "The blue dye is from the FCU", I replied, "It means that the casing has broken".

The FCU, or Fuel Control Unit, was a mechanical device which ensured that the correct amount of fuel was delivered to the combustion chamber of the engine. It was purposefully designed by Cessna to leak a blue dye in case it ever broke, so that it would be obvious during an inspection. The FCU was an incredibly complicated device which contained various different valves and mechanical levers. It was designed to adjust the fuel flow depending on the power lever position, amongst many other factors such as the altitude, temperature and engine indications. The designer of this FCU really was a genius, as this was all done mechanically, without any electronic input whatsoever. "And do you know how the FCU works?", asked Rik. I paused, hesitated, then told him the truth. "Err...I'm not quite sure", I replied. Rik laughed, "That makes two of us then!". Rik was a practical pilot. As long as you knew *what* the outcome of a system failure would be, he couldn't care less if you knew *how* the system actually worked.

The ground crew bought us the passenger manifest, a document which had details of the weights of all of the passengers and their baggage. Once the manifest was received, Rik shouted "Boarding!", to the ground crew, to indicate that we were now ready for the passengers. As FO, it was my job to use the information from the manifest to calculate the weight and balance of the aircraft. I wrote down the weights from the manifest onto the weight and balance form, then got out my pocket calculator. I needed to be quick with the calculations as the passengers were coming, however not too quick that I might make a mistake. After adding up all of the weights and moments, I was relieved to see that both the weight and the arm (centre of gravity), were within the limits of the aircraft. If they weren't, then I would have needed to start the weight and balance again from scratch!

PT ASI Pudjiastuti Aviation Weight & Balance Form

REGISTRATION NO: BVD   CESSNA 208B GRAND CARAVAN
DATE / TIME: 2/3/15   FLIGHT NO / CUSTOMER:
FROM: WIMM   TO: WITC

Instructions:
1. Determine aircraft and configuration, enter empty weight, arm and moment in appropriate column.
2. Enter all passenger and load data into columns and calculate moment.
3. Add all weights and all moments for takeoff. Divide moment by weight for arm.
4. Check load position on chart page 2.   5. Subtract fuel used and moment.
6. Determine landing weight and moment. Divide Moment by weight for arm.
7. Check load position on chart page 2.   1 kg = 2.2 Pounds

Load Calculation	Weight	Arm	Moment
Empty Weight	5157	190.15	980,604
Useable Fuel	1300	203.77	264,901
Pilots	340	135.50	46,070
Row 1 (1 - 3)	510	174.00	88,740
Row 2 (4 - 6)	340	210.00	71,400
Row 3 (7 - 9)	340	246.00	83,640
Row 4 (10 - 12)		282.00	
Row 5 (10a - 12a)	510	344.00	175,440
Zone 1		172.00	
Zone 2		217.80	
Zone 3		264.40	
Zone 4	120	294.50	35,340
Zone 5		319.50	
Zone 6		344.00	
Pod A (230 lbs maximum)		132.40	
Pod B (310 lbs maximum)	240	182.10	43,704
Pod C (270 lbs maximum)	130	233.40	30,342
Pod D (280 lbs maximum)	20	287.60	5,752
Ramp Weight	9007	202.72	1,825,933
Start & Taxi	-35	203.77	-7,20
Takeoff Weight & Moment	8972	202.72	1,818,801
Fuel Used	-350	203.77	-71,320
Landing Weight & Moment	8622	202.68	1,747,481

PREPARED BY: APPROVED BY:
White Original: Origin Airport   Blue Copy: Aircraft

Above: The weight and balance form which we needed to complete before each flight. By adding the moments together and dividing by the total weight, we could calculate the arm (centre of gravity) of the aircraft.

The passengers arrived at the aircraft just as I was signing the completed weight and balance form. I gave the form to Rik to countersign, then stood by the rear aircraft door to meet and greet the passengers as they boarded. After the last passenger boarded the aircraft, I briefly stepped inside the cabin to check that all the passengers were belted up, then went back outside to close the door and signal to the ground crew to remove the tail stand of the aircraft. I completed the final walk around and climbed up into the cockpit. As Rik was going to be the PF (Pilot Flying) for the first flight, it was my job to brief the passengers...in Indonesian. This was the moment that I had been dreading!

I put on my headset and pressed the PA button on the intercom. I then picked up the briefing card (a script written by the company in Bahasa Indonesia) and slowly began to recite the "Before Departure" briefing over the intercom to the passengers. "Selamat Siang...para penumpang...yang terhomat...selamat datang...di Susi Air". Roughly translated: "Good afternoon, please can I have your attention, welcome aboard this Susi Air flight". It took me almost a minute just to say this first sentence and I'm pretty sure I balls up the pronunciation of every single word. I could hear the passengers laughter from behind me. Rik, who was also laughing quite unashamedly, stepped in and made the passenger briefing for me. It took him about 20 seconds to complete the full briefing and he didn't even need to look at the briefing card!

After Rik started the engine, I set up the weather radar and entered the Bluesky flight plan. We completed the Before Taxi checklist and I requested the taxi instructions from ATC. We then continued with the rest of the checklists whilst Rik taxied to the runway for take off. Rik flew the aircraft whilst I monitored him and operated the radio. The first flight was uneventful. The weather was surprisingly good for that time of day; there weren't many CBs...at least not yet. Rik landed in Silangit, taxied to the apron and shutdown the engine. I hopped out of the aircraft and checked that the ground crew had installed the tail stand, shortly before opening the rear door so that the passengers could disembark. The ground crew handed me the manifest for the next flight and I completed the weight and balance form. Rik completed the ATC flight plan form and called for boarding. Now it was my turn to fly!

As the passengers were boarding, I gave Rik a quick departure briefing. He seemed happy enough with what I said. I completed the final walk around and climbed back into the aircraft. Rik gave the briefing to the passengers this time, (which was a relief to myself), shortly before starting the engine. We completed the Before Taxi checklist and Rik asked ATC for our taxi instructions. I carefully taxied the aircraft to the holding point of the runway whilst we completed the Taxi and Line Up checklists. ATC gave us our take off clearance and I lined up on to the centre line of the runway. I slowly advanced the power lever forward whilst applying back pressure to the control column, before asking Rik to set the take off thrust. As we accelerated down the bumpy runway, I allowed the nose wheel to hover just a few inches above the tarmac. At about 65 knots, our main wheels lifted off the ground and I smoothly rotated to 8 degrees nose up. At 400 feet I lowered the nose slightly to accelerate and retract the flaps, whilst turning on track for Medan.

Asides from my foreign language skills, Rik seemed impressed with my performance so far. My handling of the aircraft was fairly smooth and I was following all of the correct procedures. I was actually quite proud of myself. I briefed the approach into runway 05 to Rik, and we commenced our descent into Polonia. One of the points that Rik mentioned to me during the briefing, was that he wanted me to land at a point which was much further from the usual touchdown zone of the runway. When landing on a large runway, it is common practice for all aircraft, both big and small, to pass over the threshold at 50 feet and touch down 300 metres later. However the taxiway to vacate the runway at Polonia was all the way at the end, and the runway was nearly 3 km long! If we landed on the 300 metre touchdown marker, it would take us a very long time to vacate the runway, meaning any aircraft behind us would need to go around.

"I want you to aim *after* the last touchdown marker", said Rik over the loud sound of the engine. "Understood.", I replied. And this brings me to the next lesson of the book.

LESSON 8: BE CAREFUL WHAT YOU SAY TO YOUR COPILOT

Above: Final approach to runway 05 in Polonia airport. Due to the distance of the taxiway, we needed to aim for a touchdown point further down the runway than that of a large aircraft.

Rik wanted me to land *after* the last touchdown marker on the runway (900 metres from the threshold), however he didn't say *how far* after. Based on my very limited experience, I knew that I could stop the aircraft in about 600 metres or so after landing, without slamming on the brakes. We were a bit heavy, so I planned for 700 metres to be safe. Based on that, I decided to aim for a point approximately 200 metres after the last touchdown marker. However something which I forgot to consider, was that Rik would have had very little confidence in a brand new Caravan pilot being able to touchdown and stop the aircraft with any large amount of accuracy. Unbeknown to me at the time, he was expecting me to touchdown *just* after the last touchdown marker. (He would have been better off just telling me to land *on* the last touchdown marker).

As I manoeuvred the aircraft onto final approach, I asked Rik for flaps 30 and the Finals checklist. We appeared to be on profile; not too high, not too low. Rik kept silent, so I assumed that he was happy. If Rik was happy, I was happy. My first passenger flight appeared to be going quite well, I thought. It wasn't until after we passed over the threshold of the runway that Rik informed me otherwise. "You're getting too high!", he told me. I reduced the power slightly and steepened the approach, so that we would land closer to the last touchdown marker. 10 seconds later, he shouted, "You're still too high!".

Still now, even to this very day, this would be the worst landing that I would ever make in my entire career as a pilot. With Rik's final words of that flight, just 50 feet above the runway, I panicked. I immediately jerked the power lever back to idle, causing the prop to disk. I needed to pitch down to stop the aircraft from stalling. Rik immediately moved the power lever forward to arrest the descent, causing the prop to surge. Now, just 20 feet above the runway, still with a high descent rate, both myself and Rik pulled the control column back to prevent going nose first into the tarmac...

...Bounce!

After what could be best described as being the first "impact", the spring loaded suspension of the main landing gear launched us back up into the sky. We were now pitched nose up with a dangerously low speed. I immediately pitched down and increased the power to prevent us from stalling. Perhaps he was just lost for words, however for some reason Rik still hadn't instructed me to hand over control to him. Given the situation, I would have been only too glad to do so. We bounced down the runway a few more times, eventually landing for good.

The worst part of that flight wasn't necessarily the landing itself. The worst part was after we had parked and shut down the engine. As the Caravan was an open cockpit, all of the passengers could see the pilots. Even to this day, I still remember turning around and seeing all 12 passengers stare at me in utter disgust. I apologised to them in Indonesian. I honestly felt so ashamed. However Rik seemed to have a sense of humour about the whole situation. "Your third landing was the best!", he remarked with a grin on his face. Rik asked the base engineer to take a look at the axial of the main landing gear for signs of damage. Fortunately the Caravan was specifically designed by Cessna to take a great deal of punishment. The landing gear was fine. Any other aircraft would have probably been written off. It would be another hour before our next flight. Myself and Rik walked back to the terminal for lunch.

Our next flight was to Meulaboh, and this time we would have a very special guest onboard; the Governor of Aceh. The Governor was a very high ranking Indonesian politician. He was the dictator...I mean leader...of the 5 million plus residents of the semi autonomous province of Aceh. Due to Susi's connections with the political elite, it wasn't uncommon to have such high ranking officials on our flights. (Some of my colleagues have even flown the Indonesian President himself). I was going to be the PF for this next flight. After all of the pre flight paperwork was complete, I stood by the rear door to meet and greet the VIP and his entourage. I completed the final walk around and climbed back up into the cockpit for the third time that day. Rik turned around to me and smiled. "New flight, new start", he told me. I smiled back. He was right. Mistakes happen. We should always learn from our mistakes, but never dwell on them.

The flight to Meulaboh went quite smoothly. There were a few CBs enroute, however nothing too major. My landing in Meulaboh was definitely a massive improvement. I managed to touch down where I needed to, with the main wheels gently "kissing" the tarmac. Rik looked at me. "Told you!", he said. This was certainly a confidence booster. I taxied to the apron and shutdown the engine. I had drank a bit too much coffee before the flight and by this point my bladder was almost bursting. I really needed to take a leak. I asked Rik where the toilet was located in the airport. "It's in front of the terminal", he replied, "but you really don't want to go there". Well unless I was going to unzip my flies and piss on the apron in front of the Governor of Aceh, I really didn't have much of a choice.

I needed to wait a few more seconds after shutdown before opening my door, in order to avoid getting burnt by the red hot engine exhaust. (The exhaust pipe of the Caravan is located on the FO's side of the aircraft). As soon as I was confident that my flesh wasn't going to get welded onto the exhaust pipe, I opened my door and lowered the ladder. I then promptly walked into the terminal to find the toilet. The terminal itself, much like the entire airport in Meulaboh, was quite small, so there wasn't any chance of getting lost. I made my way into the single story terminal building, past the only security guard in the entire airport, and then out through the main entrance. It was from there that I found the door to the one and only toilet in the entire airport.

As soon as I opened the door, I instantly understood what Rik was talking about. For those readers who have watched the movie "Trainspotting", do you remember the scene where Ewan McGregor walks into "the worst toilet in the whole of Glasgow"? Now imagine something similar, however instead of there being an actual toilet, there was nothing more than a large hole in the ground. I'm not even going to mention what was on the floor surrounding this hole, however you can use your imagination. Let's just say, I needed to be very careful where I stood. And this brings me to the next lesson.

LESSON 9: ALWAYS CARRY ALCOHOL GEL WITH YOU IN INDONESIA

After I had finished what I needed to do, I looked around for a sink to wash my hands. Of course there was no sink. There was a tap located on the bottom of the wall, however not a drop of water came out. I now understood why the toilet was in the state that it was. Due to the precarious way in which I needed to position myself over the hole in order to avoid stepping in something very bad, I needed to place my hands up against the grimy, piss-soaked walls. My hands were very sticky. There was no soap and no water. I didn't even have any alcohol gel or wet wipes to clean with. My OCD began to kick in.

I remembered that there were some wet wipes in the cockpit of the aircraft. I would need to promptly walk back to the aircraft, whilst avoiding touching anything. I carefully unbolted the door of the toilet and walked outside. About 50 metres away from me, just outside the main entrance of the terminal, was the Governor of Aceh. The local press, delighted that such a high ranking official would visit Meulaboh, had been waiting for his arrival. He was surrounded by a camera crew and a journalist was interviewing him with a microphone for the local news. Half way through his interview, the Governor made eye contact with me. Shit! How was I going to make it back to the aircraft? He was standing right in front of the entrance to the terminal! To make matters worse, he began walking up to me...and he was being followed by the press. It appeared that he wanted to shake my hand in front of the cameras!

The Governor approached me with his hand held out. Standing behind him were approximately 10 journalists, some of whom were still filming. What happened next was one of the most difficult decisions that I had ever needed to make in my entire life. Do I contaminate the Governor of Aceh with the dried urine on my hands, or do I embarrass him in front of the media by refusing to shake his hand? I hesitated...and then held my hand out. He wrapped his hand firmly around mine, whilst looking very seriously towards the cameras. He had absolutely no idea. I looked towards the cameras also, with an awkward smile on my face.

I walked back to the aircraft with my head held low. That was the second time that day that I had felt utterly ashamed of myself. I thoroughly cleaned my hands with the wet wipes and started the weight and balance calculations. I had one more flight left to Polonia, then the day would finally be over.

CHAPTER 15

FIRST TOUR

A couple of days after my somewhat eventful first day of line training, I was scheduled to fly again from Medan Polonia in the morning. This time I would be flying to the island of Simeulue with Ned, the Captain from my observation flights. Unlike my previous flights with Rik, most of our passengers, both there and back, were bules. Simeulue is popular with professional surfers from all over the World, as the waves can grow to epic sizes. We needed to remove a column of seats from inside the cabin in order to fit all of the surfboards from the passengers.

The approach into Simeulue was quite interesting, as it involved circling around the island and then descending inland between some very tall palm trees. The sea was a translucent turquoise, the trees were a bright green and the sand was a brilliant white. It really seemed like an island paradise. The flights, both there and back, went very well. Something which I did notice however, was that I felt a bit uncomfortable flying across the ocean. On reflection, this was partly because we were flying a single engine aircraft and I didn't have too much faith in the 6 person life raft that we were carrying onboard our 14 seater aircraft. However it was also partly due to the optical illusion of the sea looking like the sky, which is especially prevalent in hazy conditions. If you didn't focus on your instruments it would have been very easy to become disorientated. In fact, this disorientation between the sea and the sky is suspected to be one of the reasons why so many light aircraft go missing over the Bermuda Triangle.

Above: Flying on top of the clouds to Simeulue. Or were we? Was that the sea or sky above us? (On this occasion, my camera was upside down, not the aircraft).

I returned back to the hotel after my flight to Simeulue. I would need to pack my suitcase for the following day. I had been scheduled for a 4 day tour in Bengkulu, one of the satellite bases of Medan. I would be flying with a young Norwegian Captain by the name of Stian. We were scheduled the following morning for a "ferry" flight from Medan to Padang. This ferry flight was for repositioning purposes only; there wouldn't be any passengers. From Padang we would collect our first passengers and fly them to Muko Muko, before flying another batch of passengers from Muko Muko to Bengkulu, where we would be staying for the next 3 nights.

Prior to my tour of Bengkulu, Rik had advised me to bring a book to read. This was partly because there was very little to do in Bengkulu, and also partly because Rik knew that Stian was introverted. I mean, really introverted. I met Stian in the minibus on the way to the airport. He seemed pleasant enough, however he was virtually silent. Every time I tried to strike up a conversation with him, he would reply with the most minimal information and without any expression, then end the conversation abruptly. Don't get me wrong, I was far from being an extravert myself, especially back then. But Stian was a whole new level. The ferry flight to Padang was over 2 hours long. Asides from the necessary SOP "call outs", virtually no word was said for the entire flight. In the end, I gave up trying to socialise.

After landing in Padang, we picked up our first passengers. We were scheduled to fly these passengers down the coastline of Sumatra to Muko Muko, a large town located approximately 80 miles South of Padang. I was PF for this flight. On final approach to the runway in Muko Muko, I could see what appeared to be a small dark spot located about halfway down the runway. I thought nothing of it, and continued the approach. It was only after touching down that I could see what the dark spot actually was. It was a tortoise! I didn't even realise that they had tortoises in Sumatra, but yes, there was a fucking tortoise crossing over the middle of the runway, and as you can probably imagine, he wasn't going anywhere fast. I applied maximum reverse thrust and braking. Stian took the controls and swerved to the right of the slow moving reptile. We were still moving at around 30 knots or so by this stage.

Fortunately our wheels managed to remain on the tarmac without running over the poor little chap. Once safely clear, Stian gave the controls back to me and I taxied to the apron. I was actually quite glad that we encountered that runway incursion, as it appeared to have finally broken the ice. "Wow! Did you see that?", commented Stian enthusiastically. "Yeah that was pretty awesome!", I replied, "I'm guessing he's still going to be crossing the runway for our next take off". We both laughed for about 10 to 15 seconds, then Stian suddenly fell silent again. His face was once again absent of any form of expression. He looked over to his left and stepped outside of the aircraft. I cracked on with the weight and balance so that we could depart as soon as possible. We had just one flight left to Bengkulu.

After boarding our final passengers of the day, we taxied out to the holding point of the runway for our departure. Sure enough, the tortoise was still crossing the runway. As we were backtracking the runway, Stian, who was PF, momentarily stopped the aircraft next to the tortoise so that I could take a look. His mouth was wide open, gasping for air, and he was frantically trying to cross over the runway as fast as he could, one arm at a time. The poor guy was trying his best to get out of our way. It wasn't his fault that he was slower than a 56K modem with the phone of it's hook. Stian made a judgment call. Rather than delay the flight, he would simply take off slightly to the right of the centreline. By now, the tortoise was towards the edge of the runway anyway.

The flight to Bengkulu was about 40 minutes long. After the passengers had disembarked, I helped Stian secure the aircraft. Stian installed the chocks for the wheels, whilst I covered the pitot tubes of the aircraft (the probes which measure the air speed). Stian then secured the propeller of the aircraft with a cable, so that the wind couldn't cause the 1.3 metre long aluminium propeller blades to strike an unsuspecting person on the head. After securing the aircraft, I followed Stian through the terminal building to the arrivals hall, where we met Yesaya, our driver. Yesaya, like many Susi Air employees, was originally from Pangandaran. He was quite a cheerful guy. Yesaya drove us straight back to the pilots house, located about 10 minutes away from the airport.

The pilots house was a small, single story building located in a quiet, residential neighbourhood. Desi, the cici (housekeeper), came outside to meet us when we arrived. Myself and Stian were the only people staying in that house. Bengkulu was a very small base for Susi Air; there was only 1 Caravan and 2 pilots based there at any one time. Stian, who had been based in Bengkulu numerous times before, went straight to his bedroom. I noticed from outside his open door, that he had a fairly large bedroom with an en suite bathroom. Not a bad place to stay, I thought. Next to the kitchen, Desi walked towards (what I thought) was a cupboard, and slid open the door. She smiled at me, "This is your room", she said. I walked up to the sliding door to find a very small room with a mattress on the floor. "Err...thanks", I replied. I asked Desi where the bathroom was. She pointed at Stian's room. It appeared that I would need to knock on Stian's door every time that I would need to use the toilet or take a shower.

Yesaya and Desi said goodbye to us and drove off in the minibus. I explored the house. It didn't take too long. There was a small kitchen with a gas stove and a fridge, a living area with a table and 2 chairs, and our bedrooms. I walked outside to see if there was anything interesting to see; just a load of houses spread out over a vast distance. It was only 2pm and I was already bored out of my brains. I knocked on Stian's door to ask if I could use his shower. It was about thirty something degrees outside, there was no air conditioning and I was still wearing my pilot's uniform. I took my wash bag and a change of clothes into Stian's bathroom, and shut the door. I turned on the tap to the shower, however no water came out.

I got dressed back into my uniform and opened the bathroom door. "Stian, how do you turn on the shower?", I asked. Stian walked into his bathroom to investigate. "Maybe the circuit breaker to the pump has tripped", he replied. Stian showed me the circuit breaker box outside the front of the house. He opened the box and reset the tripped circuit breaker. I thanked him and walked back into the bathroom to take a shower. I managed to get a drizzle of cold water out of the shower head for about 2 minutes, before the circuit breaker for the pump tripped again. I shouted out to Stian that it had happened again. "Wait one moment!", he shouted back, "I'll unplug the charger for my laptop and reset the breaker!". 30 seconds later, the water began to dribble out again. Sure enough, it appeared that recharging a laptop whilst taking a shower, was enough to trip the circuit breaker for all of the electrics in the house.

I finished my shower and changed into shorts and t-shirt in the bathroom. I opened the bathroom door and took my things back to my bedroom, whilst being careful not to disturb Stian, who was now laying on his bed whilst watching a movie on his laptop. The bathroom arrangement was a bit awkward. Later that evening, whilst myself and Stian were eating the dinner which Desi had cooked for us previously, I asked him what he did to kill the time in Bengkulu. There weren't any shops or restaurants nearby. There wasn't really anything to see or do. "Normally we just watch movies and series on our laptops", he replied. Stian introduced me to the Susi Air custom of movie swapping. Whenever pilots were based in remote locations with very little to do, and slow internet, they would swap their external hard drives or USB sticks with one another to share movies and TV series. "Have you ever watched Breaking Bad?", asked Stian.

I would spend the next couple of days flying just a few hours in the morning, followed by chronic boredom in the afternoon and evening. We would depart Bengkulu at 7am each morning, then fly to Muko Muko, then Padang, then back again along the same route. By 12pm we would finish work and spend the rest of the day in a run down house in the middle of no where, plagued by power cuts and water shortages. However despite this, I must admit, I did enjoy watching the first season of Breaking Bad.

Above: Curug Embun, located in the middle of the rainforest.

LESSON 10: WHEN IN A REMOTE LOCATION ALWAYS ASK THE LOCALS FOR ADVICE ON THINGS TO DO

You can only watch so many TV series and movies on your laptop before boredom will take over. On the morning of day 3, on the way to the airport, I was talking to Yesaya the driver. Yesaya told me about a waterfall about 1 hour drive outside of Bengkulu, by the name of "Curug Embun". The rock pool at the bottom of this waterfall was suitable for swimming, especially on a hot day. Finally, something to do! Myself and Stian arranged with Yesaya to go there in the afternoon once we had finished work. Desi and the ground crew would come with us as well. Now this was more like it. I didn't travel 8000 miles to Indonesia to stay indoors watching my laptop all day!

Needless to say, the 1 hour trip to Curug Embun was definitely worth it. It was great to finally leave Bengkulu and explore the wilderness of Sumatra. The water, covered by the canopy of the trees, was refreshingly cold. We all jumped into the rock pool to cool off from the equatorial heat. Myself, Stian and the ground crew jumped straight into the deep end, whilst Desi and Yesaya paddled in the shallows. Everyone had a smile on their face. I even saw a resemblance of a grin from Stian, who usually had a poker face. In many ways, being in a small base had its perks. In the larger bases, the Indonesian staff and expat staff would rarely socialise with one another. However in the smaller bases, you were more like one big happy family.

I floated in the water, admiring the natural beauty of the waterfall, situated in the middle of the rainforest. I thought to myself; if I had visited Indonesia as a tourist, would I have even known about this place? Probably not. And that's the great thing about living and working in another country, as opposed to visiting that country as a tourist. I was very lucky indeed.

CHAPTER 16

SUSI AIR ON HOLIDAY

One of the best perks of being a Susi Air pilot were the holidays. Asides from all of the time off that we had from work, there were always plenty of locations nearby which were worthy of a look.

After returning to Medan from my tour in Bengkulu, I would be staying in a different hotel. (Apparently Susi stopped paying the bills of the previous 4 star hotel, however not before racking up an enormous amount of debt). The new hotel was as cheap as could be; the rooms looked like they hadn't been cleaned since the hotel was first constructed thirty something years ago. Fortunately it would only be temporary. Rik and the district manager, Fitri, were already in the final stages of signing a rental agreement for a new house for the pilots.

I had the following day off work. My day off would coincide with the days off of Francois and another FO. Not wanting to waste this day off at home watching TV, we decided to instead spend this time on the island of Simeulue. We managed to get some standby tickets to fly with Susi Air in the morning, and then return the same day on the afternoon flight. When we arrived in Simeulue we asked the Susi Air representative at the check in desk if he could help us book a taxi so that we could go to the beach. The bad news was that there weren't any taxis in Simeulue, and the beach wasn't walking distance either. The good news however was that he instead gave us the keys to the Susi Air minibus so that we could drive ourselves around the island for free. It was time for a road trip!

Francois had done some research on Simeulue beforehand. About 30 minutes drive from the airport was a beach which was suitable for snorkelling. Most of the beaches in Simeulue had very little shelter from the open ocean, with waves growing in excess of 4 metres in height. This was of course great for professional surfers, however as amateurs, we probably would have drowned if we'd tried to surf there. Despite this, there was at least one beach which was sheltered by a coral reef. There were no waves, so of course surfing was out of the question, however it was a great place to snorkel and discover various different species of aquatic life.

We spent a couple of hours in the water, both swimming and snorkelling. I saw plenty of brightly coloured corals, together with several species of small fish. I didn't see any large fish unfortunately. The water was reasonably clean by Indonesian standards. It was quite relaxing. I spent half the time just floating on my back. I asked the others if they had seen anything interesting in the water. Francois told me that he saw a crab, a sea slug and countless small fish. But like me, he didn't see anything particularly large in the water.

In some ways though, that was quite reassuring. Now I could just float on my back without needing to worry about anything below me, biting me. Although there were indeed sharks in Indonesia, they were usually small reef sharks, and even then, they were very rare. I continued to float flat on my back on the surface of the 3 metre deep water, with my arms and legs spread wide out. My fingers and toes were spread out too. I didn't have a care in the World. After all, I didn't need to worry about any large, predatory fish in the water below me, did I?

Well actually, it turned out that we should have indeed been worried about large, predatory fish. We would later learn just a week following our snorkelling trip, that a huge, 4 metre long tiger shark had been spotted off of the coast of Simeulue, close to the location where we'd been snorkelling. Don't get me wrong; I love sharks! They're an important part of our ecosystem and I also enjoy diving with the smaller varieties. But this was a fucking 4 metre long tiger shark! And we weren't diving down to his level, we were instead floating on top of the water with a huge sign saying fucking eat me! As we floated on the surface, he may well have been lurking below us, watching us with his large, scaly eyes. Needless to say, we dodged a bullet that day.

We left the beach in the early afternoon and headed back to the airport. It was now my turn to drive. I didn't want to say to the others at the time, for fear of embarrassment, however I wasn't particularly confident driving a car, let alone a minibus. You see, I'd only very recently passed my driving test and I hadn't driven a car since then. As bizarre as it sounds, I actually had a Commercial Pilots Licence long before I had a drivers licence. I started the engine of the minibus and put it into first gear, before slowly releasing the clutch to the biting point. I released the parking brake and we slowly began to accelerate. I didn't stall the engine! I was actually pleasantly surprised. I slowly drove the minibus along the off road track leading to the main road.

Eventually we came to the junction of the main road which would take us to the airport. I gently applied the brake whilst stepping down on the clutch. I looked carefully in both directions; the road was clear. I slowly pulled out on to the main road. The minibus shook a few times...then stalled. I quickly started the engine again. The others didn't seem to think anything of it. I continued driving down the long, straight road, eventually getting into fifth gear and a speed of around 90 kph (60 mph). I was now starting to feel a lot more confident driving.

Everything was going just fine until we came up to a group of kids on a motorbike ahead of us, driving ridiculously slowly on the road. When I say that they were kids, I mean the oldest one was probably 10 at the most. And there were 3 of them driving a full sized, adult motorbike on the road! They weren't wearing helmets either. I immediately slowed down from 60 mph to 30 mph. The road was long and straight and there was clearly no oncoming traffic. I put it into third gear and began overtaking them on the opposite side of the road. Much to my annoyance, the kid driving the motorbike then began to speed up, blocking me from overtaking. We proceeded to drag race against each other for a few more seconds, however it was apparent that their bike could accelerate a lot faster than our minibus. I braked and manoeuvred back on to my side of the road, behind the kids on the motorbike. They then slowed down again to 30 mph. By now, all 3 kids were pissing themselves laughing.

Francois also saw the funny side of what they were doing. Unfortunately at the time, I didn't. Those muppets were going to end up causing an accident. This was quite possibly the first time that I had ever experienced road rage. I banged the horn multiple times. What was wrong with their parents? This is the reason why most countries don't allow children to drive on the fucking road! Frustrated, I tried over taking them a few more times, with the same result. I was usually very mild mannered back then, however I now found myself in a situation where I needed to remind myself several times that it was neither socially nor legally acceptable to run the little brats over. I was not in a good mood.

However the joke was on them. After about 10 minutes of playing these games, they ran out of petrol. Apparently their parents didn't teach them how to read a fuel gauge either. They slowly pulled over to the side of the road in the middle of nowhere, several miles from the nearest petrol station. I pulled up next to them to see if they were ok. The motorbike kids appeared saddened at their unfortunate dilemma. With sorrow in their eyes, they looked at us for help. We looked at each other...and then burst out laughing. I promptly drove away, leaving them to walk. It served the little brats right. We continued driving to the airport to catch the last flight back to Medan. We were all working the following day.

I would continue to fly from Polonia airport for the remaining 10 days of my 3 week tour of Sumatra. It was an eye opening experience. The weather, especially for the afternoon schedule, was usually horrendous. Large deviations off course were needed to navigate around the most severe of the thunderstorms, whilst being mindful not to stray too close towards the high terrain. CFITs, or Controlled Flight Into Terrain, were always a major threat. Every year in Indonesia, an average of 2 to 3 aircraft, ranging in sizes, crash into high terrain. Medan alone has lost 2 aircraft for such a reason; one Garuda Indonesia A300 and one medium sized turboprop aircraft. (It perhaps didn't help that Medan ATC gave the Garuda A300 radar vectors into the surrounding mountains).

Above: The island of Samosir, in Lake Toba. The lake is larger than the whole of Singapore!

At the end of our 3 week tour of Sumatra we would be given 1 week off before our next tour. Myself, Francois and Ricardo had arranged to meet Rik and a few other pilots in Samosir, the island in the middle of Lake Toba. We would stay there for a few nights, then return back to Medan so that we could fly to our next base. In my case, I was going to be based in Jakarta the following week. We booked some standby tickets with Susi Air to Silangit. From there, we would first take a taxi to Parapat, where the harbour was located, then take the boat across the lake to Samosir and meet the others in the lakeside hotel which we had booked.

After landing in Silangit we found a reasonably priced taxi to take us on the 2 hour drive to the harbour. It was the middle of the afternoon in the equator, yet the temperature was in the early twenties. This refreshing change of climate was partly due to the elevation of Lake Toba (which was about 3000 feet), and also partly due to the very deep, ice cold water. We boarded the taxi boat to Samosir, along with a further 15 or so passengers. The trip was about 20 minutes long. The boat took us directly to a small jetty which connected with the back garden of our hotel. In the distance I could see Rik and the other pilots chilling on sun loungers along the lake front, drinking beers. Before we even checked in to our rooms, we went over to join them for a beer. This is what holidays are about!

The following day Rik had arranged for us all to go on a motorbike trip around the island of Samosir. There were 8 of us in total. After breakfast, we would first ride our bikes to the Batak Museum (a traditional village displaying the history of the native Batak tribe of Northern Sumatra). From there, we would continue to ride 50 km (35 miles) around the circumference of the island, stopping somewhere for lunch on the way. Like driving a car, I was also pretty clueless about riding a motorbike. I was given an automatic scooter to ride. It was probably for the best.

The Batak Museum was an interesting experience. Our tour guide took us around the village, explaining to us about the history and culture of the Batak people. The Bataks were native Sumatrans whose history can be traced back approximately 2,500 years. Like many civilisations across the World, they had a somewhat dark history, which our Batak tour guide was only too happy to teach us. With a grin on his face, he explained to us what the punishment would have been for theft, back in the day. He explained that firstly, they would have kept the alleged thief in a small cage prior to his trial. In absence of any form of a prison back in those days, the punishment upon conviction was invariably death. However the way in which they went about the execution was particularly cruel. Whilst laying back on a stone block, the eyes of the condemned prisoner would be gouged out, and then a mixture of chilli and lime juice would be poured into their eye sockets. Later, they would be disembowelled and have their (still beating) heart yanked out from inside their chest cavity.

Above: The condemned prisoner awaiting execution. Photo taken at the Batak Museum in Samosir.

Don't get me wrong, my own country had a pretty dark history with hanging, drawing and quartering, not to mention having people burned alive at the stake. However this sociopath appeared to be unusually proud of this history, especially given that they still did this up until a century ago. Struggling to hold back on his laughter as he was explaining the method of execution, our Batak guide finally proclaimed to us all, "But at least they couldn't see themselves getting disembowelled! No eyes!". His final statement was met with silence and tumble weeds. We looked at each other. Okaaay then. We decided to make our way for the exit, however our guide quickly stopped us. With a creepy grin on his face, comparable to that of Jack Nicholson in the Shining, he informed us, "You have only paid for the entrance fee, the fee for the tour guide is extra!". Not wanting to be accused of theft, and the penalty which potentially came with that accusation, we decided to cough up the extra money.

We spent the next couple of hours riding our bikes around the rest of the island. Rik was speeding ahead of us all, whilst myself and Francois were trailing behind. We stopped by a restaurant for lunch, then continued around the circumference of the island, eventually arriving back to our hotel. Now it was time for beers and a swim! Our hotel had a diving board above the lake. I dived head first into the lake...and immediately regretted that decision. The air was forced out of my lungs from the shock of the ice cold water. It was colder than a polar bear's feet! Lake Toba is over 500 metres deep, meaning that the vast majority of the water mass would never see the light of day. Regardless of how warm it was outside, the lake itself would always be refrigerated. It took a while to get use to, but eventually my body temperature dropped so much that I didn't notice the cold any more. We continued to dive and swim in the water for another 30 minutes or so. Afterwards I promptly dried off and laid in the sun, before the hypothermia kicked in.

We spent the rest of the day sat there in the sunshine next to the lake, drinking beers and admiring the scenery. It was hard to believe that we were actually getting paid to be here!

CHAPTER 17

A BRIEF GUIDE TO JAVA

Although far from being the largest island in regards to land mass, Java has the largest population of all of the other islands in the Indonesian archipelago. Over half of Indonesia's 260 million inhabitants live on this relatively small patch of land, giving it a population density similar to that of Bangladesh. It has a similar level of pollution and poverty also. For these reasons, Java is perhaps one of the least scenic of the main islands. It may not be the most popular of islands for sight seeing, however it is home to the capital city of Indonesia; Jakarta.

Above: The main destinations from Jakarta base. Pangandaran is 10 miles East of Nusawiru.

Some Susi Air pilots loved Jakarta. Personally I wasn't one of those pilots. Although there were indeed some reasonably nice locations to live within the nation's Capital, there was still a great deal of traffic and pollution. Sure, some Susi Air pilots would request to be based there so that they could live a relatively normal, Western life, in the more upmarket areas of Jakarta. But if you were seeking adventure and wanted to experience the natural beauty of Indonesia, Jakarta definitely wasn't for you. The Susi Air training base in Pangandaran was also located on the island of Java. Pangandaran, or "Pangas" as it was abbreviated by Susi Air pilots, was a relatively small fishing town at the time that I first joined Susi Air. However over the coming years, Pangandaran would gradually swell in size to become a medium sized city.

The island of Java is littered with (very) active volcanoes. As previously mentioned in the chapter "A Brief Guide to Indonesia", 3 separate volcanic eruptions in Indonesia have killed a total of 798 people between 2010 and 2018. All of those volcanoes were located either in, or nearby the coast, of Java. Asides from the obvious danger that these volcanoes pose to people on the ground, they also pose a major threat to aircraft in flight. Even without a full scale eruption, many of these volcanoes will spew enormous amounts of ash into the atmosphere on a regular basis. This very fine ash will melt onto the hot turbine blades of a jet or turboprop engine, potentially causing the engine to fail. In 1982, a British Airways Boeing 747 flying over Java, had all 4 of it's engines fail for this very reason!

I would be based in Java for the following 2 months. During this time I would learn a lot from my Captains. However first I needed to make a brief stop in Singapore…

CHAPTER 18

THE SINGAPORE AIR SHOW

After returning back to Medan from my trip to Lake Toba, I received a phone call from the Susi Air OCC (Operations Control Centre). My schedule had changed. Instead of flying directly to Jakarta for my next tour, OCC instead wanted me to fly to Singapore Changgi airport. From there, I would meet with Asif, the Base Manager of Jakarta. Asif and myself would be tasked with collecting a Susi Air Caravan which was on display at the Singapore Air Show, and subsequently flying it back to Jakarta. Wow, I thought. This was going to be an interesting trip!

I was booked a ticket for the 6am flight the following morning to Singapore. As I wouldn't be returning to Medan, I took my suitcase and belongings with me. After a 2 hour flight, I arrived at Changgi airport, cleared immigration and collected my suitcase. Now I just had to figure out where to meet Asif. I had his mobile number, but I didn't have any credit to call him outside of Indonesia. Fortunately Asif had a Singaporean SIM card. He sent me a text message with his location; the Starbucks in the Arrivals Hall. I went over to meet him. He seemed like a nice enough chap.

Asif had been flying with Susi Air for several years. He was also one of the few pilots in the company who were qualified to fly the Piaggio Avanti (the strange looking aircraft with the back-to-front wings). In fact the Avanti was pretty much the only aircraft he'd been flying in recent years. He hadn't flown the Caravan much at all since he qualified to fly the Avanti. He delegated pretty much all of the tasks of Base Manager to his deputy, Ahmed. Ahmed would plan the busy schedule of the Jakarta pilots, whilst Asif just picked up the extra pay cheque for being the Base Manager.

Regardless of how unfair that may have seemed, they both seemed happy enough with that arrangement.

Above: The Singapore Air Show ground display, located in the military aerodrome, 2 miles South of Changgi airport.

Asif led me outside the terminal building to meet our driver. Our driver was dressed in a suit and was holding a sign with both of our names. He took us to our car...a black Mercedes S-Class. We really were getting the VIP treatment! Our driver took us through the security checkpoint for the Singapore Air Show, located on the military aerodrome just a couple of miles South of Changgi, and dropped us off in the VIP area. He gave us our VIP passes. With these passes we could go pretty much anywhere that we wanted. Amongst the crowds of wealthy aircraft owners, a representative from Cessna came out to meet us. "You're welcome to stay in the Cessna VIP lounge whilst you're waiting", he said with a smile on his face. We followed him to the Cessna VIP lounge. It was the size of a large house and was virtually empty. There were sofas with an 80 inch screen TV, a dining area with a buffet and even bedrooms with en suite bathrooms so that we could rest!

I left my suitcase in one of the bedrooms and joined Asif for breakfast and coffee in the dining area. Asif explained to me the itinerary of the day. We would need to wait until the Air Show finished at 5pm before we did anything. After the crowds had dispersed, and it was our turn to taxi, we would then take off from the runway on the military aerodrome. From there, we would need to fly to the Singapore Seletar airport, about 10 minutes flight away, so that we could clear customs and immigration. Then we would begin our 3 hour flight to Jakarta Halim airport, arriving at around midnight. It was going to be a very long day for us, especially given that we had both been awake since 4am that day. But we had plenty of time to rest.

Myself and Asif ventured outside of the VIP lounge to browse all of the aircraft on display. Our Caravan was parked directly outside of the Cessna VIP lounge. However there were dozens of other aircraft on display. Civil and military aircraft, both large and small. For an aviation geek like myself, this could be best described as "plane porn". The best part was, we still had about 7 hours to kill before we needed to fly! Asif had a quick browse of the other aircraft with me, however didn't show quite as much enthusiasm. He headed back to the VIP lounge after about 30 minutes.

I took my time browsing the other aircraft. Meanwhile, various jet fighters from around the world were flying overhead in formation, performing various aerobatic manoeuvres for the spectators below. In the VIP area of the ground display, I saw many high ranking foreign diplomats, military leaders and airline bosses. Whilst strolling around the top brass in my pilots uniform wearing a VIP pass, I must admit, I felt quite important. And to think just a few months ago I was selling fruit and vegetables door to door, having all but given up my hope of becoming a commercial pilot! Life can sometimes be full of surprises.

I returned to the VIP lounge for lunch. I had quick chat with Asif, who was at this point just chilling on the sofa watching a movie on the widescreen TV. He asked me to go outside and pre flight our aircraft. I took the aircraft key from the Cessna representative and walked out to our Caravan. As I approached our aircraft, I noticed that the vast majority of the crowds were just walking by, for the most part, ignoring it. To be fair, there were far more interesting aircraft on display than our Cessna Grand Caravan. However something which I did notice, was that as soon as I unlocked the aircraft door and climbed up into the cockpit, some of the passers by stopped and began to take photos. It's one thing viewing a static aircraft display, but many people prefer a more interactive viewing experience. They seemed fascinated as I switched the battery on and extended the flaps of the aircraft.

After switching the battery off again, I began the pre flight inspection around the exterior of the aircraft. A family approached me and asked me if they could take a photo. "Yeah sure thing!", I replied, "Would you like me to take a photo of you all together?". "Well actually...can we take a photo with you next to the aircraft?", asked the Dad. I was slightly confused. Why would they want a photo of me? The family quickly surrounded me whilst the Dad started taking photos of us all next to the Caravan. A few moments later, another family approached me, asking the same. Unsatisfied with simply taking a photo of the aircraft, they seemed to also want a photo taken with a pilot. Eventually there was a small line of people queueing next to me, waiting to have their photos taken. I must admit, I was loving the attention...at least for the first hour.

Later on, as the crowds began to disperse, I was approached by a camera crew for the Chinese news broadcaster, CGTN. The news correspondent asked me if I was happy to give a short interview. He wanted me to explain to his viewers how the Caravan worked. I paused for a moment. I definitely wasn't an expert on the Caravan. I hadn't even completed my line training yet! What was I supposed to say? The correspondent smiled, "Just explain engine!", he abruptly shouted, before shoving a microphone in my face. I figured that being a news broadcaster in China, their audience would have been in the hundreds of millions. I chose my words carefully so as not to say anything fundamentally incorrect. "Sooo...the fuel goes into the combustion chamber of the engine...where it is ignited...and then the fire drives a turbine...and that turns the propeller".

The correspondent, who by now had a very serious expression on his face, nodded repeatedly, pretending to understand what I had just said. "And what happen then?!", he shouted. I paused again so as to choose my words carefully. "Err...the propeller spins and produces thrust...and then the aeroplane moves forward", I said. The correspondent then pointed at something inside the engine cowling. "What that do?!", he shouted. I stood there blankly. What does that thing do? Fuck knows! I cleared my throat. "Oh that...well...that is a necessary component of the engine", I replied. Satisfied with my answers, the correspondent then turned around to face the camera with a serious look on his face, then started shouting in Mandarin. Even to this day, I still have no fucking idea if that video was ever aired on Chinese state television. I certainly hope not.

At 5pm the security began to usher the remaining visitors off the apron, so that the aircraft on display could depart. Asif came out to the Caravan. He had a quick inspection and gave me a briefing for our next flight. "The shortest flights are always the hardest, especially when flying through busy airspace", he advised. Our 10 minute flight would involve transiting through the airspace of Changgi airport, navigating around the dozens of large airliners which were landing and taking off. Asif wanted to do the first flight himself, which meant that I had the misfortune of speaking to the very busy and impatient Air Traffic Controllers. To make matters more interesting, Asif didn't have a headset with him. We would need to switch the cockpit speakers on, and I would need to speak to ATC through a hand held microphone. This was going to be interesting.

After performing the final walk around, I climbed into the cockpit and asked ATC for the departure clearance. We were going to be number 14 for departure. After a 20 minute wait, ATC gave us clearance to start the engine. We taxied to join the queue of other aircraft waiting at the holding point of the runway. After take off, the fun began. "Papa Kilo Bravo Victor Bravo, maintain runway heading, contact Changgi Departure on 124 decimal 6". 10 seconds later on the next frequency; "Papa Kilo Bravo Victor Bravo, climb 4000 feet, turn right heading 350 degrees, contact Singapore Centre on 127 decimal 3". My head was spinning. Asif, who was far more accustomed to flying through Singaporean airspace, saw that I was struggling and took over the radios. He was flying the aircraft with his left hand whilst speaking on the hand held microphone with his right hand. To my surprise, he even managed to spark up a cigarette during our chaotic 10 minute flight!

After landing in Seletar airport, Asif taxied the aircraft to the apron and shutdown the engine. We secured the aircraft and entered the VIP terminal. "Before we clear customs and immigration, we need to pick up Susi's shopping", instructed Asif. "Huh?", I replied, "Susi's shopping?!". So it turned out, that much to Christian's disappointment, Susi was addicted to shopping. I mean really addicted. Sometimes shopaholics will buy random shit that they don't need...in small doses. However in Susi's case, there was somewhere in the region of 1500 to 2000 lbs of shopping, in various bags and boxes, waiting to clear customs. The contents of these bags and boxes ranged anywhere from clothing to kitchen appliances. Standing next to the monumental pile of cargo, (which was almost blocking the entrance of the immigration office), were 4 members of Susi Air staff, who needed us to take them back to Jakarta. We needed somewhere in the region of 1750 lbs of fuel for our flight to Jakarta. Best case scenario, we would have been about 1000 lbs over weight...possibly a lot more. And this brings me to the next lesson of the book.

LESSON 11: IT'S IMPORTANT TO BE ASSERTIVE...BUT ALSO TO KNOW WHEN TO BACK DOWN

I looked as Asif. "You know we're going to be overweight, right?", I asked. "It's fine", replied Asif. I looked carefully at his facial expressions. He knew full well that there was a problem. "Would *you* phone up Susi and tell her that you're leaving her belongings behind?", he asked me. He made a fair point. Usually in commercial aviation, pilots are protected if they refuse to follow unlawful instructions from the management. But we were an Indonesian based, bush flying operation. Although technically we should have been legally protected if we refused to over load the aircraft, the reality is that we probably would have been kicked out of both the company...and the country, if we had left Susi's shopping behind.

I wish I could say that the extra weight was the only problem that we had. Unfortunately it wasn't. Susi's shopping was very bulky and there was barely enough room in the cargo pods and cabin to store it. As a result, the rear of the aircraft was crammed with very large, heavy boxes, including various kitchen appliances, which would have blocked our escape from the rear emergency exits. To make matters worse, we could only use the rear doors for an evacuation after ditching, as the front pilot doors would have been completely submerged underwater. We had a 3 hour flight across the ocean and we were flying a single engine aircraft. We were effectively now flying a death trap.

Did I voice my concerns to Asif? Absolutely. But ultimately, he was a management Captain with years of experience, and I was the new guy. To this very day, I still ask myself if I could have been more assertive in regards to leaving cargo and people behind. However I am convinced that if I had gone so far as to refuse to fly, firstly Asif would have just flown the aircraft by himself, and secondly, this would have been the last chapter of this book. There wouldn't have been any sequels to Papa Kilo. There would have been no more stories to tell, because I would have been fired after just 10 weeks. So if you're enjoying this book, stop judging my decision to fly an over weight aircraft with no emergency exits. I risked my personal safety so that you could have hours more entertainment ahead of you. *You're welcome.*

I did offer to calculate the weight and balance, however Asif preferred not to know. In his mind at least, ignorance was bliss. Besides, if I were to have calculated the weight and balance with any level of accuracy, I would have needed to unload all of the cargo and weighed every bag and box by myself. It was clear that nobody else was going to help. The Susi Air staff boarded the Caravan using the front pilot doors. They squeezed themselves into the 2 front rows of passengers seats. The poor guy sitting in the one remaining seat in the second row, found himself surrounded by a mountain of shopping bags. He didn't appear to be particularly comfortable.

I completed the final walk around and climbed into the cockpit. I would be the Pilot Flying this time. During take off, when rotating at about 70 knots, I was pleasantly surprised to find that the aircraft did indeed lift off the tarmac, albeit very slowly. We gradually climbed to an altitude of 9,500 feet. Asif was intending on climbing to 11,500 feet originally, but I gave up when the rate of climb of our over-weight aircraft plateaued at just 300 feet per minute. The night sky was pitch black, as was the sea. The haze and clouds obscured the light from the stars and moon above us. 30 minutes into the flight, we suddenly went from smooth flight to severe turbulence. Asif checked the weather radar. It appeared that we had unknowingly flown through the centre of a thunderstorm. We couldn't see a damn thing. Asif left the weather radar on for the remainder of the flight.

I looked at the map on the GPS; we were over 100 miles away from land. If we had an engine failure, we would have needed to ditch the aircraft in the pitch black, stormy ocean below us. We would have had no emergency exits above the water line. Our best hope would have been to hold our breath and wait for the seawater to fill the cockpit, so that the pressure would equalise and we could open the cockpit doors. Of course we didn't even have a life raft, so we may as well have just stayed inside the sinking aircraft to avoid prolonging the agony of drowning. Asif looked at me. "You mind if I smoke?", he asked. He may have been my boss, but I needed to restrain myself from telling him to fuck right off. The last thing we needed right now was a fucking cabin fire! We were over an hour away from anywhere that we could land, and this guy wanted to spark up a cigarette in a confined space packed with (quite possibly) flammable cargo? Seriously? Cringing, I forced a smile and replied back, "Would you mind just waiting until we get on the ground?". Asif seemed pissed off with my reply. However at that point, I couldn't have cared less.

I spent the remainder of the 3 hour flight contemplating my experience so far at Susi Air. On the up side, it was one big adventure! I wouldn't get to see and do all of these amazing things if I wasn't flying for Susi Air. No trips to the remote parts of Indonesia, no bush flying, no VIP passes to the Singapore Air Show. However on the down side, I really needed to think carefully about the safety side of things. Flying an over weight, possibly out of balance, single engine aircraft with no working emergency exits, over the middle of the ocean at night time, was far from being safe. Would this just be a one off occurrence? Or would I be pushed into doing things like this on a regular basis?

Only time would tell.

CHAPTER 19

ARRIVING IN JAKARTA

Even to this very day, I struggle to understand how each of the bases of Susi Air could have been so fundamentally different to one another. In many ways, each base was like a different company, with Susi Air being the umbrella corporation at the top. I had spent the previous month reporting to Rik, one of the best Base Managers who I would ever meet in Susi Air, in regards to organisation, safety and empathy for others. Now, here in Jakarta, I was about to witness quite possibly the worst management in my entire 4 years as a Susi Air pilot.

Myself and Asif landed at Halim airport just after midnight, following our 3 hour flight from Singapore. Whilst the ground crew were off loading Susi's shopping from our aircraft, I checked the online roster for the following day on my phone. Ahmed, Asif's Deputy Base Manager, had rostered me to fly the next day at 6am, less than 6 hours from now! In aviation, we have strict regulations in regards to minimum rest time. Under Indonesian law we needed at least 9 hours rest inbetween flying duties, and to be fair, that wasn't much time compared to the regulations of most other countries. I assumed it must have been a rostering error and bought it to Asif's attention. "I don't deal with the rostering, just call Ahmed", he said. I phoned the number written on the bottom of the roster. I looked at Asif, "There's no answer", I said. "Well...just call him again", replied Asif. Asif, despite picking up the extra pay cheque each month for being the Base Manager, didn't appear to be particularly interested in my dilemma.

Did Ahmed not realise that I would be flying late at night before he rostered me to work early the next morning? Or maybe he just didn't care?

I was getting the impression that Asif and Ahmed couldn't care less about the rules...or safety for that matter. Yes we're in Indonesia, yes we're bush pilots. Rules are sometimes bent, I get that. But let's just forget the regulations for a moment and exercise some common sense here. Realistically, myself and Asif wouldn't even be leaving Halim airport until 1am that evening. I would be staying in Patria Apartments, about 20 minutes drive away from the airport. I would then need to check into my room and I probably wouldn't even get to sleep until 2am. I would then need to leave Patria the following day at around 4:30am, which meant that even if I skipped breakfast, I would need to wake up at 4am. So I'm supposed to fly an aircraft having had just 2 hours sleep the night before? Seriously?!

After phoning Ahmed numerous times with no success, I phoned OCC. Fortunately someone answered. They agreed to find someone else to fly the morning schedule the following day. Now I could finally relax. I took a taxi from Halim airport to Patria Apartments. I was staying on the 26th floor in a small 2 bedroom apartment. My room had no window and didn't appear to have been cleaned after the previous guest. I carefully wiped the previous guest's pubic hair off of the bed sheets using some tissues. The tiny bathroom, measuring about 1.5 metres by 1.5 metres including shower, sink and toilet, was an absolute state too. The drain was clogged with hair and half the floor was submerged under a one inch deep pool of stagnant water, with a layer of foamy scum floating on the top. I decided to leave my toothbrush in my suitcase after I brushed my teeth. I didn't want my toothbrush to touch anything in that bathroom.

I woke up the following day. It was pitch black. I checked the time on my phone; it was 10am. Of course, my bedroom had no windows. I had no way of telling if it was day or night. I opened my door and was instantly blinded by the intense sunlight which was apparent throughout the living area of the apartment. I checked the roster on my phone. Ahmed had scheduled me to fly at 12.30pm that same day, with himself as the Captain. I noticed something else on the monthly schedule. I hadn't been rostered for a single day off in the 3 weeks that I was to be based in Jakarta! The same appeared to be true for all the other pilots, both Captains and First Officers. At the bottom of the weekly schedule I saw that Ahmed had written an instruction in large red, block capitals; "IF NOT ROSTERED TO FLY, YOU ARE ON STANDBY FOR THE MORNING, AFTERNOON AND EVENING". What? So we needed to make ourselves available for duty 24 hours a day, 7 days a week? This was getting ridiculous. But what really pissed me off was the fact that this was so unnecessary. There were just 2 Caravans based in Jakarta, yet there were 7 sets of crew on the roster. There was a surplus of pilots compared to most bases, yet they were too disorganised to appoint at least one day off for us a week, as per the law?

I had a quick shower and got dressed into my uniform. There was no food in the apartment and I didn't know of any cafes with edible food nearby. I didn't even know if the company was arranging my transport from Patria to the airport. The District Manager, who was supposed to organise these things, never replied to my messages. Not wanting to have any last minute surprises, I booked a taxi to Halim airport so that I could arrive early and get some food. The closest thing Halim airport had to edible food was KFC. It wasn't exactly the breakfast of champions, however I hadn't eaten since the afternoon before, and frankly, I was beginning to get "hangry" (hunger related anger). After finishing my breakfast, I headed to the crew room, located behind the Susi Air VIP lounge. It was there that I would first meet Ahmed.

Now I know what you're thinking. Based on everything that I have said so far, you probably think that I'm not going to say anything nice about the guy? Well actually, after meeting Ahmed in person, I would say quite the opposite. He was a likeable guy. He was actually quite welcoming and friendly. Sure, it was evident that he was about as useful as a helicopter ejector seat, in regards to managing the base. But he was very sociable and appeared to have a positive attitude. Ahmed, who was in his early twenties, had been flying for Susi Air for roughly 2 years, quickly rising through the ranks. You could perhaps argue that he rose *too quickly* through the ranks.

He was upgraded to Captain after just a few months as an FO. Shortly after his first command, he was upgraded again to "Training Captain", and then subsequently appointed to the Deputy Base Manager position in Jakarta. And this brings me to the next lesson of the book.

LESSON 12: NEVER LET PERSONAL AMBITION OVERTAKE YOUR LEVELS OF EXPERIENCE AND COMPETENCE

Everybody likes to be promoted, especially when we are young and ambitious. However sometimes when we are working in safety related industries such as aviation, it pays for us to take our time when climbing up the ladder. I'm using Ahmed as just one extreme example here. During Susi Air's rapid phase of expansion, shortly before I joined the company, it was common place for FOs to be upgraded to Captains with very little experience or training inbetween. As you can probably imagine, when flying in a region of the World as hazardous as Indonesia, with high terrain, severe weather and incompetent ATC, this was a recipe for disaster. I would soon realise after my first flight with Ahmed, that he probably shouldn't have been a Captain, let alone be given any position in training or management. I don't mean to be harsh with my words, and I have taken every care to change his real identity in this book to avoid any embarrassment to himself. However some things really need to be said.

Ahmed and myself were to fly 4 sectors that day. From Halim airport, we would first fly to Cilicap and back, then fly to Nusawiru and back. Each flight would be approximately 1 hour in length. The first thing that I would notice from flying with Ahmed, is that he would rush everything, without thinking about the consequences for safety. Whilst still in Halim, I began calculating the weight and balance of the aircraft as we were boarding. I was still filling out the weight and balance form as the last passenger had boarded. "What are you doing?", asked Ahmed. "Just finishing off the weight and balance", I replied, "I should be finished in about a minute".

My response appeared to have triggered Ahmed. Although he came across as being a relatively nice guy when we first met 30 minutes ago, he suddenly began behaving like an absolute dick...in front of the passengers. "I don't care!", he shouted, "We have to go now!". I paused for a moment to consider what he was asking me. On the one hand, he was completely wrong. Asides from our scheduled departure time not being for another 10 minutes, the weight and balance was a necessary legal document which needed to be completed for all flights with commercial passengers. However on the other hand, he was the Captain. Reluctantly, I left the weight and balance and instead focused on the final walk around. As soon as I climbed into the cockpit, he immediately started the engine before I even had a chance to raise my ladder and close the door! What the actual fuck? I was right next to the fucking exhaust pipe of the engine!

However this was just the beginning. Prior to taxiing the Caravan, a 30 second "warm up" period was required in order for the weather radar antenna to stabilise. It was important not to move the aircraft before the warm up period had finished, as it could damage the antenna. However Ahmed thought that he knew better. Not only did he taxi the aircraft before the warm up had finished, he abruptly stopped the aircraft for a brake check. Now don't get me wrong, checking your brakes before taxiing is always good practice, however you don't just stamp on the brake pedals, violently jerking all of the passengers forward! It was safe to say by this stage, the $22,000 onboard weather radar was now completely fucked. And the Bluesky flight plan? That important device onboard the aircraft which allowed our position and data to be tracked in the event of an emergency? Forget it. "It's not important", said Ahmed, "You can enter the flight plan after we take off". Ahmed then continued with what was quite possibly the fastest taxi that I had ever seen in a Caravan, in close vicinity to other aircraft and obstacles. If we had had a brake failure at that point, we would have been screwed.

Shortly after departure, Ahmed engaged the autopilot. We continued our climb to 11,500 feet. Looking outside, I could see some CBs ahead of us, however of course we couldn't see anything on the weather radar. "The mechanics in this base our useless", remarked Ahmed, "The weather radars never work on these aircraft!". I thought of a few words to say back to him, however I decided to instead bite my tongue. I was still new in the company. Around 40 minutes into the flight, we approached the top of descent for Cilicap. Ahmed immediately set 1100 feet on the altitude bug, then started to descend. This would have been perfectly acceptable if we were going to remain visual, however we blatantly weren't. There was a thick layer of cloud separating us from the high terrain below.

I checked the Minimum Off Route Altitude (MORA) on my chart. Although we had passed over the high mountains behind us, we still had a MORA of 5400 feet for our sector. I bought this to Ahmed's attention. He didn't seem too pleased with my observation. "It's fine!", he snapped. Well ok I thought, if he was going to stay on the exact same track that he flies on a regular basis, and he knew from previous experience that this track would give us sufficient terrain clearance, there wasn't a massive problem. It wasn't necessarily right, but at least it was safe.

However passing 2000 feet, we were still flying through cloud. To my surprise, Ahmed then turned the aircraft to the left of the track, so that he could join a final approach for runway 13, whilst still flying through cloud. This was getting serious. It's one thing flying below the MORA when you're sticking to a track which you know will guarantee clearance of terrain and obstacles. But Ahmed was now flying the aircraft from the known, to the unknown. Concerned, I challenged Ahmed, "Can you at least level off at this altitude? I can't see a thing!". Ahmed told me that he could "see the ground". Although we could indeed see "patches" of ground directly below us, we couldn't see anything in front. And it was the terrain and obstacles in front of us which we needed to worry about! We popped out from underneath the cloud at about 1000 feet, only to find that we had overshot the runway. "Go around!", I yelled. However instead of going around, Ahmed aggressively banked the aircraft back towards the extended centre line of the runway. We were still flying at nearly 170 knots at this point, over twice the speed for final approach!

Ahmed violently pulled the power lever back to idle, causing the prop to suddenly disc. He aggressively pitched up to arrest the rate of descent, whilst slowing down abruptly. I could feel myself being flung forward into my shoulder harnesses. The passengers must have been scared out of their wits! As the speed decayed, Ahmed called for flaps 10. Before I had even taken my hand off the flap lever, Ahmed immediately called for flaps 20, then flaps full. Passing 100 feet above the runway, he suddenly pushed the power lever forward, causing the prop to surge. This was pretty damn far from being a stabilised approach! He touched down with the majority of the 1400 metre runway behind him, before applying maximum reverse thrust and braking.

At the end of the runway he abruptly turned the aircraft around 180 degrees, causing the tail of the aircraft to act as a centrifuge for the unsuspecting passengers sitting in the back, before back tracking to the apron. I looked at his face. He appeared to be very pale. He knew full well that he had fucked up the approach, and that he should have gone around. However that was going to stop him from saving face. "Dan, why did you ask me to go around?", he asked, "That approach was fine! Just fine!". His incompetence and arrogance were endangering people's safety.

I had another 3 flights with Ahmed that day. Unfortunately he would roster me to fly with him again for another 4 occasions during my 3 week tour of Jakarta. It would be the same story each time; he would rush the turnarounds on the ground and do some other, very questionable things, in the air. For the most part, he would still be pleasant enough to fly with when he wasn't endangering people's safety. However whenever you would need to challenge him on something important, he would revert back to behaving like an absolute dick again. It appeared that he needed this ego in order to conceal his lack of confidence with his own flying and management abilities. He knew full well that he had no business being in the left hand seat.

But it wasn't just his fault. The company was at fault too. When Ahmed first joined Susi Air as an FO, he would have had many people supervising his performance, whilst providing him with large amounts of critique and discipline. However the more that he was promoted, the less people there were to supervise him. The reality was, he had very little knowledge and skill when he was first upgraded to Captain, and he didn't have much in regards to self discipline either.

A PERSONAL NOTE ON THIS CHAPTER

It is important to remember that this all happened a <u>very</u> long time ago. I am confident that today, Ahmed is a far more mature, experienced and humble pilot. I have taken every effort to protect his real identity and I quite genuinely wish him all the best for his future. However, after much consideration, I still feel that it was important to use him as an example of how <u>not</u> to behave as a pilot.

CHAPTER 20

MICROBURST

Following my first flight in Jakarta with Ahmed, I would fly with various different Captains. Fortunately, unlike Ahmed, these Captains would be highly skilled and far more safety conscious. They would also have a natural tendency to teach the copilots who they were flying with. With the assistance of these highly skilled and experienced Captains, I would perfect the fine art of "cloud surfing" around the numerous CBs (cumulonimbus clouds) and towering cumulus clouds which we would encounter en route. I would also gain confidence in decision making, following a weather related diversion from Cilicap to Nusawiru. Asides from the learning experience, most of these Captains were an absolute joy to fly with.

Shortly before the end of my 3 week tour of Jakarta, I was rostered to fly with a Danish Captain by the name of Jens. This would be the second time that I would be flying with him, having been my Captain on the previous flight where we diverted to Nusawiru. As much as I enjoyed flying with the guy, I would soon learn that we would have some extraordinarily bad luck whenever we were rostered to fly together. Unbeknown to us at the time of our departure from Halim, we were about to witness the most ferocious weather phenomenon that either one of us had ever seen before.

Our afternoon flight from Halim to Cilicap was for the most part uneventful. Jens was the PF for this flight. We needed to avoid some CBs en route and also during descent, which was normal for that time of day. However there was nothing out of the ordinary. Approaching Cilicap we could see that there was a large CB nearby. Although taking off and landing in the vicinity of CBs is best avoided if possible, we still needed to be realistic. Due to the nature of the weather in many parts of Indonesia, if we stopped taking off and landing every time we saw a CB, we would have rarely flown at all. However unbeknown to us, there was something unusual about this particular CB, which we wouldn't find out until after we had landed. And it was just as well that we found out <u>after</u> we had landed, otherwise we probably wouldn't have survived to tell the tale.

As Jens parked on the apron and shutdown the engine, we could hear thunder in the distance. It appeared that the CB nearby was now developing into an active thunderstorm. The ground crew wheeled out a large, 200 kg steel step ladder to our aircraft for the refuelling. However we couldn't refuel with a thunderstorm in the vicinity, as the static could have potentially ignited the fuel. Jens informed the ground crew that they would need to delay the refuelling. It appeared that we were now going to be late. However we would soon find out that being late was going to be the least of our worries. Just a few moments after Jens had asked the ground crew to standby with the refuelling, a flash of light blinded us all, which was immediately followed by a deafening sound, similar to that of a cannon being fired right next to our ear drums.

BANG!

A bolt of lightning had just hit the surface of the apron, no less than 100 metres away from us! The two ground crew, Jens and myself looked at each other, then immediately ran inside the small, single story terminal building for cover. We had just come pretty damn close to getting fried! However that was just the beginning. A few seconds later, and I really mean just a *few* seconds later, the wind went from perfect calm to approximately 60 – 80 mph. Following this sudden, violent burst of wind, torrential rain flooded the ground. In less than a minute, the weather had gone from being just fine, to something resembling a hurricane! Neither Jens nor myself had ever seen anything like it.

Although neither myself nor Jens had seen this severe weather phenomenon before, we had both learned about it, long before either one of us had ever joined Susi Air. It was called a microburst, and it was responsible for countless aviation accidents involving both small and very large aircraft. Usually a thunderstorm will dissipate it's water content through rain, gradually. However in the case of a microburst, all of the water vapour will condense at the same time, causing a very heavy, 6-10 mile high column of water to collapse, crashing down on to the Earth's surface. The result is an incredibly violent, vertical down draft with speeds in excess of 60 mph, which spreads out horizontally as it strikes the Earth's surface. It is a very rare phenomenon indeed, even for Indonesia. But it is also deadly. Even a large airliner cannot out climb a microburst, even with all engines at max thrust. Our Caravan had no chance of escaping it's wrath...which was disturbing, given that if we had landed just 2 minutes later we would have almost certainly died, taking our 12 passengers with us.

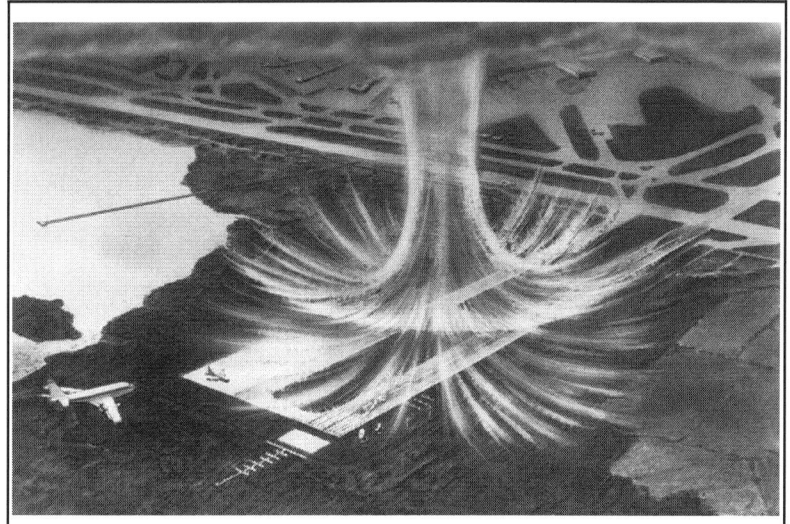

Above: An illustration of how a microburst can bring down an aircraft. Image credit NASA.

From inside the relative safety of the terminal building, we continued to watch the incredible fury of mother nature. Throughout the hurricane level wind and torrential rain, we saw lighting bolt after lighting bolt strike the tarmac of the apron outside, the sound almost blowing out our ear drums. By this point, the ground was completely flooded. If we had touched the wet surface outside, we probably would have been electrocuted from the lightning strikes. This created a problem, as it was soon apparent that we had left the very large, heavy, steel step ladder outside, next to our aircraft. It weighed about 200 kg. In fact it was so heavy, that it needed to be wheeled by two people. However it soon became apparent that it wasn't where we had left it. In fact, it was no where in sight! Jens looked at me and said one word, "Shit". Yep, those were my thoughts exactly. And this brings me to the next lesson of the book.

LESSON 13: NEVER RISK YOUR SAFETY TO SAVE SOMEONE ELSE'S PROPERTY

It wasn't until the microburst ceased, approximately 15 minutes later, that we found out where the step ladder had gone. There were a few light aircraft parked on the far side of the apron. The 200 kg step ladder was now embedded into the wing of a PA28! It appeared that the ladder had struck the aircraft with such force, that it had sliced through the metallic wing like a knife through warm butter. Needless to say, the aircraft's owner was pissed off with myself, Jens and the ground crew. "Why did you just leave the ladder out there!", the owner screamed, whilst waving his arms about. "Errr...did you not see the lightning hit the ground?", I sarcastically replied. Jens, being a bit more diplomatic than myself, gave him the contact details of Susi Air, so that he could arrange compensation.

Yes, if we had time, we should have secured the ladder. But we didn't. And I'm sure as hell not going to endanger my safety, or anyone else's for that matter, in order to protect someone else's property. And it appeared that the senior management of Susi Air agreed with me. After they investigated the incident, we were both absolved of any wrong doing that day. And rightly so.

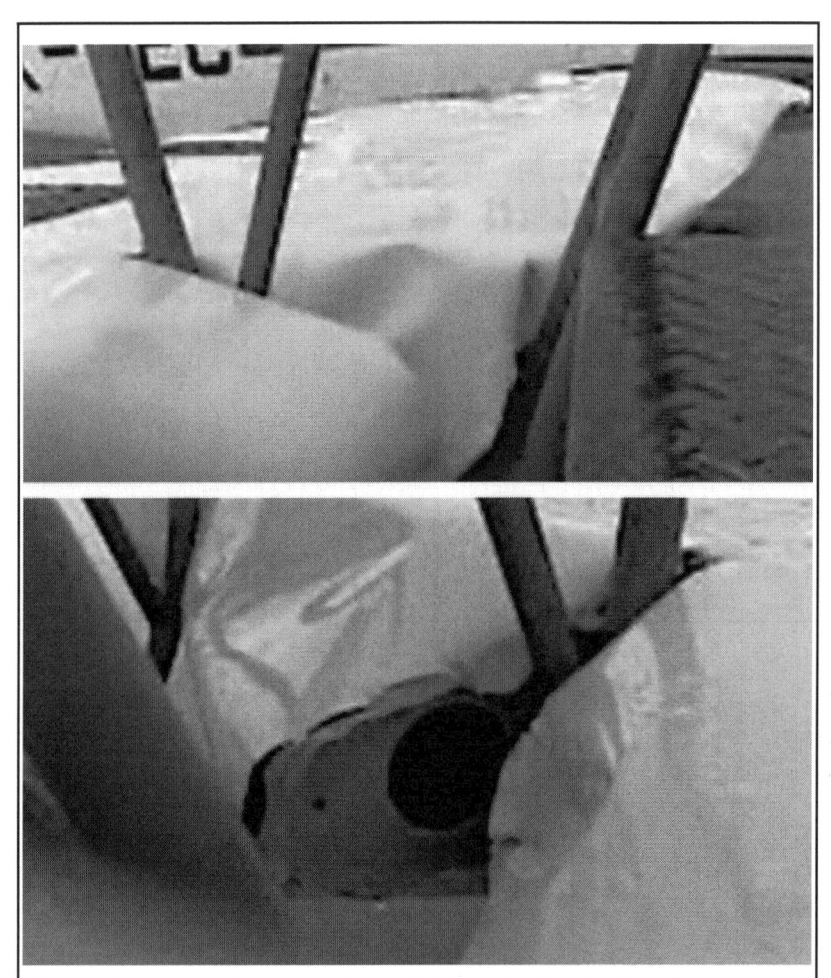

Above: This is what happens when a 200 kg refuelling ladder slams into an aircraft wing at over 60 mph. Needless to say, the owner was a tad pissed off. (Apologies for the poor resolution, I had a Nokia 3110 at the time).

CHAPTER 21

TRAINING ASSOCIATE

As much as I enjoyed flying with many of the Captains in Jakarta, I was beginning to grow a bit tired of flying to the same destinations over and over again. Towards the end of my 3 week tour in Jakarta, as my experience and confidence began to increase, I began to crave more of a challenge. I didn't want to take off and land on large, flat, tarmacked runways all the time. I wanted to take off and land on short dirt strips, sloped up the sides of mountains. After all, this was the reason why I came to Indonesia. I was hoping that my next tour might be in Papua.

Unfortunately Mr Cheung had other plans for me. At the time, there was a chronic shortage of instructors in the Training Department. So much so, that Cheung had now resorted to forcing FOs like myself, who had previous instructing experience, to help out as "Training Associates". As a Training Associate, or TA, it would be my task to conduct the simulator training, including the recurrency training of the Captains. Yep, that's right. Cheung wanted First Officers like myself to train and assess Captains. The fact that I had less than 200 hours flying experience on the Caravan didn't appear to dissuade Cheung from assigning me this duty. Cheung asked the rostering department to send me to Pangandaran for 3 weeks following my tour of Jakarta. Papua was going to have to wait until next time.

I was rostered to fly one way from Halim to Nusawiru with Tod, the Chief Flight Instructor. We were going to fly 8 Susi Air Captains for their annual recurrency training in Pangandaran, including Rik from Medan and Asif from Jakarta. The other 6 Captains were based in Papua. As we were pre flighting the aircraft, I noticed that Tod was behaving somewhat bizarrely.

He kept talking about things which didn't really make any sense to me. One of the incoherent sentences which I distinctly remember Tod telling me, was that "Cessna should build a tap into the side of the engine so that we can refill our bottles with water". He then stared at me blankly, eyes wide open, waiting for me to respond to his statement. "Err...yeah that sounds like a good idea Tod", I replied. I didn't know Tod particularly well at the time, so I just assumed that he was a bit special. However looking back, I probably should have taken his incoherent ramblings a bit more seriously. Something wasn't quite right with him. Which brings me to the next lesson.

LESSON 14: NEVER BE AFRAID TO ASK YOUR COLLEAGUES HOW THEY ARE FEELING, EVEN IF THEY ARE MORE SENIOR THAN YOU.

As the recurrency Captains boarded the aircraft, I noticed Tod pacing up and down the tarmac of the apron. He appeared to be talking on his phone. However as I looked closer at his hand, it soon became apparent that there was no phone. He was just randomly talking to himself. This was perhaps the point at which I should have stepped in and started to ask some important questions. However he was the Chief Flight Instructor, and I was the new guy. I should have stepped up, but I felt too embarrassed to ask him if he was ok. I completed my final walk around and off we went. Once we levelled off at our cruise altitude of 11,500 feet, Tod informed me that he was going to take a short nap. He gave me both the controls and the radios, then closed his eyes. Well that probably explained his bizarre behaviour, I thought. He was just tired.

No problem then. I'll just fly by myself and wake him up when it's time to descend, I thought. Using the "Heading Select" mode of the autopilot, I surfed around the various towering cumulus clouds in front of us, with Tod asleep in the left seat. However as we approached the top of descent, he didn't seem to want to wake up, despite me shaking his arm. He told me that he was awake, but he still had his eyes closed and was muttering something about the "Sky being too blue today". Okaaay then, I thought. I began our decent into Nusawiru and got the attention of one of the Captains sitting in the first row behind me. You really couldn't have picked a better time to have a pilot incapacitation; I had 8 different Captains onboard to choose from! However Tod didn't appear to want to leave his seat willingly, and he also weighed around 18 stone (about 120 kg). Dragging him out probably wasn't going to be an option.

It appeared that I was going to be landing that aircraft single pilot. With the Captains in the front row monitoring my actions, I carried out the descent and approach checks by myself. Passing 1000 feet, I needed to ask Tod to switch on the Ignition and move the "Inertial Separator" to "bypass", as these were located on his side. However other than that, I was able to fly the aircraft by myself from the right seat. As Tod was still semi conscious, and the 2 Captains sitting in the front row were monitoring my actions, I continued to call out what I was doing. Fortunately the weather was fine. And to be fair, the Caravan was specifically designed for single pilot operations anyway. Landing in Nusawiru was straight forward enough. After landing, I taxied to the apron and shut down the engine.

Tod was still insisting that he was fine. He said that he was "just a bit tired from the watching the propeller spin around all day". I secured the aircraft with the help of Rik, then we all headed out to the front of the terminal where 2 minibuses were waiting to take us all to Pangandaran. I was sat next to Tod for the journey. "Are you going to visit the medical centre when we get to Pangas?", I asked him. With his eyes closed, he slowly muttered, "No...I'm just dehydrated...the engine wouldn't give me any water to drink". Okaaay then, I thought. "Tod, I really think you should see someone when we get back", I said. So after seeing a "doctor" when we arrived to Pangandaran, it turned out that the poor guy had actually contracted Dengue fever, and his strange behaviour was due to him being delirious.

Tod would be off work for the following week, which was a slight problem for the recurrency Captains as he was the only instructor who was actually authorised to conduct their Pilot Proficiency Checks. Bart was currently flying on the line in Medan after being "fired" by Cheung following a disagreement. The other Flight Instructors appeared to have quit the Training Department in an attempt to escape Cheung. The only instructor left in the Training Department was Mitch, who despite being the Chief Ground Instructor, was still a First Officer himself and couldn't conduct any flight training. Unfortunately the 8 Captains who were taking their recurrency training weren't going to be leaving Pangandaran anytime soon.

The following morning I went to Cheung's office so that I could receive his instructions. He asked me to spend the day conducting the simulator training for each of the recurrency Captains in the PA28 simulator. It seemed a bit daft for a junior FO like myself to train the recurrency Captains in the simulator, many of whom had been in the company for several years. However what made this especially daft was that the simulator was for a completely different type and class of aircraft to the Cessna Grand Caravan. Mitch showed me how to switch on and operate the simulator. From there, I was on my own.

I walked over to the lobby of the Susi Air Hotel to meet with the Captains. Slightly embarrassed, I explained the instructions that Cheung had given me. Fortunately, they seemed to see the funny side of the situation. This was just as well, given that I would be flying with 6 of them in Papua. The first Papua Captain, who had been flying for Susi Air for about 6 years, walked with me to the simulator room. With a grin on his face, he looked at me and joked, "You may be my instructor now, but don't forget that I'll be *your* instructor in Papua". Jokes aside, he was right. I decided that the least awkward way of conducting the simulator session was to simply ask each of the Captains what they would like to practice, then I would simply observe them without giving any instruction.

Pretty much all the Captains asked for the same thing. They wanted to practice some holds and approaches by sole reference to instruments, i.e. nothing to see out of the window. And to be fair, even though the aircraft was completely different, there was still some beneficial training purpose in regards to practising these procedures. Unsurprisingly, the Papua Captains performed very well in regards to track and altitude keeping. They had years of flying experience and required a great deal of skill to operate in that particular part of Indonesia. The same was true for Rik too. He also had years of flying experience and performed very well.

The only Captain who concerned me during the simulator training was Asif. For each of the Captains, I failed the Attitude Indicator during the hold. The Attitude Indicator, commonly known as an Artificial Horizon, is an instrument which shows the pitch and bank of the aircraft. It was a relatively minor failure, as any competent pilot could simply control the pitch and bank using reference to the other instruments onboard. 7 of the recurrency Captains successfully managed to control the aircraft with this minor failure, whilst maintaining very high standards of track and altitude keeping. Asif on the other hand managed to put the aircraft into a spiral dive towards the ground. I paused the simulator just before he impacted the terrain, in order to avoid any further embarrassment to himself. "Can we try that again?", he asked. Well you can't bloody try it again in real life! Can you? (I refrained from saying that last part out aloud).

The Captains were in ground school the following day with Mitch. Usually recurrency training takes about 3 days to complete, however in their case it was going to take a lot longer. The only other person asides from Tod, who was qualified to conduct Pilot Proficiency Checks at the time, was Christian, and he was currently away on business. The recurrency Captains weren't going anywhere until Tod regained his health. This would create a backlog in training, as 4 senior FOs were about to commence their Upgrade training to become Captains, shortly after the recurrency Captains had arrived. Desperate for instructors, Cheung "unfired" Bart, and invited him back to the Training Department to work full time. Meanwhile, I was spending most of my time twiddling my thumbs. I wasn't a Flight Instructor on the Caravan. There wasn't much that I was qualified to do within the Training Department, other than switch on the PA28 simulator.

Although I must admit, even though at times working as a TA was about as interesting as watching paint dry, I did enjoy working with Bart. I helped him out with odd jobs around the office. I learned a lot from him too. I was also his FO when the time finally came to fly the recurrency Captains back to Jakarta. He actually gave me my first "upgrade evaluation" during this flight. He told me that I needed two of these evaluations from different instructors in order to be considered for the Upgrade course. It was still early days for me, however it was nice to know that at least I was on the right track!

I spent a total of 3 weeks working as a TA in Pangandaran. Fortunately though, things were about to get a lot more interesting for me. For my next tour, I would be based in Papua for 6 weeks. Now it was time for the *real* adventure to begin!

CHAPTER 22

A BRIEF GUIDE TO PAPUA

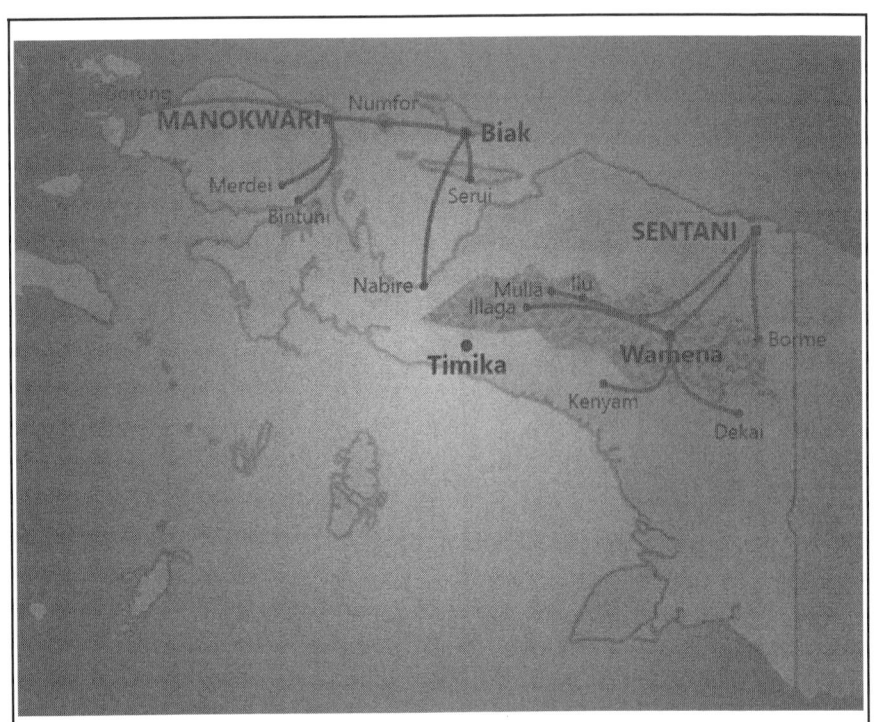

Above: The Papua Lowlands base (Manokwari), the Papua Highlands base (Sentani) and the satellite bases. Also included are a few of the many destinations that Susi Air have flown to. The majority of these destinations have been omitted from this map...there simply wasn't enough space for them all.

Papua is by far the most interesting region of Indonesia in regards to the mountainous terrain, diverse wildlife and ancient tribes. Despite the breath taking nature of Papua, there is very little tourism. It's not the easiest of places to travel to, and even if it was, the Indonesian Government heavily restricts tourism in certain areas, (usually to hide it's human rights abuses against the indigenous people of Papua). The last thing that the Indonesian Government wants is for outsiders to take photos and videos of the violence. This places Susi Air pilots, and various other expats in the mining and aviation industry, in a very unique situation. We have the opportunity to see the things in Papua which most people around the World simply wouldn't be able to see. Both the good things and the bad.

HISTORY

The island of Papua is thought to have been first inhabited around 50,000 years ago, at around the same time that Australia was first inhabited. For the most part, Papuans remained isolated from the rest of the World. Towards the end of the 19th Century, the East half of the island of Papua, (now Papua New Guinea), was colonised in parts by Germany and later Britain. The Netherlands had previously colonised the entire West half of the island of Papua, known at the time as "Netherlands New Guinea". Following the end of WW2, as Indonesia gained their independence from the Netherlands, the Dutch Government continued to rule over West Papua, with the intention of granting them independence by 1970. They argued that due to the differences in culture and ethnicity, it was unfair to expect the people of Papua to freely assimilate into the newly formed nation of Indonesia. The Dutch Government would invest a great deal of resources in order to assist the people of Papua form their own independent, democratic government.

Sukarno, the Indonesian President, continued to make claim that West Papua was part of Indonesia. With the threat of a possible war, the Dutch

Government were put under a great deal of pressure to make a deal with Indonesia. In 1962, the Dutch Government handed over administration of Papua to the UN, who in turn, handed over administration to the Indonesian Government a year later. The people of Papua were not consulted during these changes in administration. Many Papuans felt betrayed. They were previously promised independence, however instead of exercising their right to self determination, they were now under the control of a dictatorship.

In order to give legitimacy for their occupation of West Papua, the Indonesian Government, now led by President Suharto, held an independence referendum in 1969, just one year before West Papua was originally supposed to be granted independence. The referendum, known as the "Act of No Choice", involved the Indonesian military rounding up 1026 random Papuans and ordering them to vote, under gunpoint. Unsurprisingly, very few Papuans voted in favour of independence. Suharto, who was debatably even more harsh than his predecessor, Sukarno, would now brag to the rest of the World that West Papua wanted to remain a part of Indonesia. This "referendum" would trigger the beginning of many armed uprisings, massacres and (debatably) even genocide.

THE BIAK MASSACRE

There have been many instances of Indonesian authorities involved in massacring unarmed civilian populations, both in Papua and elsewhere in the Indonesian archipelago. One of the best documented and most recent accounts of such a massacre, was in 1998 on the island of Biak, West Papua. During a march commemorating the failed declaration of independence of West Papua, over 200 civilians were murdered in cold blood by the Indonesian military. Some of the civilians were shot during the march, including whilst running away. However what happened *after* the shootings was even more disturbing. Approximately 200 civilians were arrested by the military, and subsequently taken to a nearby naval base. They were then loaded onto two different ships, taken out to sea, and thrown overboard, far away from land. Some of the bodies would wash ashore over the following weeks, however most of the victims were never seen again. The Indonesian authorities claimed that the bodies washed ashore were from a tsunami which hit Papua New Guinea over a month earlier. However most forensic experts doubt the Indonesian Government's claim. What's more, the Indonesian Government never did explain what happened to the Papuans who were loaded onto their ships.

DEMOGRAPHICS AND GEOGRAPHY

Papua is home to just under 4 million people. The coastal regions of Papua are inhabited by many native Javanese. They were actively encouraged to move to West Papua under the Government's "Transmigration Program", in order to displace the native Papuans and promote the spread of Islam. The highland regions tend to be far more tribal, with the predominant religion being Christianity, which was first introduced by European missionaries. There were a total of 312 different tribes in Papua, including a small minority of tribes who have never made any contact with people from outside. Some of these tribes have since been wiped out, or are now significantly smaller. It has been estimated that well over 100,000 Papuans have been killed by the Indonesian authorities since 1969, with approximately 14,000 living in exile in neighbouring Papua New Guinea. There is certainly a strong argument that there is a genocide taking place in West Papua, albeit very gradual.

West Papua is rich in precious metals, including gold. The Grasberg mine, located in the Papua Highlands, is the largest gold mine in the World, and the second largest copper mine. Naturally, given the immense wealth involved, there are many foreign governments and corporations who are happy to turn a blind eye to the atrocities of the Indonesian authorities in West Papua, in exchange for mining rights. Despite this, most Papuan separatists see foreign workers, such as mining engineers (and Susi Air pilots), as being somewhat neutral in this conflict.

Personally from my experience, I found that most Papuans, at least those living in the more remote locations, were actually quite welcoming of pilots. They saw us as their connection with the rest of the World. Without us it could have taken several days just to walk to their nearest village. We also bought them much needed supplies and medicine. However although they were usually friendly towards us, it was important to remember that most of those remote tribes were armed with bows and arrows, and the separatist rebels were armed with guns.

You definitely wouldn't want to get on the wrong side of them.

Above: Members of the Papuan Liberation Army flying the West Papuan flag. Location unknown.

CHAPTER 23

ARRIVING IN BIAK

Following a quick visa run to Singapore and a 6 hour overnight flight, I arrived on the island of Biak in the early morning. Sometimes it's easy to forget just how massive Indonesia is; my journey to Biak was over 2000 miles long! The runway in Biak was unusually large, at around 3.5 km in length. This was nearly twice the length required for most large, passenger aircraft, and about six times the length required for a Caravan. Although the official Papua lowland base was in Manokwari, a town located about 150 miles West of Biak, Biak was still a major satellite base, with around 6 pilots based there at any one time. It was also the main engineering base for Susi Air in Papua.

Following my arrival in Biak, I was greeted outside of the terminal by a driver, who took me straight to the pilots house. It was a large house located in the centre of town, with 3 metre high walls surrounding the perimeter. On top on these walls was razor wire and the gate leading inside was made from solid steel. Susi Air appeared to take security very seriously in Biak. To be fair though, tensions were understandably high in the region from the massacre which occurred 12 years earlier. Most of the locals wouldn't have caused us any problems, however there were potentially a few people in the area who might have had other ideas.

I was greeted in the house by Surya, the cici, who showed me to my room. By now it was about 8am. "You must be tired!", said Surya. Yep, she was right. I hadn't slept in 24 hours and I was struggling to keep my eyes open. I took a shower and went straight to bed. The night before I was staying in the Patria Apartments, in a dirty room with a lumpy mattress. However here in Biak, I had a large bedroom, immaculately cleaned, with a comfy bed. Papua pilots really did get the 5 star treatment. I played some chilled out music and laid in bed. Within about 30 seconds I was in a deep sleep. I woke up around midday, when the other pilots returned from work. I made my way into the living area to meet them. There were 3 Captains and 2 FOs, not including myself. We all sat down together for lunch, then spent the remainder of the day by the beach.

The following day I was rostered to fly to the island of Serui with Dante, a Caravan Captain from South Africa. He was one of the youngest Captains in Papua, however he still had plenty of flying experience, having been flying since his teenage years. He could best be described as a "stick and rudder" pilot. He didn't care much for technology such as autopilot and GPS; he just wanted to manually fly the aircraft. I would learn a lot from him. We were rostered to fly two round trips to the island of Serui from Biak, with the first departure at 7am. Each flight was approximately 30 minutes and we were scheduled to finish at around 10am. We would then be free for the remainder of the day. This type of morning only schedule was quite typical for Papua. Many of the smaller strips had "curfews", as the wind would be too strong in the afternoon.

Above: Final approach to runway 36 in Serui. Due to the high terrain surrounding the end of the runway, a go around is not possible at low altitude.

Dante flew the first flight to Serui. Serui, (for the most part), was a Captain's only landing. Due to the high terrain at the end of the runway, it was a one way in, one way out airport. You couldn't land on runway 18 in a Caravan (although I know one person who allegedly tried) and you definitely couldn't take off from runway 36. To make matters more interesting, a go around wasn't possible at low altitude, as the Caravan's climb gradient was simply too shallow to make it over the mountains at the end of the runway. Basically, after the "committal point" on the approach, there wasn't any room for errors. And the runway was only 550 metres long!

During the cruise on our first flight, Dante briefed me the approach:

"I'm going to turn on to a 1 mile final at 500 feet. Keep a close eye on the wind, if you see we have a tail wind, tell me straight away. If it doesn't look good, I'll go around and immediately break off to the right. At 300 feet I'm going to call committed; there won't be any option to go around then."

The approach into Serui was both daunting and breath taking. It felt counter-intuitive to fly towards the high terrain on final approach, and I must admit, my heart was racing. I kept monitoring the wind for any changes, whilst Dante flawlessly kept his speed and profile. The scenery was like something out of a movie, however we were both far too preoccupied to appreciate it. Dante made a fairly assertive landing at the beginning of the runway. Given that there were buildings immediately at the end of the 550m metre runway, even the smallest "float" during the flare could have caused a serious accident. It was best to get the tyres on the tarmac sooner rather than later. Dante applied maximum reverse thrust and applied the brakes. He stopped the aircraft with about 150 metres left to spare, then back tracked to the apron, located half way down the runway.

After a quick turn around, it was now my turn to fly back to Biak. Unlike Dante, I wouldn't need to worry so much about hitting the exact touchdown zone on Biak's 3.5 km runway. However I would be taking off from Serui's 550 metre runway. This in itself came with many risks, namely aborting the take off. Usually a small aircraft like a Caravan would be able to stop on the remaining runway in the event that the take off needed to be rejected. However with very short runways, this becomes more complicated; like for the approach, committal points need to be nominated prior to take off. In our case, Dante told me that he wanted us to use a Church (which was located unusually close to the runway), as the committal point. Any problems after we past the Church, other than an engine failure, would need to be resolved in the air. If we went too far past the Church, and the engine died, we died.

At the end of the briefing, Dante told me one last thing to me, "Dan, keep both your hands on the control column during take off. Only I will have my hand on the power lever". "Understood", I replied, before commencing the final walk around. What Dante said made perfect sense. Rejecting a take off past the committal point could have dangerous consequences. Only Dante would be making the decision to abort the take off. After starting the engine, Dante taxied and backtracked runway 18. As the required turn arc was so small, due to the narrow runway, it would have been difficult to taxi from the right seat. The brakes and rudders on my side just weren't strong enough to make that kind of turn. After lining up, Dante gave me the controls. It was to be a max performance take off. We both pressed down on the brakes as I slowly advanced the power lever. I then called "set take off power", before placing my both of my hands on the control column, like Dante asked. Dante called "take off power set, T's and P's in the green" and I called "brake release". We accelerated down the runway quickly, lifting off of the tarmac with around 100 metres of runway left in front of us.

We continued the climb up to our cruise altitude of 6,500 feet. Going by Dante's example, I decided that I would also hand fly the entire flight. After all, I didn't pay 50k for my flight training so that I could push buttons on an autopilot. One of the features of Caravan was that the onboard computer could calculate the point at which we needed to descend. "We don't need this", said Dante. "You know how to calculate your descent point in your head?", he asked. I had a quick think. I couldn't recall if I had learned that during training or not. "Dante I honestly can't recall mate", I replied. "No problem, I'll teach you", said Dante, "It's 3 miles for the first 1000 feet, then 6 miles thereafter". Whilst flying the aircraft, I did a quick calculation in my head. We were 6,500 feet. So that would be 3 + (5.5 x 6). "So we begin our descent at 36 miles from Biak?", I asked. Dante smiled, "Exactly!".

After landing at Biak, Dante informed me that he was going to reduce the payload slightly for the next flight to Serui. As the day progressed, the wind speed would start to increase. It was also starting to turn to a tailwind for the approach on to runway 36. On the following flight back to Serui, whilst on final approach for runway 36, we experienced more turbulence than on the previous flight. Because Serui is surrounded by high terrain, the wind becomes distorted. This is known as "mechanical turbulence". We started off with a headwind, then a tailwind, then a headwind again. All the time I was calling out this change in wind direction and speed to Dante. At the 300 foot point, Dante committed to the approach. I continued to call out the changes in wind, whilst Dante flew the aircraft. It was exciting for me, however it was just another day at work for Dante. Despite the variable wind, Dante managed to touchdown right at the beginning of the runway. He was a pro.

Above: Final approach for runway 29 in Biak.

On our final flight back to Biak, whilst I was flying, Dante gave me a challenge. "Do you think you could land in Biak with an engine failure?", he asked. It was a 3.5 km runway; it was easy enough to make a glide approach. "We can make things more interesting", said Dante, "Let's see if you can land right on top of the last touchdown zone marker for runway 29. I'll bet you a beer!". "Challenge accepted!", I replied. The glide ratio of the Caravan was just over 2 miles per 1000 feet. From an altitude of 6,500 feet, on a long base leg of about 13 miles, Dante set 350 foot pounds of torque, to simulate zero thrust. I trimmed the aircraft for the best glide speed, which was about 85 knots for our weight, then planned the approach. "I'll make the 500 foot key point over the beginning of the clearway", I briefed, "The 1000 foot key point will be on a 1 mile left base leg." Dante nodded, "Yeah, that's sounds reasonable", he said, "But let's see if you can put it into practice".

Based on our current altitude and distance from the 1000 foot key point, I could see that we were high. I turned the aircraft away from the key point, in order to increase the track miles. Passing 2000 feet, I turned back towards the 1000 foot key point. It now appeared that we were slightly low. I immediately turned towards the 500 foot key point over the clearway on final approach. Now we were back on profile. I asked for a wind check from ATC; we were expecting a 15 knot headwind. I needed to delay the flap extension. Approaching the 500 foot key point, I began to turn towards the final approach. I asked Dante for flaps 10, then flaps 20. We were now stabilised on final approach. I looked at the last touchdown zone markers ahead of us...we were going to make it! At around 10 feet above the runway, I gently raised the nose of the aircraft to control our descent onto the last touchdown zone marker. Waiting for it...waiting for it...now! The main gear kissed the tarmac exactly on the last touchdown zone marker.

"Nicely done!", said Dante, "You owe me a beer now!".

"Wait...what do you mean?", I replied. Dante grinned. "I said that I'll bet you a beer that you <u>can</u> land on the last touchdown zone marker", he said.

CHAPTER 24

THE MULIA SHOOTING

At times West Papua can resemble a war zone. Shortly after I arrived in Biak in April 2012, unknown assailants opened fire on a Trigana Air turboprop aircraft, whilst landing in Mulia. Mulia airport, which was located on the side of a mountain in the highlands, had a committal point for landing. The gunmen waited until after the aircraft touched down before opening fire. They knew that there was no way for the pilots to go around. The pilots and their passengers, were by every definition, sitting ducks.

Above: Final approach into Mulia airport. The landing strip is very steep and surrounded by high terrain. The pilots of the Trigana Air turboprop had no where to go when they were fired upon.

The gunmen, who were believed to be located nearby on the hill to the right of the landing strip, waited for the Trigana Air to touchdown before spraying the aircraft occupants with rounds from one or more M16 automatic rifles. Both the Captain and First Officer were amongst those who were shot. The Captain, with no where else to go, swerved off of the runway and crashed into the terminal building located on the far side of the airport. One person was killed, with at least 4 people being injured. As a result of the shooting, all airlines, including Susi Air, immediately stopped flying to Mulia. The residents of Mulia were now isolated from the rest of society, with limited supplies.

The local police, military and journalists were quick to investigate who was responsible for the shooting. Mulia, like much of the highlands, was a hotbed for armed rebels. A fact which the Indonesian authorities were only to quick to point out during their initial investigation. However if true, this would have been the first time that Papuan rebels would have targeted a civilian aircraft. Previously, rebels had often targetted police, military and politicians. However there wasn't a history of violence towards civilians. Furthermore, they wouldn't have had any incentive to attack their main source of supplies into Mulia. Some journalists instead theorised that the attack was actually a "false flag" operation, conducted by Indonesian special forces, in order to justify an increased military presence in the region.

It was a well established fact, from both sides, that a unit from the "Brimob" (an Indonesian special forces regiment), were nearby the location at the time of the shooting. According to the admissions from the local police, the Brimob gave chase to the armed assailants. However despite all of their equipment and firepower, they were unable to capture or kill any of these assailants. To add a bit more gasoline onto this bonfire of a conspiracy, the Brimob also happened to be armed with M16 rifles; the same weapon which was believed to be behind the shooting. The passenger who was killed during the attack was a journalist who was reporting on the local elections. Although this furthers the conspiracy theories of the shooting being an inside job, it was unlikely that any one of the passengers could have been specifically targeted, due to the speed of the aircraft and rate of fire.

The jury's still out on this one. Even at the time of publishing this book, there is still no solid evidence which definitively points to either the Indonesian authorities, or the rebels, for being behind the attack. However in either case, it was quite right for airlines to refuse to fly to Mulia immediately following the shooting. Ultimately, we were all civilian pilots. Although there was always going to be an element of danger in regards to flying in parts of the World such as West Papua, we needed to have limits. We were unarmed and our aircraft weren't equipped with protective armour. We didn't have military escorts when we flew to remote locations like this. And even if we did, we wouldn't have even known if we could trust those escorts.

The shooting at Mulia was a hot topic for Susi Air pilots in the following weeks. All of the pilots in Biak and Manokwari couldn't stop talking about what had happened. Even the most senior of Papua Captains were shocked. We all hoped that it was just a one off incident which would never happen again. Unfortunately we were all wrong.

Welcome to Papua.

CHAPTER 25

MANOKWARI

I continued flying in Biak for a few more days following my first flight to Serui. Biak was great fun. We would fly in the morning, finish early, then head to beach in the afternoon. Fortunately my next base, Manokwari, would have a similar way of life.

From Biak, I was rostered to fly to the island of Numfor, then onwards to Manokwari. When we arrived in Manokwari, I swapped with another FO who then flew the return trip back to Biak. This was a convenient method which Susi Air used to transport pilots between different bases. After all, there was no point in taking a seat away from a fare paying passenger when we could just fly the plane ourselves! I was to spend the next 2 weeks in Manokwari, then head back to Biak for a couple of days, before moving onwards to Sentani and Wamena. This was a typical rotation for a First Officer in Papua; we would start from the easier bases in the lowlands, then onwards to the more challenging bases in the highlands.

I arrived in Manokwari at the perfect time; the other pilots had arranged a BBQ in the front garden of Captain's house. The Base Manager, a New Zealand guy called Frank, and another Captain who was also from New Zealand, Ted, had built a BBQ using an old fuel drum which they'd cut in half. They'd stocked up on the beers as well. Not wanting to be a free loader, I bought a bottle of Jack Daniel's to the BBQ, (it was duty free from my last visa run in Singapore). There were 8 Caravan pilots based in Manokwari; 4 Captains and 4 FOs. There was also 1 Porter pilot, 2 cicis, the driver and 2 pilots from other companies at the BBQ. All in all, it was a pretty good turn out.

The Captain and First Officer houses were just 5 minutes walk apart. Both houses were located in a very quiet, almost rural neighbourhood on the outskirts of Manokwari. It was quite a pleasant location with friendly neighbours...I mean very friendly. The locals politely stood outside of the gate to the Captain's house whilst we were having the BBQ, watching us. Whenever we looked in their direction, they smiled and waved at us. It was a bit weird at first, but I got use to it, as did all the other pilots when they first arrived in Manokwari. They didn't seem to want anything from us. They were just really nice people who wanted to say hi. Later, after we had eaten, we played frisby with them.

The flying from Manokwari, like Biak, was very enjoyable. We flew to some interesting destinations. My personal favourite was Merdei, a short dirt strip in the middle of no where. It was a very distinctive landing strip, which was marked with nothing more than the tyre marks of the previous aircraft which had landed there. Basically, Merdei was just a field with long grass and a few houses; the locals hadn't planned any specific runway for us to land on, let alone build anything resembling a terminal building. The take off from Merdei was especially interesting. Due to rocks and other debris at the beginning of the strip, we needed to perform an "offset departure".

Above: An "offset departure" from Merdei.

After the Captain parked the aircraft at a 45 degree angle, facing the strip, we would advance to full power, before releasing the brakes and very carefully turning the aircraft back onto the strip at high speed. Basically Merdei was a curved runway. To make matters more interesting, after lift off, we needed to immediately bank the aircraft right towards a nearby river, as we couldn't climb above the high trees at the end of the strip. We would then fly down the river until we gained enough altitude to make it over the trees. The best part of Merdei was that there wasn't a Captain's only restriction; I could both land and take off their as an FO. It was a lot of fun and a massive confidence booster. There really wasn't much room for error.

There were a few other interesting strips as well. Bintuni, like Merdei, was also quite short, and required a great deal of precision for both the take offs and landings. Like Merdei, both Captains and FOs could land there. Despite their challenges, neither of these strips had committal points for the landing. Committal points for the take offs, yes, however the Captain would always have his hand on the power lever, regardless of who was the PF. As a result, the Captain would ultimately have the decision as to whether or not abort a take off. In regards to the approach into these landing strips, it was still possible to go around at any point before touchdown. Even though the runways were very short, with very little room for error, the Captains who we flew with were more than happy to let us land. Ultimately if we messed things up, we could always go around and try again.

Some of the Captains I flew with in Manokwari loved to test us when we were flying. Sometimes they would give us engine "failures" on our descent into Manokwari airport, to see if we could make the runway. Of course they kept the engine running the whole time, however they would simulate zero thrust with the power lever. Sometimes they would test us in other ways. My personal favourite was from Oscar, another New Zealand Captain who gave me a (real) flap failure on my approach into Bintuni. As the PF, I asked him for flaps 10, then flaps 20. I saw him select the flaps each time with the flap lever. However something just didn't feel quite right. And this brings me to the next lesson of this book.

LESSON 15: NEVER MAKE ASSUMPTIONS WHEN FLYING...DOUBLE CHECK EVERYTHING

Each time Oscar selected the flaps, the aircraft didn't pitch up, as it normally would do with the extension of flaps. I looked at the flap indicator on final approach...the flaps were still fully up! I immediately executed a go around. After levelling off at 1000 feet, I turned to my left to see Oscar with a grin on his face. "Well done mate!", he said, "I wasn't sure how long it would take you to notice". It turned out that he had pulled the circuit breaker for the flap motors. He really did move the flap lever when I asked him to, in order to trick me into believing that the flaps really were being extended. This test was all in good fun, and also perfectly safe...he of course wasn't going to let me land on a short runway without flaps. Although we were both laughing our heads off after the go around, there was a very serious lesson that Oscar wanted to teach me. "Soon enough you're going to be a Captain yourself", advised Oscar, "Then you'll be flying with brand new FOs, who will be doing all kinds of weird and wonderful shit. If something doesn't feel right, check it again...and again".

In the 2 weeks that I was based in Manokwari, I would fly a lot and learn a lot. However I wasn't just improving myself through flying. Almost every day after work, myself and the other pilots would go running. We were running about 3 to 5 miles a day across the rugged terrain surrounding Manokwari. Sometimes we would arrange trips down to the beach too, so we could go swimming, or in the case of some of the other pilots, surfing. Frank warned me that the last FO who had surfed at that particular beach, fell off head first from his board and straight onto the brittle, razor sharp coral below. He sliced his back to pieces. Or as Frank quite eloquently put it, in his Kiwi accent, "He completely fucked his back up mate!". Frank and Ted were both semi pro surfers. However I was still a beginner when it came to surfing, so I just stuck to swimming in the calmer part of the water with the other pilots who didn't surf. Either way though, Manokwari was a great base for getting fit.

Following my 2 week tour of Manokwari, I was rostered to fly in Biak for a couple of days, before moving onwards to the highlands. On my final day in Biak, I was rostered to fly a double Serui. The Captain who I was flying with, another guy from New Zealand (there were quite a few in Susi Air), was a Captain in the highlands who had been sent out of base. This Captain had a lot of experience and confidence. So much so, that he let me land in Serui, which was usually a Captain's only landing. I appreciated the trust that he showed me. Fortunately, my approach and landing went well. This confidence boost was exactly what I needed before I moved onto the more challenging strips up in the highlands.

Following my final flight from Biak, myself and the other pilots ended the day with a 3 mile run in the early evening, shortly before dinner. All 6 of us went along. It was a fairly low paced, relaxing run, along a route which took us through a large park. The sun was beginning to set. We could see flocks of colourful birds fly across the crimson sky. This really was the perfect way to end my tour of the Papua lowlands, I thought. I followed the other guys through a gap in the fence in the park. I looked to my right to see the sunset...SMACK!

I'd just ran head first into a metal bar! It turned out that the gap in the fence that the others had just ran through, still had the horizontal, steel support beam connecting the 2 sections of the fence. This steel support beam, like the rest of the fence, had been painted green...the exact same shade of green as the bushes on the other side. The others knew that there was a beam there. They ducked under it. However I didn't see it coming. The force of the metal bar striking my forehead caused me to somersault backwards. The sound of my skull hitting the steel sounded a bit like a hammer hitting a church bell. Ouch! Fucking ouch! I could quite literally feel my brain ricochet against the inside of my skull.

In the background I could hear laughter. I slowly got up, clenching my blood soaked head, to see a group of local kids pointing their fingers at me, pissing themselves laughing. This was embarrassing. Trying to save face, I looked at them and laughed back, whilst hiding the massive gash on my forehead. With my head still spinning from the concussion, I slowly staggered through the gap in the fence, this time carefully lowering my head under the metal beam. The others were already miles ahead of me, completely oblivious to my unfortunate mishap. I slowly made my way back to the pilots house, covered in blood, with a bruised ego.

Ok...so maybe this wasn't the perfect way to end my tour of the Papua lowlands.

CHAPTER 26

THE HIGHLANDS

The following day after my head injury I was to fly to Sentani with an English Captain called Mark. Mark was a very likeable guy. Despite his years of flying experience, he was very humble and down to earth. I told Mark about my accident the evening before and asked him if he had any objections to flying with me. "Nah that's fine mate", he replied, "If you pass out I'll fly you to the nearest hospital". I was dressed in my pilots uniform with my head bandaged up, however the passengers didn't seem to be at all concerned about this during the boarding. Fair enough then, I thought.

From Biak, we were to first fly to a small airport called Sarmi, before continuing on to our final destination, Sentani. During our first flight, I noticed that Mark had a strong west country accent, yet he would always speak the Queen's English whenever he made a radio call. He kept switching his voice between that of a farmer and that of a British Airways Captain. It was quite interesting to listen to. I have a somewhat mixed accent; a strange combination of west country, Irish and Australian. Following his example, I actually started to do the same thing myself. In fact, even to this very day as a Boeing 737 Captain, I still mimic a very clear and calm voice with a neutral accent, whenever I speak on the radio or make a passenger announcement. So much so, that even people who know me wouldn't recognise my voice. It just makes it easier for non native English speakers to understand what I say. It also sounds far more professional. I have Mark to thank for that.

We arrived in Sentani at around midday. The pilot's house in Sentani was unique in the sense that it was the only accommodation, other than Pangandaran, which was directly owned by the company. In fact, Christian and Susi had gone out of their way to invest a lot of time and money building this house, which could best be described as an upmarket, 10 bedroom, villa. Government subsidised flights in Papua were a big money earner for Susi Air. As a result, they took very good care of their Papua Captains, especially in the highlands.

After dropping off my suitcase in my room, I walked over to the kitchen and living area which was located outside under a large shelter in the centre of the villa. There were a few large sofas surrounding a 60 inch screen TV and a massive dining table with hand carved wooden chairs. I saw Mark walk up to a fridge located next to the TV. That seemed to be a strange location for a fridge, I thought. However when he opened the fridge, it became apparent that it was stacked full of beers. No food, no soft drinks, just cans of beer. I estimated that the "beer fridge" contained somewhere in the region of 80 cans. "Can I get you a beer, Dan?", asked Mark. I had just died and gone to heaven. We walked over to the sofas where a few of the other pilots were sitting, watching an England football match on the 60 inch screen TV. "Welcome to paradise!", remarked one of the Captains, as he shook my hand. Paradise indeed.

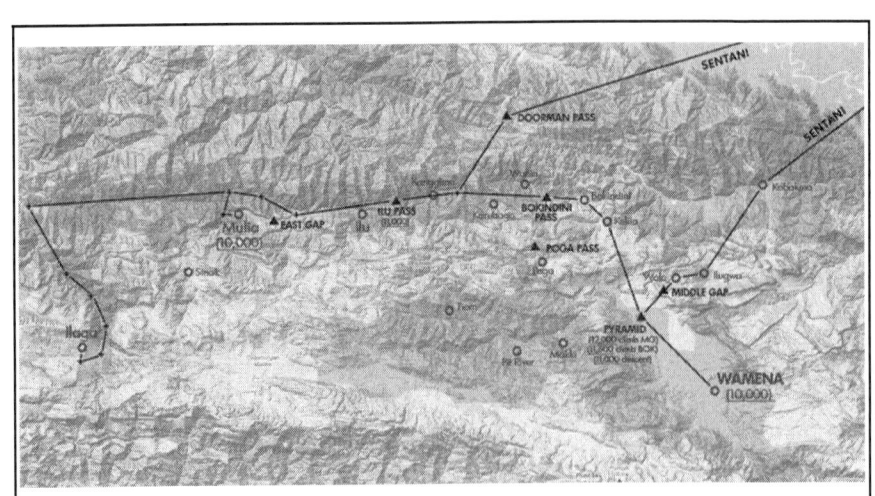

Above: The Papua highlands. Due to the high terrain, low altitude aircraft were only able to take certain routes through the valleys in the mountains.

After lunch, I began studying for my flight the next day to "Ilu". Ilu was a small town located in the centre of the highlands, serviced by a 1000 metre, 7% up slope, landing strip. I was to fly there with Simon, another English Captain, who was also the Base Manager for Sentani. Although on paper, the runway was officially 1000 metres in length, (which was fairly long for a Caravan), only the upper 2/3rds of the runway was suitable for landing. The lower part of the runway had begun to crumble away off of the edge of the cliff at the beginning of the runway. Nobody knew for sure if the force of an aircraft landing at the beginning of the runway would cause the ground to collapse. What made this strip equally as interesting, was that a straight in approach for the runway was impossible. Due to a very large mountain standing on the final approach path, it was necessary to approach sideways and then abruptly turn right in order to land. As with most other mountain strips, Ilu had a committal point for take off and landing. For all these reasons, Ilu had been classed as a "Grade 3" mountain strip. A Grade 3 meant that only specially trained, highly experienced Captains, could land there.

Above: The final approach of runway 17 in Ilu. Due to high terrain on the left, a straight in approach was not possible.

We departed Sentani at 7am the following day. Rather than carrying passengers, which is what I was previously accustomed to, we would instead be carrying a cargo of five 200 litre fuel drums. We were now flying what could best be described as a giant petrol bomb. Needless to say, Simon would be landing in Ilu himself. I would be the PM for the first flight, then PF on the way back to Sentani. The flight time was about 1 hour and 20 minutes. From Sentani, we initially flew to a waypoint by the name of "Doorman's Pass", located to the North of the high terrain. From this point onwards, we would need to fly a very specific track through various valleys in order to get to Ilu; deviating even slightly to the left or right of this track simply wasn't an option due to the high terrain. This in itself posed a number of threats, which I would later see on the return flight back to Sentani. We were flying at a cruise altitude of 12,000 feet, yet I needed to look up in order to see the tops of the mountains that we were navigating around. Some off the valleys were very narrow indeed; even the slightest error in track keeping could have caused a CFIT (Controlled Flight Into Terrain).

Above: Flying through a valley at 12,000 feet, yet we're still well below the terrain either side of us.

You would have thought that flying to a remote location in the mountains would have meant that we would be the only aircraft in the area. However that simply wasn't the case. The track which we were flying was the same track that most other aircraft needed to fly. It was a bit like driving through a narrow road in the middle of the countryside. There may have been very little there, however all of the other traffic in the area were forced to use the exact same route that we were taking, causing what could best be described as a bottle neck. To make matters more interesting, there was no radar coverage due to the high terrain. The only way to guarantee safe separation from other aircraft was to look outside and report our position on the area frequency at regular intervals. CFITs were the biggest threat to aircraft in the highlands, however MACs (Mid Air Collisions) were a close second. In our particular case, LOC (Loss Of Control) was also a major threat. If the harnesses securing the fuel drums gave way, the fuel drums could have rolled back, causing our aircraft to abruptly pitch up and stall.

Approaching Ilu, Simon initially descended down to 10,000 feet so that he could fly overhead and examine the weather. "I'm checking that there is no cloud in 3 specific areas", said Simon, "The final approach, the runway and the missed approach path". When flying close to high terrain, we must always assume that every cloud is a mountain. This is especially true in narrow valleys where there isn't necessarily much room to perform a U-turn. Once satisfied that the key areas were free from cloud, Simon descended further to observe the windsock and check that the runway was clear, before continuing outbound away from Ilu. Ilu was 6000 feet high. Passing 7500 feet, Simon made a sharp U-turn to the right down the valley, so that we were now on an extended right base for runway 17.

There was now a mountain on our left side. And it was close. I mean really close. Our wing tip was almost brushing against the trees on the side of the mountain. But Simon needed to get close. If he was too far to the right, he wouldn't have been able to align the aircraft with the runway in time. He also wouldn't have been able to go around, as the only missed approach path was a sharp U-turn to the right, back in the same direction that we had come from. An overshoot of the final approach would have proved fatal, as the valley ahead of us climbed up steeply past Ilu. Far steeper than we could climb in our aircraft. "Are you happy with the approach so far?", asked Simon. "Yes", I replied. Simon sharply banked right to align with the runway. "We're now committed", advised Simon. We appeared to be high, however this was an optical illusion due to the slope of the runway. Simon made a textbook landing on the upper, smooth portion of the runway. We slowed down very quickly due to the steep slope of the runway, before taxiing to the small, grass apron located halfway down the runway.

After we parked and shutdown, we were greeted by the locals, many of whom were armed with bows and arrows. I must admit, I was a bit reluctant to get out of the aircraft at first. Simon looked at me and smiled. "Relax, they're friendly", he said. Sure enough, they seemed pretty happy to see us. Ultimately, we were their gateway with the rest of the World. Patrolling the far side of the apron, there were a unit of about 10, heavily armed, Indonesian special forces. Since the shooting in Mulia, the Indonesian Government had tightened it's grip over the more remote parts of Papua.

After installing the tail stand, I opened the cargo door and helped Simon loosen the harnesses of the fuel drums. The 200 litre fuel drums weighed over 180kg each. They were previously loaded in Sentani by the back of a truck, which happened to be the same height as the floor of the aircraft. However there was no truck here. "Simon...how are we supposed to unload these fuel drums?", I asked. Simon smiled, "_We_ are not unloading these", he said. Outside the aircraft, I noticed that the local ramp agents had placed two tyres by the cargo door. After removing the harnesses, Simon stepped out of the aircraft and walked about 20 metres away. I followed him. From a distance, we watched the local ramp agents unload the fuel drums. It soon became apparent why they had placed the two tyres outside of the cargo door. It also became apparent as to why Simon wanted to watch them from a distance.

BANG!

The sound was so deafening that it echoed down the valley. Over 180 kg of metal and highly flammable fuel had just been launched out of the back of the aircraft, cushioned by nothing more than a couple of flimsy rubber tyres. Myself and Simon stepped back a few paces. "Hey Simon, is it a problem for that guy to be smoking as he's unloading the fuel drums?", I asked. We both stepped back a few more paces.

Above: This is how to unload a 200 litre fuel drum when you don't have a truck.

After the unloading of the fuel was complete, we helped the local ramp agents load the empty fuel drums onto our aircraft for the return flight to Sentani. I was now the PF. As I was unfamiliar with Ilu, Simon briefed me for the departure. The standard rules applied for taking off from a strip with a committal point. Simon would have his hand on the power lever at all times, whilst I would keep both hands on the control column. Only Simon would get to decide if a take off would be aborted, and the committal point would be just 50 metres into the take off roll. The steep down slope would have made it very difficult to stop. "If I abort the take off and we can't stop in time, I'll swerve right into a ditch", advised Simon. It may have sounded a tad extreme, however it was either that, or plummet several thousand feet off of the edge of the cliff at the end of the runway. It would be a max performance take off, followed by an immediate turn to the left to avoid crashing into the mountain on the other side of the valley.

Above: Taking off from Ilu. Due to the mountain on the other side of the valley, an immediate turn to the left was required.

We accelerated quickly down the runway. I applied a bit of back pressure on the control column to protect the nose wheel from the bumpy tarmac, then rotated at about 60 knots. After take off, I immediately turned left, as per Simon's instructions. During the initial climb, I remained close to the right side of the valley. Once Simon was happy that we had enough terrain clearance to manoeuvre, I made a U-turn to the left. We were now on course back to Sentani. We continued our climb to our cruise altitude of 11,000 feet.

BANG!

From behind us, I heard the sound of metal breaking. Startled, I looked at Simon. "What the fuck was that?!", I frantically asked. Simon laughed. "Ah sorry I forgot to warn you about that", he replied, "That's normal when we fly empty fuel drums". Due to the pressure difference in the climb and descent, the metallic casing of the fuel drums will buckle, causing a loud bang. We both laughed. It's perhaps not the most reassuring of noises to hear when you're flying a plane. But at least we knew it wasn't the plane itself making those noises.

The visibility in the valley had begun to deteriorate. About 10 miles ahead of us, overhead the junction for Doorman's Pass, we could see a CB on the weather radar. I looked outside. We appeared to be clear of terrain to the left, and that was also the direction that we needed to turn in order to get back to Sentani. However the visibility was marginal. "Would you like me to turn to the left of track to avoid the CB?", I asked Simon. "Absolutely not!", Simon replied, "Do you know how high the terrain is over there?". I was a bit startled from his response. "So we just fly through the bad weather ahead of us?", I sheepishly asked. "Absolutely", replied Simon, "You may think you're clear of terrain here, but the visibility isn't great. There's a lot you can't see." Simon was absolutely correct. And this brings me to the next lesson of the book.

LESSON 16: PRIORITISE WHEN DEALING WITH THREATS

In an ideal world, we would never fly through bad weather, however sometimes we simply don't have a choice. Later on in my career with Susi Air, when I gained more experience and became a trainer myself, I would always teach new pilots about the three major threats in Indonesia, or as I liked to call them, "the 3 Ts". Terrain, Traffic and Thunderstorms. Flying through a thunderstorm <u>might</u> cause an accident. Flying close to other traffic will <u>probably</u> cause an accident. However flying into terrain will <u>definitely</u> cause an accident. If you ever find yourself in an undesirable situation where you are presented with multiple threats at the same time, the 3T model of decision making will always help you to prioritise. Unless you are 100% sure that you can remain visual, or can climb above the Minimum Off Route Altitude, there will be times that you just need to stay on that magenta track line and fly straight through the centre of that storm, or worse still, towards another aircraft. When flying in the Papua highlands, where the terrain was far higher than we were able to fly and the airspace was congested with other aircraft, these decisions needed to be made on a regular basis.

Flying in the Papua highlands was challenging enough for pilots flying relatively new aircraft. All of the Caravans and Porters in the Susi Air fleet were equipped with 2 GPS units, to ensure both accuracy and also reliability in the case that one GPS unit were to fail. We also had the luxury of following pre existing tracks which we knew would guarantee terrain clearance.

But let's remember for one moment, that pilots had been flying low altitude aircraft through those Papuan valleys since the end of WW2. Like us, those vintage pilots would have had no ground based navigation aids or radar service. However unlike us, they wouldn't have even had GPS! How on Earth did these pilots safely fly through these valleys? The answer is, they didn't. Prior to aircraft being equipped with GPS, aircraft were crashing in the highlands every other month. The valleys were quite literally littered with wreckage from vintage aircraft, most of which were never seen again due to the thick jungle canopy. Not only was navigation in the highlands challenging without GPS, the pilots didn't necessarily know *what* they were navigating around in the first instance, as much of the region hadn't yet been accurately charted. One wrong turn into a narrow valley or a momentary contact with a cloud, could have proved fatal.

It was important for us not to take all of this knowledge and technology for granted. Our lives literally depended on it.

CHAPTER 27

WAMENA

Over the following week I would fly to various mountain strips from Sentani. Ilu was one of my favourites, however there were a couple of other strips which were also very memorable. Borme was one such example. Borme was the steepest mountain strip that I would ever fly to during my time in Papua. With a slope of 10%, it was about as steep as a Caravan could safely land on. If it were any steeper, only a Pilatus Porter would be able to land there. The visual illusion of being too high on the approach due to the steep runway slope, really was quite unbelievable.

Above: It may look like we're too high to land in Borme, however that's just an optical illusion. Borme is 10% up slope. We're on the correct profile.

One week after my arrival in Sentani, I was to go on a 4 day tour to Wamena, the satellite base for the Papua highlands. Wamena was a city with a population of 240,000 people (including the surrounding areas), located in the centre of the mountains. It had a fairly large airport with a 2000 metre long runway. It was completely landlocked from the rest of Papua; the only way to access Wamena was by aircraft. You may be asking yourself how and why there would be such a large settlement in such a remote location with no infrastructure connecting it to the rest of Papua? The simple answer to that question was the mining industry. As a result of shipping workers, supplies and product, to and from the various mines up in the mountains, the mining industry ultimately transformed what was originally a small, remote village, into the city that it is today.

I would be travelling to Wamena with Pete, a young Canadian Captain who was also the head of operations for the highlands. Pete had done very well for himself. He had joined Susi Air when he was in his late teens, just before Susi Air had imposed a minimum age restriction of 21 years. He quickly rose up through the ranks, gaining a reputation with Christian and Susi as being somewhat of a pioneer. Whenever Susi Air wanted to open up a new base somewhere, they would send Pete over there to determine the best destinations, routes and scheduling. Later in his career, after he had some experience flying in Papua, Pete would be a key player in designing the route guide and training syllabus for new Captains and FOs. He was about my age, however he had a lot of experience in both flying and management.

The morning flight to Wamena was just over an hour. The area surrounding Wamena airport was very busy, with aircraft taking off and landing every couple of minutes. Due to the high terrain surrounding Wamena, radar vectors were not possible. The larger aircraft needed to strictly follow a pre determined GPS track and descend in a hold, regardless of whether they were visual or not. However for smaller, more manoeuvrable aircraft like ours, we could simply ask for a straight in visual approach, effectively skipping the queue. We could descend at angles far steeper than that of the larger jet aircraft. After landing, we taxied to the apron and shut down. We off loaded our suitcases from the aircraft and gave them to the driver, who subsequently drove them to the pilots house. However we wouldn't be going home just yet. We first needed to make a return flight to Dekai, a short strip located to the South of the mountains.

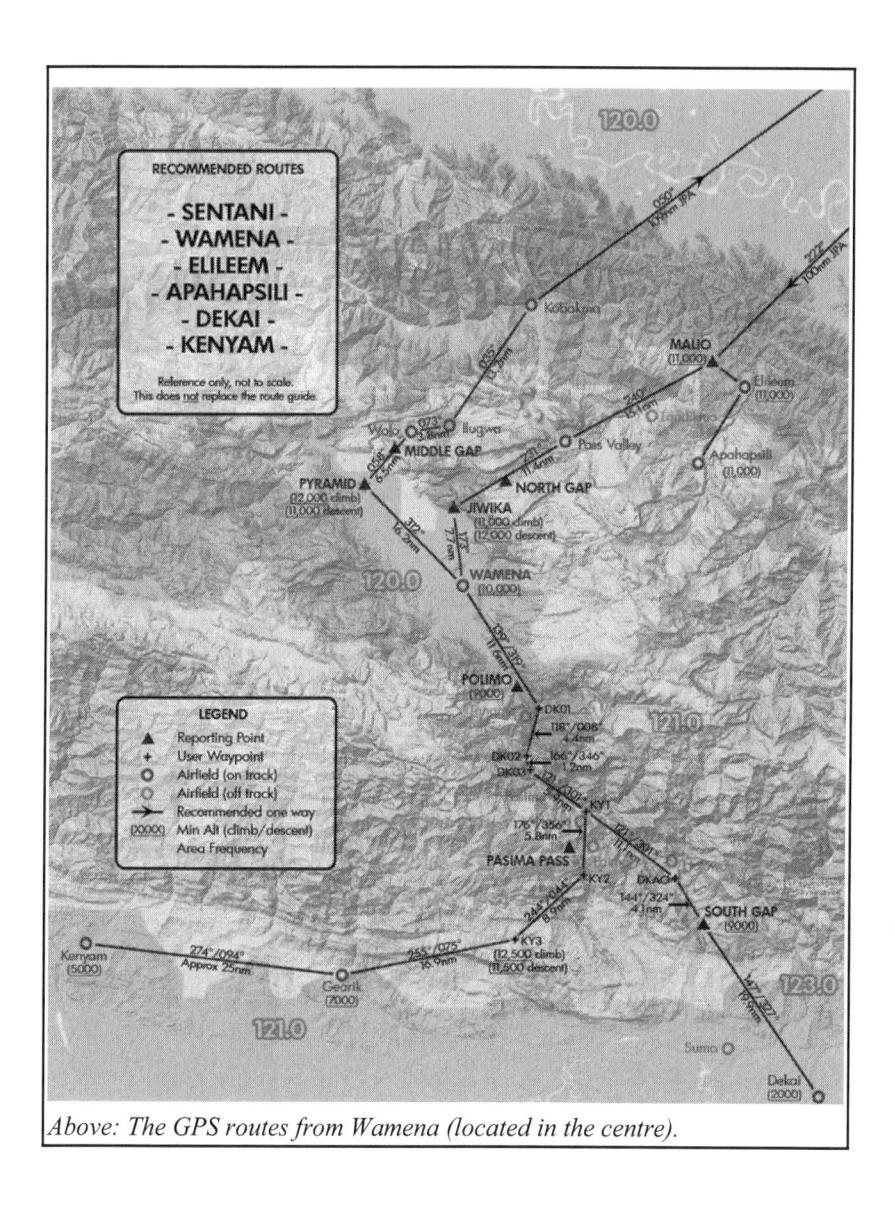

Above: The GPS routes from Wamena (located in the centre).

The flight to Dekai was about 1 hour there and 1 ½ hours back. We returned to Wamena just as the weather had begun to deteriorate. As Wamena was surrounded by high terrain, it created what could best be described as a "bowl". All of the water vapour accumulated inside of this bowl throughout the day, creating low visibility and cloud in the afternoon. We would need to stay on the GPS track until we became visual. We would first need to fly overhead Wamena and descend in the hold, one by one, along with all of the larger aircraft. We would be joining the back of the queue. To make matters more interesting, we were getting low of fuel. Due to the short length of the strips that we would fly to, and the need to tanker fuel for both the trip there and back, we were limited with the fuel that we could take. During our descent overhead Wamena, we were getting uncomfortably close to our 400 lbs of reserve fuel. Fortunately, by this point, we had just become visual with the ground. We were number 3 to land, following a turboprop on downwind and a 737 on final.

After landing, we taxied to the apron and shutdown. The driver took us straight to the pilots house, located about 10 minutes drive from the airport. We were sharing this house with Duncan, a Porter pilot from New Zealand who was based full time in Wamena, and his German Shepherd, "Bear". Bear was just a couple of years old when I first met him. He may have been a puppy, however he still managed to deter any would-be burglars. In the past, the pilots house was being robbed every other month by a local gang in Wamena. Duncan's response to this was to cover the fences surrounding the house with razor wire and buy himself a guard dog. It seemed to work.

As Pete walked through the door to the pilot's house, Bear ran out to meet us. With open arms, Pete kneeled down and embraced the highly excitable puppy. "Oh! Who's this? Who's a good boy? Have you missed me?", said Pete in a high pitched voice. Bear then started chewing on Pete's arm. "Ow ow, stop that!", shouted Pete. Duncan came to the door and laid down the law. "Bear! Stop!". On hearing Duncan's voice, Bear immediately ceased and sat to attention. I quickly walked through the front door. Standing in the living area of the house, Bear came over to investigate me. He circled me a few times, sniffing me. Satisfied that I wasn't a home intruder, he retreated back to Duncan. "Don't worry, he's harmless", said Duncan, as Bear walked back to Pete and started chewing on his leg. Dogs, like toddlers, go through a biting phase when they're younger.

The cici showed myself and Pete to our rooms. Duncan invited us to have beers around his friend's house later that afternoon. His friend, Noel, was the pilot of a PAC 750 single engine turboprop. He had been based in Wamena for several years with another airline. He was by every definition a career bush pilot. He was in his late 40s and had around 15,000 hours of bush flying on his CV. He loved flying in the remote areas of Papua and had absolutely no intention of ever flying for an airline. Noel was great fun to hang out with. As I would later find out however, he was also fucking nuts when he was drunk. But in the best kind of way.

The driver took us all to Noel's house, located about 15 minutes drive away. As we arrived, Noel casually walked out to greet us with a beer in his hand. "Let's get this party started!", he shouted, half cut. After he shook hands with Pete and Duncan, he approached me to shake my hand. "We haven't met before, have we?", asked Noel. "No it's my first time in Wamena", I replied. "Well you're going to need a beer then!", said Noel, "Welcome to hell!". We followed Noel into his house and he opened up his beer fridge. "OK so what would you guys like?", asked Noel, "We have Anker, Anker or Anker". There were literally about 100 cans of Anker beer is his fridge. This guy was an absolute legend.

We sat down on his sofa with the beers and started talking about work. Bush flying wasn't just a job for many pilots, it was a hobby. Noel had all kinds of crazy stories to tell. One story which really stuck in my mind was when he was flying Caravans in the past. One time he needed to open the door of his aircraft on final approach and look outside as he couldn't see through his front window due to torrential rain. Caravans don't have windscreen wipers and even the smallest amount of rain can obscure your view outside of the window. "I had my left hand on the control column, my right hand on the power lever and my feet on the rudders!", he said, "I had to use my fuckin' elbow to push the door open!". (Regardless of whether that story was actually true, I wouldn't recommend trying that in real life).

Myself and Duncan were enthusiastically listening to Noel's stories, however Pete seemed somewhat bored. It became apparent that there was some friction between himself and Noel. Pete was young and somewhat reserved, whilst Noel was much older and brash. However they were both highly experienced pilots and accustomed to being their own boss. Whilst myself and (to a certain extent) Duncan, looked up to Noel, Pete really didn't. Sensing the dissent in Pete's attitude, Noel changed the conversation to myself. "So how many hours have you clocked up so far?", he asked me. "Just coming up to my first 1000 hours!", I replied enthusiastically. "Once you get 1500 hours, send me a message and I'll see if I can get you a job with my company", he said. Pete seemed absolutely incensed with Noel. He was very much a company man, and didn't seem to appreciate someone trying to poach is copilot in front of him.

Around 7pm, our driver came back to collect us. Duncan asked Noel if he wanted to go back to ours for dinner, much to Pete's dismay. "We've got steak tonight!", said Duncan, "Imported from Australia!". Terry quickly agreed. We finished our beers and got in the minibus. About 5 minutes into the journey, the driver abruptly stopped in the middle of the street. A group of locals were standing in the middle of the road carrying sticks and they appeared to be deliberately blocking us. "What's going on 'ere?!", asked Noel. Shit. Was this a robbery? Somewhat drunk, Noel opened the door of the minibus and marched over to the locals. "Noel get back in here!", shouted Duncan. One of the locals walked over to Noel with a stern look on his face. Standing right next to each other, they both stared each other down for a good 10 seconds or so...before bursting into laughter. Noel shook his hand and got back into the minibus. The other locals smiled and moved to the side of the road so that we could drive through. To this very day, I still have no fucking clue what that was all about.

The following morning, myself and Pete flew to Ilaga, a mountain strip about 1 hour flight from Wamena. Ilaga was similar to Ilu; it had a high elevation, a steep slope and a committal point. The landing strip was a bit shorter than that of Ilu, which combined with the 7500 foot elevation, made it more of a challenge. Both there and back we were flying passengers. In Ilaga, some of the passengers were carrying various weapons; bows and arrows, machetes etc. You know, the usual things you'd expect people to carry on a plane. Unsurprisingly, Pete asked them to leave their weapons in the cargo pod underneath the aircraft. They all seemed like nice enough people, but to be fair, we were flying an open cockpit aircraft. There was no barrier between them from us.

Most of the younger passengers were dressed in Western clothes, however some of the elders were dressed in traditional clothing; in other words nothing but a Koteka. A Koteka is a tube which is placed around the genitalia of the men. Other than a Koteka, the elders weren't wearing anything, which was actually quite brave given that the temperature in Ilaga was around 15 degrees centigrade. I felt a bit chilly wearing trousers and a pilots shirt to be honest.

The flights that we were operating were subsidised by the Government, however our passengers still needed to pay something. And in the absence of a ticket desk in Ilaga, that meant that the pilots would need to take cash payments. One of the elder passengers wearing nothing but a Koteka, approached Pete to buy a ticket. I wondered where he kept his cash, as he didn't have any pockets. However I would soon find out. The elder briefly removed his Koteka and grabbed some bank notes from inside, before offering them to Pete. Pete quickly pretended to be busy inspecting the aircraft and instead asked him to give the money to me. I reluctantly took the money and added him to the Passenger Manifest. "Err...thanks", I said. Pete looked at me with a grin.

Later that day, back in Wamena, we took Bear out for a walk with Duncan. It was actually quite interesting to walk down the road with a German Shepherd. Wamena usually had a high rate of gang related crimes, especially robberies. However nobody would dare go near us as we walked down the road. Despite being just a puppy, everyone seemed to be petrified of Bear. I would later take Bear out for walks myself. After my 4 day tour of Wamena had finished, I continued flying in Sentani for another week, before returning back to Wamena for one last 4 day tour.

By the end of my 6 week tour of Papua, I had been based in 4 different locations and flown to over 30 different landing strips, whilst clocking up about 110 hours of flight time with 14 different Captains.

I had learned a lot in those 6 weeks.

CHAPTER 28

STORM OF THE CENTURY

The end of my tour in Papua coincided with my 6 month bi-anniversary since I had first arrived in Indonesia. These 6 months had been very eventful. I had flown to some landing strips sloped up the sides of various different mountains in Papua, been interviewed on Chinese TV at the Singapore Air Show, experienced a microburst first hand and flown single pilot with a Captain who was delirious from Dengue fever. I had even had shit thrown at me by a troupe of monkeys. Following my 6 week tour of Papua, I now had 2 weeks off. It was time to take a well deserved holiday in Bali.

I flew direct from Sentani to Denpasar, Bali, where I spent the next week in a backpacker hostel getting drunk with random travellers. Later I went to Singapore for a quick visa run, before flying to my next base; Jakarta. Flying repeatedly from Halim to Nusawiru and Cilicap was a bit of a come down from flying in Papua. However it was only for 3 weeks. The rostering department had assured me that they would send me to a new base afterwards. I was convinced that after Papua, my tour in Jakarta would be uneventful and boring. However it would turn out that I was wrong.

On my first day back in Jakarta, I was rostered to fly with a Captain who I had previously met in Medan. He was an English Captain called Ross, who was out of base for a couple of weeks, covering another Captain who was on holiday. We were to fly two return flights to Cilicap in the afternoon. Ross, unlike most the other pilots, was in his late 30s. Despite his considerable flying experience, he had no ambition to fly for an airline. He enjoyed bush flying in Indonesia far too much. With his seniority came a great deal of confidence. He had a similar attitude to Bart from the Training Department. He simply didn't take any shit from the management. And in hindsight of what was about to happen, I really am grateful that I was rostered with him, and not some other Captain who blindly followed orders from the management.

After completing our first flight to Cilicap, we needed to refuel for our return trip back to Halim. Usually most Captains wouldn't have taken any more than 1100 lbs of fuel for this 1 hour flight, as if we were to take much more than that, there was a risk that we need to off load passengers and baggage due to the weight. However Ross knew better than that. "Did you see the cloud building up on the way here?", Ross asked me. "Yeah I did", I replied, "You want to take some extra fuel?". I was expecting him to say an extra 150 lbs or so. "We'll take 1500 lbs for the way back", he said. I looked at the Manifest. We had a load of 1050 kg. "Err...that would mean we would need to offload passengers and baggage", I said. Ross laid down the law. "It's either 1500 lbs of fuel, or we don't fly at all", he said.

Admittedly, my initial reaction to this was that Ross was being unreasonable. I mean yes, we should take (some) extra fuel for bad weather, however within reason. We were still a commercial operation and those passengers had already paid for their tickets. However he was the boss. I calculated that we would need to offload 2 passengers and all of the baggage, and informed the ground crew. We would need to take the offloaded passengers and baggage on the next flight, which would be in 3 hours time. Those passengers must have been absolutely livid. I think the management would have also been absolutely livid.

I was the PF for the next flight back to Halim. There were CBs in the vicinity of both Cilicap and Nusawiru. Half way into the flight, it became apparent that our en route alternate airport, Bandung, was completely submerged under an active thunderstorm. This wasn't particularly unusual, as Bandung sat in the middle of a bowl surrounded by high terrain. The weather was usually bad there in the afternoon. We continued the flight to Jakarta. Approaching the top of descent, whilst flying through cloud, we both looked at the weather radar. Up until that point, I had never seen anything like it. I had previously seen horrendous weather in both Sumatra and Java, but this was different.

Covering not only Jakarta, but the surrounding areas, was a solid block of magenta, with a diameter of about 50 miles. Usually storms are 5-10 miles in diameter. This must have been a mistake, I thought. "I think we're picking up ground returns with the weather radar", I said to Ross. Ross adjusted the tilt of the weather radar, so that it would point further towards the sky as opposed to the ground. "Nope, that's real", said Ross. We both paused. What we had in front of us, could have been best described as a super cell. Not only did it stretch 50 miles in diameter, it rose up to about 60,000 feet in height. It appeared that due to an unfortunate combination of various meteorological factors, several smaller storms had all merged into one. Not only did this cell cover our destination airport, Halim, it also covered our alternate airports of Pondok Cabe and Soekarno-Hatta. We now had nowhere left to land!

We broke out of the cloud and could now see the storm visually. The massive dome of black cloud expanding both vertically and horizontally reminded me of the movie "Independence Day". Ross looked at me, "Are you glad that we took the extra fuel now?", he asked. We had a serious problem, because even returning back to Cilicap or Nusawiru would have been a problem. We saw the CBs on departure. The weather would have been getting worse there too. There was only one thing that we could do...hold. And this is where the extra 400 lbs of fuel that Ross wanted to tanker, came in good use. There wasn't a single airport in West Java that we knew of, where the weather would be suitable to land.

We continued orbiting visually outside of the super cell. Usually thunderstorms dissipate within half and hour or so, however after holding for 30 minutes, it became apparent that this simply wasn't the case. There was still a solid block of magenta, 50 miles in diameter, covering all the airports in Jakarta. Using our Bluesky device, I sent a message to the Susi Air OCC, asking them for weather reports for Bandung, Cilicap and Nusawiru. There was no reply. Christian and Susi had spent a large amount of money installing this system on their aircraft, yet apparently forgot to hire a competent person to monitor this system. We asked ATC to find out the weather for those airports, however they were too busy communicating with the dozens of other aircraft which were now stranded mid air. Something which was especially disconcerting was hearing the crew of a Lion Air Boeing 737 who had just gone around, shout "Mayday Mayday!" whilst declaring a fuel emergency. We were on our own.

Myself and Ross discussed our options:

OPTION 1: FLY BACK TO CILICAP / NUSAWIRU

This seemed like a tempting solution at first. However as far as we could have known, we may well have had the same problem there in regards to the weather. The only difference being is that we would have then had 350 lbs less fuel in our tanks, and no instrument approach for guidance in the bad weather.

OPTION 2: LAND OFF FIELD

In very exceptional circumstances, landing in a random field away from an airport is also an option. We could have conducted a "precautionary landing" over the various fields below us to inspect for threats such as rough ground and electricity pylons, before landing. However it was apparent that the only fields below us were small rice padis. There would have been a serious chance of flipping the aircraft over during landing.

OPTION 3: FLY STRAIGHT THROUGH THE CENTRE OF THE STORM

The weather was horrendous in Halim, however at least we had an ILS (Instrument Landing System). This ILS would have provided guidance for us towards the runway, which was important given that we wouldn't have been able to see a single fucking thing outside! The obvious downsides of flying straight through the centre of a super cell, included severe turbulence leading to LOC (Loss Of Control), hail stones, lightning strikes, microbursts, torrential rain and low visibility.

Needless to say, we didn't have any ideal options. However the weather wasn't getting better and our fuel was gradually depleting. A decision needed to be made. We both agreed that we would attempt the approach.

PAPA KILO – DAN RICHWORTH © ALL RIGHTS RESERVED

Now you're probably thinking to yourself that Ross would have taken the controls from me and flown the approach himself, given the adverse weather conditions. But no. And this brings me to the next lesson.

LESSON 17: WHEN YOUR WORKLOAD IS HIGH, USE YOUR COPILOT!

Ross wanted me to land in Halim, and rightly so. That's not because my handling skills were better than his, in fact quite the contrary. He had years of experience flying the Caravan, whilst I had just 6 months. However by allowing me to fight for control against the severe turbulence, he knew that his mental capacity would have been freed up to concentrate on making important decisions. This delegation of tasks to improve ones own SA (Situational Awareness), is one of the fundamental principles of CRM (Crew Resource Management). There are 2 pilots there for a reason.

Above: This photo was taken by a friend staying in Patria Apartments, Jakarta, on the same day as my flight from hell.

Ross made an announcement to all of our passengers in Indonesian, warning them that we were about to fly into bad weather. With the autopilot still engaged, I briefly turned to the passengers and gave them a reassuring smile and thumbs up, in a lame attempt to keep them calm. They weren't having it. Before we had even entered the storm, we began to experience some minor turbulence. Some of the passengers began screaming. Wow, I thought. If they found that bit scary, they were going to be in for a nasty shock.

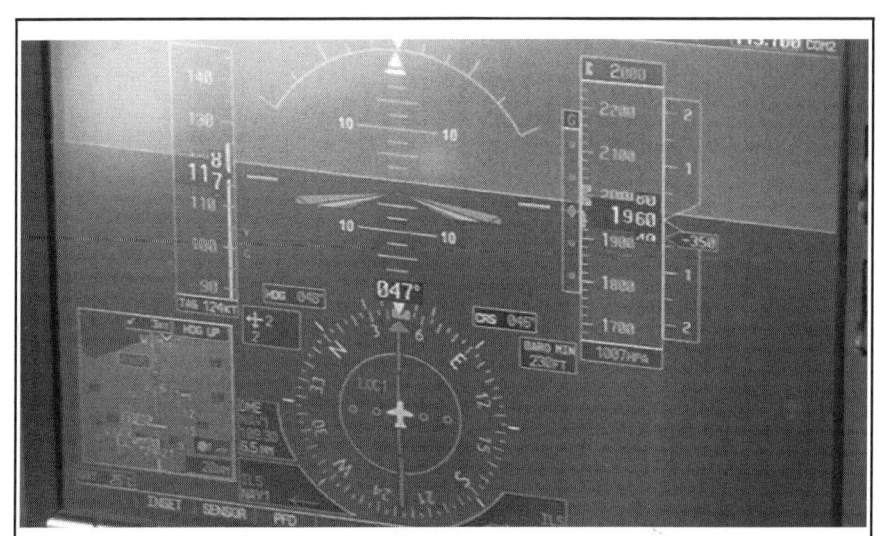

Above: An ILS approach from the G1000 Primary Flight Display. A green diamond on the altitude display shows the glide slope (too high or too low), and a green line underneath the arrow shows the localiser (too left or too right).

We were cleared by ATC for the ILS approach. As the turbulence became more severe, and the autopilot began to struggle, I disconnected and flew manually. I really needed to fight just to keep the aircraft straight and level, let alone turn onto the localiser for the ILS approach. As previously agreed with Ross, I would fly the approach as fast as possible to reduce the possibility of a stall. We would make it a flaps 20 landing. Whilst descending on the glide slope, the left wing violently dropped. I could hear screams of "Allah!" coming from the passengers in the back. I picked the wing up and continued the approach. I needed to make rapid adjustments to the controls and power lever to maintain our air speed, localiser and glide slope. We were now encountering heavy rain and lightning.

Contrary to what you may think, a lightning strike wouldn't electrocute us; the easiest way for the electricity to pass was around the metallic airframe, not the human flesh and bone inside. In fact, with the exception of some electrical failures, lightning strikes are fairly benign in metallic aircraft. The main problem with lightning, as I was about to find out, is that the bright flash temporarily blinds you. "Keep your head down!", shouted Ross. With my vision gradually improving, I continued to focus on my instruments. I didn't dare look outside again. It was hard work, however I still managed to maintain the localiser and glide slope within 1 dot of deflection.

However we still had a major problem coming up. As previously mentioned in the last chapter, there are no windscreen wipers in the Caravan. Even the slightest bit of rain will stick to the windows and obscure visibility, and we were flying through torrential rain. It was like we were flying underwater. This really was a problem, as although we could fly the approach with the instruments, we still needed to see outside in order to land. In normal circumstances, we would need to make visual contact with the approach lights or runway before we reached the "Decision Altitude", which was usually 200 feet above the runway for an ILS. However this wasn't a normal circumstance. If we were to have gone around, we would have needed to do the approach all over again, with the same outcome, only with less fuel.

Unbeknown to me at the time, I was about to fly my first (unofficial) CAT III ILS. A CAT III ILS is a type of approach which is made in a large airliner, landing in fog. The autopilot is programmed to judge the "flare" using the radio altimeter. The aircraft then lands automatically, without manual assistance from the pilots. However in our case, we didn't have such automation, or a radio altimeter for that matter. In normal circumstances, what we did would have been a big no no. In normal circumstances. However this was an emergency and we really didn't have any other options. From my right side, I could see the runway edge lights. From his left side, Ross could also see the runway edge lights. We knew that there was tarmac somewhere inbetween these lights. I reduced some power and raised the nose of the aircraft. I only had the barometric altimeter for reference and that wasn't particularly accurate. With a low rate of descent, we waited until the main wheels hit the tarmac.

SPLASH!

We had touched down...on a flooded runway! I applied maximum reverse, however didn't dare touch the brakes. We were now aquaplaning down what could best be described as a shallow river. The strong, variable crosswind from side to side, didn't help matters. Without the traction from our tyres, I needed to stamp on the rudder pedals just to keep the aircraft from blowing off of the runway.

We gradually came to a stop, then very slowly taxied off of the runway. However our sense of relief was short lived. Bolts of lightning were hitting the apron ahead of us. Once we were outside of the aircraft, a lightning strike would have indeed electrocuted us. We parked and shutdown the engine. I turned around to see the passengers. They were naturally quite upset. I quickly got out of the aircraft and put the tail stand in, so that the passengers could disembark. They ran to the terminal building as quickly as they could. Ross secured the aircraft. Then we both ran inside the terminal ourselves. We managed to get inside just minutes before a bolt of lightning struck one of the other aircraft parked on the apron.

Ross's phone rang; it was Christian. He wanted to know when we would be able to fly back to Cilicap. "The flight's cancelled", said Ross, before abruptly hanging up. We shared a taxi back to Patria apartments and spent the remainder of the day drinking beers. Even Ross, with all of his experience, hadn't seen anything like it. We were both pretty fucked up from our ordeal. Watching the news on TV, the reporters described the widespread devastation caused by the storm, from the flooding to the power cuts. They called it *"badai abad ini"*, or in English, "The storm of the century".

They were right.

CHAPTER 29

A BRIEF GUIDE TO KALIMANTAN

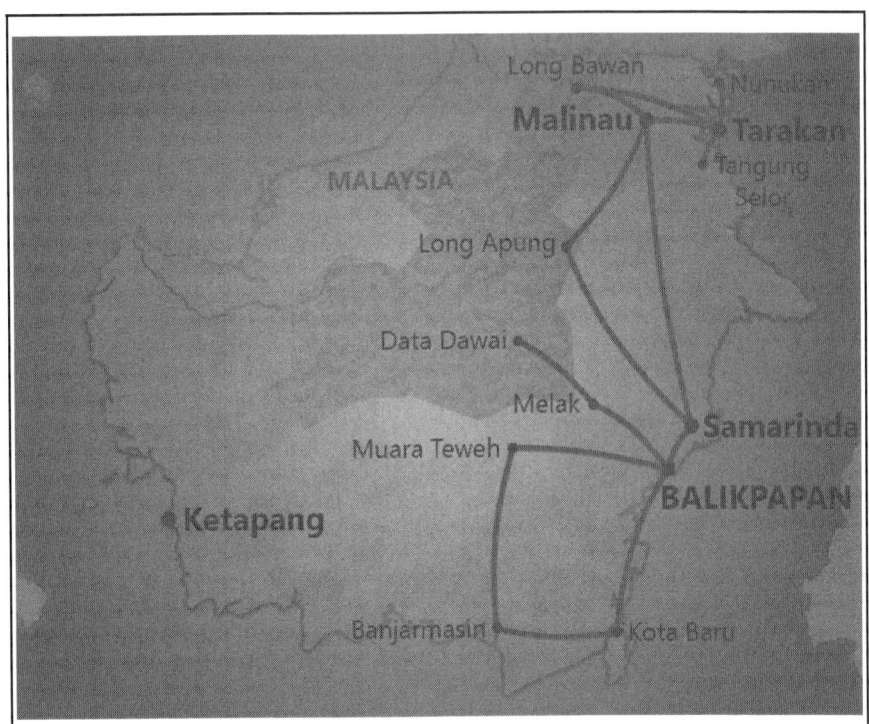

Above: The main base, Balikpapan, the satellite bases, and the destinations that I flew to as a First Officer in Kalimantan.

Kalimantan is the Indonesian part of the island of Borneo, which shares a border with Malaysia. The main Susi Air base was Balikpapan, with Samarinda, Tarakan and Malinau acting as the satellite bases. Ketapang, on the West side of Kalimantan, acted as an ad hoc base for temporary flying contracts, however it was usually operated from the base in Jakarta, not Balikpapan. We had 3 low grade mountain strips in Kalimantan; Data Dawai, Long Ampung and Long Bawan.

HISTORY

The native people of Borneo are the "Dayaks", who were comprised of various different tribes. The Dayaks predominantly occupied the inland regions of Borneo as opposed to the coastal regions, relying on the numerous river systems for food, water and transport. Over time, travellers from both India and other parts of Indonesia, would gradually colonise parts of Borneo from the 5th Century onwards, eventually dividing the island into numerous different kingdoms.

The Dutch would later colonise what would be known today as Kalimantan, in the 17th Century. Whilst the British would colonise the North portion of the island, which is now part of Malaysia and Brunei. Today, like most parts of Indonesia, Kalimantan is predominantly Muslim, albeit very moderate. The native Dayaks, like the Papuans, are predominantly Christian, due to the influence from European missionaries during Dutch rule.

DEMOGRAPHICS AND GEOGRAPHY

Kalimantan is almost the same land mass of Sumatra...in other words, it's huge. However the population of Kalimantan is about a quarter that of Sumatra, at around 14 million people. Despite this relatively sparse population, Kalimantan has a serious environmental problem. Large amounts of rainforest are burned down on a regular basis to clear space for palm oil plantations. Asides from the widespread destruction of the native fauna and flora, the pollution from these fires creates a thick, hazy smog across Kalimantan and, (much to their disappointment), neighbouring Malaysia. We saw these fires all the time whilst flying in Kalimantan.

Above: Burning down the rainforest to make way for palm oil. Whilst flying over Kalimantan, it wasn't uncommon to see a dozen or more of these fires at any one time.

The North of Kalimantan, across the Malaysian border, is mountainous, whilst the more Southern regions are relatively flat. On the East coast of Kalimantan are some great spots for scuba diving. One such spot is the Derawan Islands, located nearby Tarakan. The mountains, rainforest and coral reefs should have made Kalimantan a major tourist attraction, however very few tourists would come to visit during my time in Susi Air.

BALIKPAPAN

Balikpapan is a small city with a population of approximately 500,000 people. A large number of foreign workers live in Balikpapan, usually because they work in the oil or aviation industries. As a result, there is an abundance of high quality hotels, bars and restaurants in the city. (Debatably) next to Bali, Balikpapan is probably one of the most Westernised parts of Indonesia. Balikpapan had a reputation in the Susi Air network as being the "Party Base". I would soon see why.

CHAPTER 30

ARRIVING IN BALIKPAPAN

Following the end of my tour in Jakarta, (followed by another quick visa run to Singapore), I flew to Balikpapan to begin my 6 week tour of Kalimantan. I arrived at the airport at around 7pm on Friday, however there wasn't a driver waiting for me outside. There wasn't any answer to the contact numbers listed on the base intranet site either. I took a taxi to the address provided on the base intranet site. The house was empty, however I managed to find a whiteboard with names and room numbers. Balikpapan was a large base, and there were a total of 4 houses for the pilots, named as A, B, C and D, all within walking distance from one another. According to the whiteboard, I was to stay in C house, the same house that I was already in, in room 2, located upstairs.

It seemed a bit bizarre that there was nobody else in this house. It also seemed a bit bizarre as to why none of the managers were answering their phones. I decided to go for a walk to explore the local area and visit the other houses. I started with D house, which was located across the road. The lights were off. Nobody was there. I then walked up to A house, about 2 minutes walk away. Same again. Then I walked in the opposite direction, about 5 minutes away, to B house. Again, same story. To make matters slightly worse, the street lights were out and I couldn't see anyone else whilst I was walking, Susi Air or otherwise. There were literally no signs of life anywhere.

Out of ideas as to where to find human contact, I phoned up Gavin from my Initial course, who I knew had been based in Balikpapan before. When I told him what was going on, his first reaction was to laugh. Apparently the same thing happened to him when he first arrived in Balikpapan. If you arrived in Balikpapan on a Friday evening, you'd be on your own. All of the drivers, cicis and managers were off, and all of the pilots would go out to the local Novotel for dinner and drinks. The neighbourhood in general was very quiet, and at night time, without any lights, resembled something out of a zombie apocalypse (just minus the zombies). I needed to wake up at 5.30am the next day for my flight in the morning, so joining the other pilots at Novotel was out of the question. I managed to find some slices of bread in the kitchen of C house. That was going to be my dinner for the evening. I was a bit pissed off with the situation to be honest. Bored, with nothing else to do, or other people to talk to, I set my alarm and went to bed.

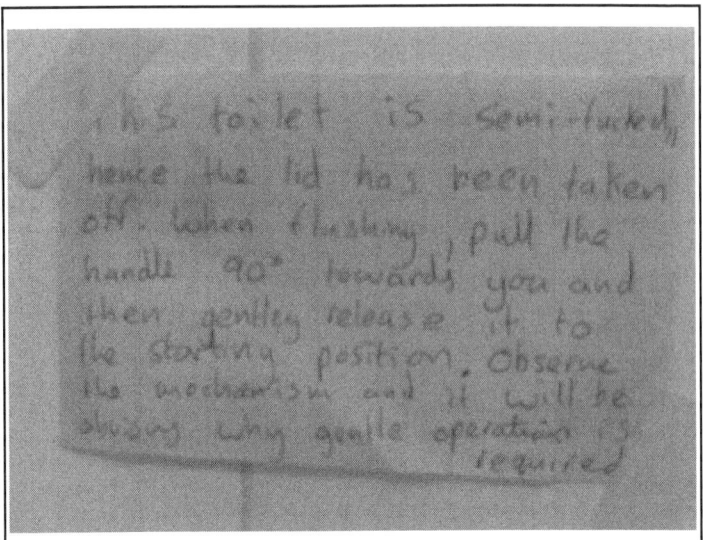

Above: A concerning message which I found stuck to the bathroom wall in C house.

I woke up the following morning with a knock on my bedroom door. It was the driver. "Cap, you ready to go?", he asked. I frantically searched in the dark for my phone. Had my alarm not gone off? I checked the time. It was 5.15am. The pickup was supposed to be at 6am! Slightly confused, I showed the driver the time on my phone. The driver looked back at me in shock. "Oh...no...the time is 6.15am", he said. Crap. Unbeknown to me at the time, Balikpapan was in a different time zone to Jakarta. Well this was a pretty crap way to begin the first day at my new base! "I am really sorry!", I said to the driver, "Give me 5 minutes and I'm ready!". I quickly got dressed into my uniform, ran to the bathroom to brush my teeth and then ran downstairs to the lobby.

Laying on the sofa in the living room was Darryl, the Captain who I was supposed to be flying with. "Mate, I'm really sorry!", I said. Darryl, who was still laying on the sofa playing with his phone, briefly looked at me. "Nah don't worry mate, these things happen", he replied. He actually seemed pretty chilled about the schedule. Darryl was from New Zealand and had recently upgraded to Captain. He was pretty down to Earth...which was just as well given the circumstance. We got into the minibus and headed to the airport. We were to fly 4 sectors that morning; Muara Teweh, Banjarmasin, Kota Baru and then back to Balikpapan.

The airports that we flew to weren't particularly challenging. All of the airports were located on reasonably flat ground, with low elevation. The shortest runway, Muara Teweh, was 900 metres long. Both Balikpapan and Banjarmasin were large airports with 2500 metre long runways. The weather for the most part was good. We stayed visual throughout the entire day; at least until the last flight. Whilst flying on our last sector from Kota Baru to Balikpapan, we could see on the weather radar that there was some weather ahead of us. It was too hazy for us to visually see the weather, however it appeared that there was a CB or thunderstorm overhead Balikpapan. As we got closer, we could see that there was indeed a small thunderstorm over the approach path for the ILS for runway 25, however it was relatively small and appeared to be dissipating.

Darryl, who had previously come across as being relatively relaxed the whole day, now appeared to be worried. I wasn't entirely sure why. We had plenty of fuel and we had Samarinda as an alternate just 20 minutes away. I was PF for that flight. "I'm going to slow down to save fuel", I said. "Yeah that's a good idea", replied Darryl, "I'm going to ask ATC to check the weather for Samarinda". We had 650 lbs of fuel left in our tanks. If we wanted to preserve our reserve fuel, we would need to divert to Samarinda before the fuel had reached 550 lbs. That meant that we had about 20 minutes to make a decision as to whether to commit to land in Balikpapan, or divert to Samarinda. It appeared to be a relatively easy decision to make, as the thunderstorm had all but dissipated. At least it was an easy decision for a copilot to make, however this brings me to the next lesson of the book.

LESSON 18: NEVER UNDERESTIMATE THE BURDEN OF COMMAND

It's very easy to make decisions when you yourself don't need to take final responsibility for the consequences of those decisions. Being a new Captain isn't easy. I can tell you now, several years later, as someone who was both a new Captain of a Caravan and also a new Captain of a Boeing 737, every small decision that you make will become exponentially more difficult to make, compared to when you were still a First Officer. Looking back on our flight, Darryl did everything right. He ensured that the fuel was preserved by slowing down the aircraft and he also checked the weather at the alternate. And rightly so. However he seemed unusually nervous. And I now understand why.

Unlike Java and Sumatra, Kalimantan had reasonably good weather. Kalimantan was not only Darryl's first base as a Captain, it was also his last base as an FO. He simply wasn't accustomed to seeing bad weather. However *I* had just come from a tour in Java, where I had the misfortune of needing to land in the middle of the worst storm that I would ever see in my entire career! This (ex) thunderstorm in Balikpapan, which by this point had now completely dissipated, meant very little to me in comparison. Even if it were still dangerous to fly through, which it wasn't, we already knew from ATC that the weather in Samarinda was just fine. It was a very easy decision to make...at least for me. But I wasn't the boss of that aircraft. I wasn't the guy who had the final responsibility for the safety of all of the passengers onboard. Although I wanted to influence Darryl into shooting an approach, I needed to be extra careful not to come across as too pushy. As Darryl's copilot, this was not my decision to make.

I looked across at Darryl. "Are you happy to shoot an approach?", I politely asked. Darryl seemed a bit reluctant at first. I was very careful not to push him. To be fair, diverting to Samarinda would have also been a perfectly safe decision to make, albeit very time consuming. "We'll try one approach", said Darryl, "However if we go around, we're diverting immediately towards Samarinda". Personally I think that was a good decision to make. Darryl asked ATC for radar vectors for the ILS, whilst I flew the aircraft. Needless to say, there was a bit of turbulence on the approach path, however nothing too serious. We encountered a bit of rain, however it dried up in time for us to see the runway before the "minimums" call. We landed without incident.

And so this is where a bit of empathy comes in handy. I think even with my recent experience with severe weather, I too would have been nervous had I been sitting in the left seat as a new Captain in this scenario. After we had parked and shutdown the aircraft, I humbled myself and spoke to Darryl about what had just happened. "If I can be completely honest with you mate, I'm actually quite glad that you were the Captain for that flight, and not me", I told him. Darryl smiled, "If I can be completely honest with you, I'm actually quite glad that I had you for my copilot", he said.

What I said was completely true. There are times when we sometimes forget that with any promotion, in any type of career, there also comes extra responsibility. Being a new Captain is difficult enough, without having a pushy First Officer next to you who thinks that they know it all.

CHAPTER 31

THE LONGEST FLIGHT OF MY LIFE

Life in Balikpapan was great! Usually after flying we would go out for dinner and drinks. Because Balikpapan was a relatively large base in regards to the numbers of pilots and engineers based there, together with the abundance of bars, restaurants and shops, you could always find something to do with someone. On Fridays we would all go out for dinner and drinks together in one large group. Every other day there would also be a BBQ at D house. There was never really a dull day.

Every once and a while, some pilots would be sent out of base for a 4 day tour in either Malinau or Tarakan. Malinau especially, was quite a contrast to the liveliness of Balikpapan. It was a small town in the middle of nowhere. There wasn't any internet in the pilots house or even a mobile phone signal, which was somewhat unusual, as this wasn't even the case with the bases in Papua. There were no bars or restaurants nearby, nor interesting landmarks to explore. However although Malinau lacked any form of entertainment on the ground, the flying was certainly more interesting compared to that of Balikpapan. The base in Malinau serviced two mountain strips; Long Bawan and Long Ampung. Even without flying to these mountain strips, the routes were much shorter and hence more interesting, compared to the routes from Balikpapan. All routes except for one however; Malinau to Samarinda. At 1 hour and 40 minutes, this was the longest scheduled flight in the Susi Air network.

One week following my arrival in Balikpapan, I was rostered for a 4 day tour in Malinau with a South African Captain called Johan. Johan was a pilot who naturally commanded a lot of respect. He was fairly stocky and appeared to be much older than most of the other pilots. He was the most senior Susi Air pilot in Balikpapan, and also a Training Captain. He was a fairly quiet, mild mannered guy. However he also came across as being the kind of person who you wouldn't want to get on the wrong side of. Everything about this guy, from his appearance to his mannerisms, implied that he was an authority figure.

We would first fly to Samarinda and then to Malinau, for the first day of our tour. In the following days, we would fly to various different airports nearby Malinau. The schedule was quite long; we would fly an average of 8 sectors per day. Johan let me land at both Long Bawan and Long Ampung. Both of these mountain strips were unique in there own special way, however for me, Long Bawan was the most notable. At the time, the runway in Long Bawan was bent. The first part of the strip was rough and sloped up, then abruptly turned to the right at the top of the slope. As a result, it was necessary to apply a large amount of right rudder after touchdown in order to keep the aircraft on the runway. It was actually a lot of fun landing there.

Above: Final approach for runway 22 in Long Bawan. Due to errors made during construction, the runway abruptly bended to the right after touchdown.

Above: Final approach for runway 22 in Malinau. It was common to see low level cloud and patches of fog in the morning.

On our fourth and final day in Malinau, we were scheduled to fly a return flight to Long Bawan, followed by a one way flight to Samarinda and then back to Balikpapan. After returning back to Malinau from Long Bawan, we picked up our lunch at the airport, which had been made by the cici in Malinau. We didn't have time to eat this on the ground, however we would have plenty of time to eat for our 1 hour and 40 minute flight to Samarinda. Our lunch consisted of fried noodles with chicken and vegetables, and a side salad. It both looked and smelled pretty damn good! We boarded the passengers and took off from runway 04 in Malinau, with Johan as the PF. Unbeknown to me at the time, this was to be the beginning of the longest flight of my entire career. Ok...not literally the longest ever in regards to hours and minutes. But even to this very day, it certainly felt like the longest.

At the top of climb, Johan engaged the autopilot and started eating. I waited until he had finished, then started eating myself. Usually in aviation, there are some very strict rules in regards to both pilots eating the same meal. In most airlines, the Captain and FO are supposed to eat different meals which were prepared independently of each other, in order to avoid both pilots contracting food poisoning. However this wasn't most airlines...this was Susi Air. And although it was technically still a rule as per our Company Operations Manual, it was never actually implemented.

About 10 minutes after I had finished eating, I felt a little light headed. At first, I assumed that I must have just been tired and that the altitude had also had an adverse affect. However as the minutes passed, I began to feel the blood drain away from my head and limbs. I slowly looked at Johan. "Johan, are you feeling ok?", I asked. Johan, who was in the middle of reading a book, looked at me confused. "Yeah I'm fine", he said, "Why do you ask?". "I really don't feel good", I replied, "Do you think there was something wrong with the food which we just ate?". Johan at first appeared concerned, then brushed it off. "No I definitely feel ok", he replied, before looking back down at his book. "You're probably just tired", he said. We continued to sit in silence for another few minutes.

And that's when it hit me. I felt like my internal organs had just been minced up in a blender. Without being too graphic, let's just say that I needed to clench my arse cheeks *very* firmly together, in order to avoid anything coming out. This was now pretty damn urgent. "Johan, I really don't feel well!", I said, "Can you just land somewhere!". Johan, engrossed in his book, appeared to be getting a bit annoyed with my interruptions. "Can't you just hold on until we land in Samarinda?", he asked. Samarinda was still over one hour flight away. "I really don't think I can!", I replied. Johan had a quick look on the map page of the Multi Function Display, for other airports nearby. We were about 30 miles away from Kalimarau, which was a relatively large airport. "Do you know how much it would cost the company if we diverted there?", asked Johan, "You're looking at a couple of grand at least". "Johan please!", I begged, "This is really urgent!". Johan looked at me, sighed, then checked the weather for Kalimarau on it's ATIS frequency.

Kalimarau was overcast in thick cloud. The cloud base was close to the minimums for the approach. "Well we can't land there then", announced Johan, "You're just going to need to hold it in until we get to Samarinda". And with that news, I lost all hope of being able to contain my insides. For long ferry flights, it wasn't unheard of for some Caravan pilots to shit in a sick bag in the bag of the aircraft, then subsequently open the upper cargo door to throw the contents out. I looked behind me. This flight was fully booked. All 12 passenger seats were taken. Would they have minded if their copilot casually walked to the back of the aircraft and shat in a plastic sick bag? Probably yes. However the question was, would that have been better or worse than shitting my pants? This wasn't an easy decision.

Johan had increased the speed to maximum cruise power, however this would have only shed a couple of minutes off of the flight time. I wondered to myself; if the worst came to the worst, and I couldn't hold it in until after we landed, would I need to resign from Susi Air? Surely there was no way that I could expect to continue to work for a company after an incident like that? I looked at the timer on the Primary Flight Display in front of me. It showed the seconds tick pass. The longer I stared at this timer, the longer it appeared to take for each second to pass. I needed a distraction in order to make the time pass quicker. This was hell. It really was hell. And this brings me to the next lesson of this book.

LESSON 19: WHEN IN INDONESIA, NEVER EAT THE SALAD.

Johan looked at me. "How is it even possible that you're ill and I'm not?", he asked, "We ate the *exact* same thing". "I don't know mate", I replied. Johan paused in thought. "Wait...you didn't eat the salad...did you?", he asked. I quietly nodded. Johan shook his head at me in disappointment. "I would have thought that after 8 months living in Indonesia, you'd know better!". The lettuce that I had eaten was most likely washed in tap water. I had probably just contracted some water born illness. "The salad is for decoration only!", lectured Johan, "You should know this by now!".

We eventually landed in Samarinda. Against all of the odds, I managed to clench my cheeks together hard enough to prevent anything from coming out...for the entire 1 hour and 40 minute flight. The second that Johan shut down the engine, I grabbed a pack of tissues from inside the flight deck and promptly waddled to the staff toilet by the control tower. My sense of relief was overwhelming. The longest flight of my life had eventually come to an end. After publishing this somewhat embarrassing story, I hope it is now apparent as to why I have changed my real name in this book.

CHAPTER 32

THE GREY AREA

A couple of days after my tour of Malinau, I was rostered to fly with Kyle, another Training Captain in Balikpapan. We were to fly a total of 4 sectors that day; first to Melak, then to Data Dawai and then back again along the same route. I'd met Kyle previously. He was quite a lively, sociable guy. He had a fair amount of experience flying in Susi Air.

We departed Balikpapan at 7am that morning to begin our 40 minute flight to Melak. Melak was a medium size airport with a 900 metre long runway. The terrain surrounding Melak was, for the most part, flat. However our next destination, Data Dawai, was far more interesting. Data Dawai was a mountain strip. It was surrounded by high terrain and the 750 metre runway was sloped by 5%. It was a one way in, one way out airport, and also had a committal point for take off and landing. Although it wasn't quite as challenging as the strips in the highlands in Papua, it was the most challenging that we had in Kalimantan. As I hadn't flown there before, Kyle landed in Data Dawai himself. However he told me that he would let me land there the next time we would fly together.

During the turnaround in Data Dawai, Kyle gave me some words of warning. "Keep a very close eye on the ground crew as they load the aircraft", he told me, "Sometimes they sneak on extra payload". Due to the length of the runway and surrounding high terrain, we were limited to a payload of just 500 kg, about half that of what we would usually take. Many Susi Air pilots had suspected for a while that some ground crew were getting paid to smuggle extra cargo onboard, without declaring it on the manifest. This was incredibly dangerous, as too much weight could have meant the difference between clearing the high terrain on our departure, or flying straight into it.

I stood next to the cargo pod and added up the weights of all of the suitcases and parcels that the ground crew were loading onboard. It was the same figure that had been declared on the manifest. However I noticed that there were a few extra parcels in the baggage cart which they hadn't loaded onboard. "Where are the other parcels going?", I asked the ground crew. One of the ground crew looked at me and smiled. "These are for another airport Cap!", he said. That was a blatant lie; Melak was the only destination from Data Dawai at the time. I knew full well that they would have loaded the extra payload had they not seen me watching. I told Kyle about the extra parcels. He sighed. "I'll file another safety report when we get back", he said, "The important thing is that they didn't load them onboard this time".

Above: Taking off from runway 02 in Data Dawai. Due to the slope of the runway and the high terrain behind us, it was not possible to take off in the opposite direction.

As Kyle had flown the first 2 sectors, I would now be flying the last 2 sectors to Melak and then back to Balikpapan. The departure from Data Dawai was just as interesting as the approach. It seemed counter intuitive, however it was necessary to turn to the left immediately after departure, in the same direction as a large mountain. We would then need to continue the turn by 270 degrees, eventually overflying the airport again. A turn to the right after departure may have seemed like the obvious choice, however if we did this, we wouldn't be able to climb high enough to clear the high terrain to the East of the airport.

On our final sector, there were some scattered clouds at around 2000 feet altitude, surrounding Balikpapan airport. They were stratus clouds; i.e. they were long and wispy, not tall and fluffy. As they were scattered, it was quite easy to fly above these clouds and still remain visual with the ground. Not that we really needed to stay visual though, as Balikpapan was a large airport with an instrument approach. Legally speaking, as we were flying a single engine aircraft, we were supposed to remain visual when carrying commercial passengers. However this wasn't always possible.

ATC cleared us to descend to 2000 feet for radar vectors for the ILS 25 approach. Kyle looked disappointed. "We keep telling these guys that we're not supposed to fly IFR!", he angrily shouted. IFR, or Instrument Flight Rules, basically meant that we could legally fly through cloud and poor visibility. Approaching 2000 feet, ATC instructed us to fly on a downwind heading of 090 degrees. A heading which took us straight through a small cloud. Kyle was pissed off. "Unable to accept that heading due to cloud!", he barked at ATC. Don't get me wrong, I appreciate that he was the Captain, and had far more experience than myself at the time, however personally I thought he was making a mountain out of a mole hill. The minimum radar altitude was 2000 feet. We were at a safe altitude to assure terrain clearance. Flying through a few stratus clouds wasn't going to do us any harm. And this brings me to the next lesson of the book.

LESSON 20: NEVER LET YOURSELF GET SANDWICHED BETWEEN LOW CLOUD AND HIGH TERRAIN

Although technically not legit, accepting radar vectors for an ILS approach was perfectly safe...not to mention practical. However if you really wanted to be that pedantic about a few stratus clouds, you could have always asked ATC to climb to a slightly higher altitude. Unfortunately, Kyle decided to do the exact opposite. "Sorry mate", said Kyle, "I'm going to have to take the controls from you". "Okaaay", I replied, slightly confused. Kyle chopped the power and dived underneath the clouds in front of us, descending to an altitude of 1300 feet. The immediate area surrounding Balikpapan was reasonably flat...by Indonesian standards. However there were still small hills and radio masts which needed to be avoided. The minimum radar altitude was 2000 feet for a reason.

Above: A pilot believes that they can safely fly below the clouds. Unbeknown to them, the ground slopes up. If they can't safely perform a U-turn, they will need to climb up again through the cloud. However they will not be able to see any terrain or obstacles in this cloud.

"Kyle, I really don't think this is a good idea mate!", I said. "No it's fine mate", replied Kyle, "We need to stay visual". We were about 15 miles away from the airport, skirting just a few hundred feet above the terrain and obstacles below us. The irony was, the reason why IFR wasn't allowed for single engine aircraft, was in case of an engine failure. However if all of a sudden, everything were to go quiet in front of us, we would have actually been much better off at 2000 feet in cloud! If we had an engine failure now, we would have had just a few seconds to pick somewhere to land. "Bravo Victor Delta...errr...confirm current altitude?", asked ATC. Kyle immediately took the radios. "We're at 1300 feet to remain VISUAL!", he shouted at ATC. I looked at Kyle. "Mate, I really don't feel ok with what you're doing right now", I said, "I really think you should climb".

By this point, I was seriously considering to say something which I might have later regretted. There was a well known phrase in Susi Air, which had rarely ever been used in the past, due to the severity of the consequences of all parties involved; "CAPTAIN, YOU MUST LISTEN". As per Susi Air regulations, if a First Officer were to use this phrase, the Captain would now be legally obliged to follow the First Officer's instructions, provided that it was the safest course of action. It was incorporated into the Susi Air SOPs in order to avoid a rogue Captain from endangering the aircraft. However any use of this phrase mandated a safety report and subsequent investigation. Depending on the outcome of that investigation, either the Captain, or the FO, would probably get fired. I decided to bite my tongue.

I still wasn't particularly happy with Kyle hedge hopping around the terrain below us. I decided to take the diplomatic approach. "Is it maybe possible for me to ask ATC for a climb to 3000 feet?", I asked, "Then you would be clear of cloud". Kyle paused, then agreed. I think he had finally realised that he had misjudged how high the terrain was below the cloud. Kyle handed the controls back to me, and I climbed to 3000 feet with permission from ATC. Whilst on an extended base leg, when we had the runway in sight, Kyle requested a visual approach. We landed without any further dramas.

After the passengers had disembarked, Kyle, although still friendly, casually down played the entire incident. "These things happen mate", he said. I think Kyle sensed that I wasn't particularly happy with what had just happened, however he did seem to want to make it up to me. "I think you've got some good flying skills", said Kyle, "I'll write an upgrade evaluation for you when we get back". He'd only seen me fly 2 sectors. He was very clearly using his position as a Training Captain in order to bribe me for my silence. However this would have been my second upgrade evaluation, and I needed two evaluations in order to progress to the upgrade assessment.

So I smiled and kept my mouth shut.

Over all, I think Kyle was actually a skilled and knowledgable pilot. However from what I could see, he had one fundamental problem. He wasn't flexible. He was so absolute in his opinion about always flying visually, that he couldn't adapt to different situations. Ultimately, he let a very minor issue involving a few clouds, affect his ability to recognise a far more serious threat...the fucking ground!

CHAPTER 33

A BRIEF GUIDE TO TIMOR

Timor is in many ways similar to Papua. It's an island which has been carved in half, with Indonesia taking the West half, and the East half now an independent nation. Like Papua, Timor has also seen a great deal of violence; most notably with the occupation of East Timor by the Indonesian military, and subsequent massacres and genocide. Despite the disturbing history of violence, it's actually a very scenic island with unspoilt coral reefs and white sandy beaches. However even today, after the conflict, it's still far from being a safe place to visit as a tourist.

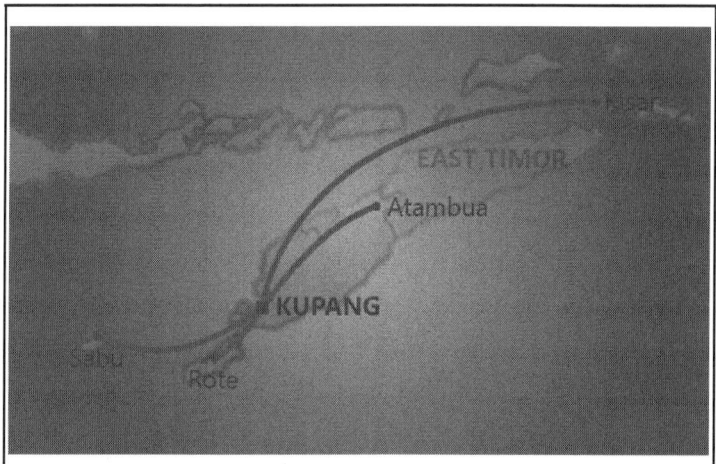

Above: Kupang base and destinations. The routes were carefully designed to always maintain glide range with land, and also to avoid flying over East Timor.

HISTORY

Prior to the European colonisation of the 17th Century, Timor was just as divided as it is today. The two main tribes which inhabited Timor were anything but united, with the Atoni tribe settling predominantly in West Timor and the Tetum tribe settling predominantly in East Timor. The only similarity between those two tribes was the island on which they both lived. Other than that, they had completely different cultures and even languages. They shared no common history.

The Portuguese were the first Europeans to colonise the island of Timor, however the Dutch began to colonise Timor shortly after. Portugal and the Netherlands would fight each other for control over the island of Timor over the following 2 centuries, before finally agreeing to split the island 50/50. As the island had previously been divided demographically, prior to the colonisation, agreeing on a clear border between these two European empires was actually quite straight forward.

Like most of Indonesia, both sides of Timor were occupied by the Japanese during WW2. The Dutch half of Timor in the West became part of Indonesia, following Indonesia's independence from the Netherlands. However the East half of Timor continued to be governed by Portugal up until 1975. As Portugal was experiencing various political problems back home, they decided to pull their military out of East Timor, giving the natives an opportunity for independence. However this dream of independence was short lived, as President Suharto sent in the Indonesian military to take control of East Timor. This occupation of East Timor would last 24 years and cause the untimely deaths of approximately 15-25% of the population.

THE CONFLICT

The Indonesian occupation of East Timor was brutal. A 2005 report from the UN Commission for Reception, Truth and Reconciliation in East Timor, estimated that the death toll during the 24 year occupation was between 102,000 – 183,000 people. Approximately 25% of those people were directly killed through conflict, with the remaining 75% dying from illness and starvation. The population of East Timor at the beginning of the occupation was only 690,000 people.

Eventually, due to worldwide condemnation, the Indonesian Government were forced to give the people of East Timor a referendum on independence in 1999. Unlike the "Act of No Choice" in Papua, this referendum was supervised by the UN to ensure that it would be conducted fairly and without the threat of violence. The people of East Timor voted overwhelmingly for independence, and the Indonesian military subsequently withdrew. President Suharto was forced to resign, and many high ranking military officers fled Indonesia in order to avoid being tried for war crimes. East Timor was temporarily administered by the UN, before gaining their full independence in 2002 as a sovereign nation.

WEST TIMOR

The Capital of West Timor is Kupang. Kupang is a relatively small city, with a population of around 350,000 people. Most residents of Kupang speak three different languages; Indonesian, Tetum (from West Timor) and Bahasa Kupang (a very unique language which was only spoken in that city). Like East Timor, the majority of the population is Christian. However religion asides, most West Timorese align themselves far more closely to Indonesia than to their Eastern neighbours. There is very little desire for independence in West Timor.

Even today, there is a great deal of tension between West and East. Many refugees fled from East Timor to West Timor in order to escape the violence. However those refugees weren't often welcomed with open arms. There is a very strong sentiment for ethno-nationalism in both the West and the East, and outsiders aren't often seen as being welcome. And yes, that hostility was sometimes directed at Susi Air pilots.

CHAPTER 34

ARRIVING IN KUPANG

Following the end of my tour in Balikpapan, I returned back to the UK for a 3 week holiday. I had a lot to be thankful for. Not only had I some unbelievable stories to tell my friends and family back home, but I also had some good news! I had been offered a place on the next Upgrade Assessment, and if successful, I would soon be training to become a Caravan Captain for Susi Air. I just had one final tour left before my assessment; 3 weeks in Kupang.

Kupang was great. It was a relatively small base, with around 8-10 pilots there at any one time. The flying predominantly involved island hopping, whilst being mindful not to fly too far out to sea. When flying single engine aircraft with commercial passengers, we legally needed to remain within glide range of land. Sometimes our planned route across the ocean would take an abrupt detour so that we could fly nearby some rocks sticking out in the middle of the sea, hence *technically* still comply with this legal requirement. However there was no way that we could have landed anywhere near those rocks. If the engine failed, we were far better off ditching in the middle of the sea.

However something which I need to give Lars, the Kupang Base Manager, a great deal of credit for, was that he took the threat of ditching in open water very seriously. Unlike the other bases in the Susi Air network, we would always carry a life raft onboard our aircraft. And unlike some of the other life rafts laying in storage at the other bases for years on end, these rafts were checked for holes on a regular basis, so we knew that they weren't just for decoration; they would actually inflate in an emergency. These rafts were also considerably larger than the other life rafts. The standard issue life rafts in Susi Air were for 6 people, however these life rafts could carry 8 people. Still, not quite enough to carry all 14 occupants of the aircraft, however it was still a step in the right direction.

The ground crew in Kupang were well trained also. Prior to boarding, they would give all the passengers a *very* comprehensive demonstration on how to inflate their life jackets and safely evacuate the aircraft in the event of a ditching. This demonstration was far more effective than the standard briefing that we would give the passengers, as we were sitting in the front of the aircraft with our backs turned to them. The ground crew were able to show the passengers what to do, face to face, speaking the same language to a far higher standard than what we could speak as foreigners. At the time, this procedure hadn't been implemented in any other base. Kupang was the first. Lars was to thank for this.

Lars' deputy was an English Captain called Terry. I'd met Terry before in Papua, when he was still an FO. He'd risen through the ranks very quickly, becoming the Deputy Base Manager for Kupang just one month after upgrading to Captain. He was in his 40s, however had the energy and enthusiasm of a university student. There was also another Captain based in Kupang who I'd previously met in Papua; Ted. Ted had been based in Manokwari for a while and fancied a change of scenery. He had moved to Kupang just a month before I had arrived. I enjoyed flying with Ted a lot. On the rare occasions that we would be rostered for a ferry flight without any passengers, he would always let me sit in the back of the aircraft and experience zero-G. Basically, whilst I was standing in the back of the cabin, he would continuously pitch down so that I would float up like an astronaut. It was great fun, although I needed to be careful not to bang my head too hard on the ceiling.

The flights to Kisar, an Indonesian island situated off of the North coast of East Timor, were quite interesting. Due to political tensions between the two countries, we needed to avoid flying in East Timorese airspace. As a result, we would need to take a massive detour out to sea, towards the islands situated North of Timor, before flying East towards to Kisar. This bizarre route almost doubled our flight time and fuel. Although we weren't flying directly inside East Timorese airspace, we were still flying nearby. As a result, we would still need to speak to East Timorese ATC. Normally when speaking to an ATC unit, it is customary to greet them in their own native language. Depending on the time of the day, we would greet Indonesian ATC with Selemat Pagi (morning), Selemat Siang (midday) or Selemat Sore (afternoon). However we had to be very conscientious not to accidentally say this to the East Timorese ATC. That would have pissed them off...a lot.

Landing at Kupang airport could sometimes be a challenge. It had a very large runway, however the crosswinds could be pretty aggressive at times. It wasn't uncommon for the surface wind to exceed 30 knots, and the surrounding terrain made this wind very turbulent. As the runway was long and wide, these crosswind landings were actually quite fun. However I definitely wouldn't have wanted to land with those conditions on a short and narrow runway. The crosswind take offs and landings were good practice before my upgrade to Captain. It was definitely a confidence booster.

After work we would sometimes go to the beach. Both Terry and Ted were obsessed with surfing. They would surf in Kupang beach almost every day. However the surrounding rocks, reefs and high waves made surfing far too risky for the rest of us novices. One of the First Officers, a New Zealand pilot called James, had recently slashed his head wide open on a reef in Kupang whilst trying to catch a wave. Myself and the others would sometimes join Terry and Ted down the beach. However for most of us, we just stuck to swimming.

Like in Balikpapan, there was one night a week in which all of the pilots, ground crew and cicis would all go out together for dinner and drinks. In the case of Kupang, it was Saturday night. And it would be the second Saturday night after my arrival in Kupang, that the shit was about to hit the fan.

CHAPTER 35

SATURDAY NIGHT

Shortly after I arrived in Kupang, Lars, the Base Manager, was going away on annual leave. He was to leave Terry, his deputy, in charge of the base whilst he was away. Shortly before Lars left the pilots house for the airport, I still remember his final words to us very clearly. "Now don't get into any trouble whilst I'm away!", he jokingly told us with a grin. We all laughed back.

Terry did a great job managing the base in Lars' absence. We were short staffed as there were currently only 3 Captains and 4 First Officers in Kupang, however Terry managed the schedule well. Most of us would be flying 6 days a week, whilst maxing out on 100 hours that month. Naturally, we were all looking forward to Saturday night, so that we could finally take a break from it all. There was only one return flight scheduled for the following morning on Sunday. Ted and another FO volunteered to fly this. That meant that the remaining 5 of us could go out and enjoy the nightlife in Kupang. (Not that there was much nightlife, but we tried to make the most of it).

In the early evening, all 7 pilots, 2 cicis and 4 ground crew went out for dinner together at a local restaurant. After dinner, it was just myself and 4 other pilots who were going out for drinks; Terry, James, Maksim and Hans. At the time, there weren't any taxis in Kupang. If you wanted to get anywhere, you needed to hitch hike and pay the driver some money. We went to the only late night bar that we knew of in Kupang, a bar called XXX. The name sounded dodgy, however it was actually quite a clean, upmarket sports bar. We bought a couple of beer towers to share between us. At the time, we were the only people in the bar.

James still had his head bandaged up from his surfing accident earlier that week. In light of his head injury, he made the wise choice to go easy on the beer that night. Maksim, a Captain from Russia, was a bit more eager with his drinks, as were myself and Terry. Hans, an FO from Germany, was slightly more reserved. However that said, we had at the very most, 3 large glasses of beer each that night. We certainly weren't drunk. Don't get me wrong, most of us at the time loved going out and partying, however there just didn't really seem like much point in getting drunk in an empty bar. At around midnight, just 2 hours after we had first arrived, we decided to pay the bill and go home.

We walked outside to find some transport. Usually, when travelling somewhere in Kupang, you could just wave down a motorbike taxi, commonly referred to as an "ojek" in Indonesia. There weren't any regulations in Kupang at the time, so pretty much anyone riding a motorbike could be an ojek. However there were 5 of us. Sometimes you could squeeze 2 people on the back of an ojek, however even then we would have still needed 3 bikes. We decided that the best thing to do would be to wait and see if we could flag down a car instead. This wasn't as easy as it sounded, as cars were rare in Kupang and the road next to the bar was far from being busy.

A local driving a motorbike came over to us to ask if we needed transport. "Where you go? Where you go?", he asked. We politely turned him down; it was better to stick together. He seemed a bit annoyed that none of us wanted to pay him to take us home. "I come back for rest of you!", he shouted, "Why you make problem?!". We told him that we were waiting for a car. Eventually, after realising that he wasn't going to get any money from us, he sped off, only to stop about 20 metres down the road. Whilst watching us from a distance, he took out his phone and called his friends. Was he asking his friends to help bring us home? Was he fuck.

In a matter of minutes, there were about 30 to 40 locals on motorbikes...and they had completed blockaded the road ahead of us! At the time, we thought he was only going to call a few friends. However it appeared that he had called half of the neighbourhood! There were only 5 of us. Severely outnumbered, and with no where to go, it was now apparent that we were well and truly fucked. "Ouch!", shouted James, whilst hopping on his right foot. It appeared that one of the bikers had just thrown a stone at James' leg. It was somewhat ironic that James, with his head bandaged up, was the only one of us to have any injuries, yet he was the first person to be targetted by the bikers. It really wasn't his week.

However the rest of us were also about to have a volley of stones, of various sizes and velocities, thrown at us by the bikers, who were standing about 20-30 metres away. We shielded our heads. Terry wasn't having any of it. "Fuckin' come over 'ere then!", he yelled. "Terry shut up!", shouted Maksim. However Terry had a valid point. These bikers, despite outnumbering us almost 10 to 1, appeared to be cowards. They had no issues in throwing stones at us from a distance, however they seemed very reluctant to actually fight us up close. I actually found that quite reassuring. At first, it appeared that Terry's challenge worked; they initially backed down and stopped throwing stones. We even saw a few of them get back on their motorbikes and drive off.

However one cheeky little git, about 5 foot 2 in height and weighing no more than 130 lbs, thought he would show off to his friends. He picked up a large rock from the side of the road with both of his arms, a rock which probably weighed more than he did. Slumped forward, he then proceeded to waddle towards us, before pathetically throwing the rock just a few metres in front of him, landing about 5 metres short of us. We looked at each other...then we looked at him. Realising that he had just made a catastrophic error of judgment, he ran back towards his friends. We chased after him.

What happened next seemed so surreal. In the distance, I could see two people on a motorbike driving towards us at about 30 mph, however at the time, everything appeared in slow motion. The passenger on the back of this motorbike was carrying a very large rock, about 1 foot in diameter, with both of his arms. I remember thinking to myself, surely he's not actually going to try to throw that at us? That rock, travelling at that speed, would kill someone. Surely they were just trying to scare us, they didn't actually want to kill us? This was very surreal indeed. I'd seen my fair share of casual violence before, however I'd never seen someone being murdered before. The back seat passenger hurled the rock in my direction. I remember lifting both of my arms up to cover my head, whilst ducking for cover.

I looked in the direction of Hans, who was running beside me. And I will never forget this. The rock, which probably weighed somewhere in the region of 30 lbs, travelling at a speed of over 30 mph, went directly into the left side of Hans' head. The force of the impact was so great, that the rock itself shattered into hundreds of pieces. Hans immediately fell backwards onto the ground. I paused. I looked at him. He lay motionless on the ground. The rock must have caved his skull in. He was very clearly dead. Myself and the others ran towards his lifeless body. Blood was spurting out of the back of his head. I knew at the time that it was futile as Hans had very clearly just died, however nonetheless, I leaned over him to check for signs of life. Wait what? He was still breathing! His skull had just been struck with a rock which was bigger than his entire head, yet he was still breathing!

Terry and Maksim tried to flag down a car whilst myself and James examined Hans' injuries. I leaned over to check the left side of his head. To be honest, I wasn't expecting to see much of his head left. However to my surprise, there were only minor cuts and bruising where the 30 lb rock had struck him. How was that even possible? Then I remembered how the rock had shattered on impact. Fortunately for Hans, it appeared that the rock was actually a piece of old cement which was riddled with hairline cracks. Although this piece of cement still delivered a massive blow to his head, frankly, I think he was lucky that he still had a head left. However it was apparent that Hans had a much more serious problem. He had struck the back of his head on the ground below him. He was bleeding rapidly and appeared to be having seizures. He was alive...at least for now. However we still needed to get him to the hospital ASAP.

By this point, after realising the severity of what they had done, the bikers backed off; at least for the moment. Fortunately Terry and Maksim managed to flag down a car. We carried Hans' into the back of the car. I went with Hans to the hospital, however there wasn't room for everyone to fit in the car. The others needed to stay behind. It was a 20 minute drive to the hospital, although it felt like much longer. I'll never forget the driver of that car. We were being attacked by a large mob and yet he was prepared to risk his own safety by stopping and helping us. I have no doubt that he saved Hans' life that night. Due to the urgency of carrying Hans inside the hospital and finding a doctor, I never did get the contact details of the driver. If on the off chance that he ever reads this book, I just want to say again to the driver, thank you for everything that you did.

The hospital in Kupang was fairly basic, however at least they were open 24 hours a day. The medical staff placed Hans' into a wheelchair and examined the back of his head. It appeared that there weren't any severed arteries of veins. They sewed up the gash to stop any further bleeding, however were reluctant to provide further medical attention. Hans began coughing up blood. There was a real chance that he had brain damage from the attack. The doctor was reluctant at first, however eventually he agreed to x-ray Hans' skull for damage.

Whilst waiting for Hans outside of the radiology room, I received a phone call from Terry. "We're in jail!", shouted Terry. It turned out, that shortly after I took Hans to hospital, the Police had finally arrived on the scene...and then proceeded to beat the living shit out of Terry, Maksim and James. One of the Police had tried to hit Terry in the throat with his baton, however fortunately missed and hit his chest instead. The Police didn't appear to be too interested in arresting the large mob who outnumbered them. Realising that they couldn't leave without arresting at least one of the parties involved, they decided to instead focus their attention on the 3 bules. Terry then gave me a heads up. "The Police are coming to the hospital to get you!", he warned. Shit! Hans was still getting x-rayed, I couldn't leave him. And this brings me to the next lesson of the book.

LESSON 21: NEVER CALL THE POLICE IN INDONESIA

The Police in Indonesia, and many other countries for that matter, are very dangerous. They are corrupt, they are violent and they have very little accountability. Sometimes in the Western World, we make the assumption that if you've done nothing wrong, you have nothing to fear from the Police. However this type of thinking in a remote part of Indonesia could potentially get you killed. You should always, and I mean always, avoid interacting with the Police, unless absolutely necessary.

I was about to get my arse kicked by the local constabulary, and there was nothing that I could do about it! Or was there? I paused for a minute and considered my options. I looked at the front entrance of the hospital. There was a CCTV camera overlooking the reception area. I casually walked over to the CCTV camera, taking a close look at the area which was being filmed. I stood in that area and didn't move. Two large men barged in through the front doors wearing civilian clothes, with guns drawn by their sides. Don't get me wrong, I don't think that they had any intention of shooting me. No no no. That would have created far too much paperwork. However I wouldn't have put in past them to pistol-whip me in the face. They took one look at me, then they took a look at the CCTV camera pointing at me. They holstered their guns. One of them walked up to me.

"We're the Police.", he said in near perfect English, "We need to ask you some questions about what happened". Careful to keep my hands in full view of both the CCTV camera and the Police, I calmly explained that I couldn't go anywhere as my friend was in hospital. The Police Officer looked at me and smiled. He knew exactly why I was standing in front of the CCTV camera. I carefully told both Police Officers everything that had happened that evening. "Yes this is what we thought had happened", the first Police Officer replied. "Wait, what?!", I asked, "Then why did you arrest my friends?". Both Police Officers laughed. The first Police Officer walked up to my face and whispered, "We don't need a reason to arrest someone". They both left the hospital.

As soon as they had left, I phoned Terry again to update him on the situation. "They just want money!", said Terry, "We're not leaving this place until they get paid!". It turned out that although the Police had been pretty brutal with them at the beginning, they were now being detained in the lounge of the Police station, as opposed to the jail cells. The Police had also allowed them to keep their phones and even made them all a cup of tea whilst they were waiting. However they made it very clear that they weren't leaving that place until "arrangements" had been made with Susi. The Police knew that Susi was rich. They didn't particularly like her either. Until the local Police in Kupang got what they wanted, Terry, Maksim and James were to be held at ransom.

I remembered that during my Initial training, when we met Christian and Susi for the first time, they had given us all business cards with their contact details. Of course this was just a polite gesture; they weren't actually expecting that any of us would ever call them! It was also now 3am. However this was pretty damn urgent. Reluctantly, I rang Susi's personal mobile number. "Who is this?!", screamed Susi over the phone. I began explaining to Susi that I was currently the only Susi Air pilot in Kupang who wasn't either asleep, hospitalised or incarcerated. Halfway through my explanation, she passed her phone over to Christian, who was a bit more sympathetic to our dilemma. He arranged for a small team of lawyers, and a briefcase carrying an undisclosed sum of money, to be flown to Kupang, from Jakarta, by Avanti.

I returned back to the radiology room to check on Hans. By this stage, he had regained consciousness. Fortunately, against all odds, both his skull and jaw were undamaged. The blood he was coughing up earlier appeared to be from a chipped tooth. He had a concussion, however was otherwise uninjured. I looked at Hans. "You really have got no idea just how lucky you are", I said. Hans smiled. Then he looked around. "Where are the others?", he asked. "Keep sitting mate", I said, "This is going to be a very long story".

CHAPTER 36

UPGRADE ASSESSMENT

Following the end of my eventful tour of Kupang, I travelled to Pangandaran to attend the Upgrade Assessment. The Upgrade Assessment consisted of 3 parts; the written exams, the simulator assessment and the final interview with the Chief Pilot. The written exams were straight forward enough. There were two exams; one for limitations and one for the memory items. The simulator assessment was a bit more challenging.

Above: The Caravan Simulator in the training building. I wouldn't recommend standing near that building in the event of an earthquake.

Christian and Susi had very recently purchased a simulator for the Caravan, with a price tag of 3 million USD. This simulator was more expensive than the actual aircraft! A significant part of that cost involved carefully transporting this simulator from the USA, where it was manufactured, to Pangandaran. The simulator was transported in parts via air to Jakarta. However from Jakarta, it was necessary to transport to Pangandaran over land. The only road at the time was bumpy as hell, and so extra care was needed not to damage any of the delicate components.

They then needed to "carefully" demolish the side wall of the newly constructed training building in the Susi Air complex, in order to move the simulator inside, before covering the massive hole with two large windows. You would have thought that they would have considered this *before* they had built the training building. You would have also thought, that with the vast sums of money they had paid, that they would have customised the instruments of the simulator so that they matched the instruments of the aircraft which we actually flew. However, unfortunately, neither was true.

My simulator assessment was interesting. I was to fly IFR between two airports in Java; Yogyakarta and Semarang. What made this particular route interesting was that there was a massive mountain standing inbetween these two airports. For this reason, a direct route wasn't possible. However even when routing around the mountain, there was a problem. According to the MSAs (Minimum Sector Altitudes) for these airports, even a route *around* the mountain would have required a minimum altitude of 13,400 feet! The Grid MORA (Minimum Off Route Altitude) provided on the IFR charts showed a similar altitude. This was too high for an unpressurised Caravan, especially for such a short flight. Flights between airports such as Yogyakarta and Semarang are a perfect illustration of the challenges that low altitude pilots face when flying in areas of high terrain. In situations like this, we really needed to think outside of the box.

The MSA is valid for a distance of 25 nautical miles from the navigation beacon. The MSAs for Yogyakarta and Semarang were too high. However were there any other airports enroute? Yes there was. There was an airport called Solo, which was located to the North-east of Yogyakarta, and the South-east of Semarang. The MSA for this airport was more favourable to our low altitude operation; just 4800 feet. The most challenging part of this simulator assessment was the planning. However once the route and altitude had been figured out, the rest of the simulator assessment was a bit easier. (Albeit the instruments were a bit different to what I was used to).

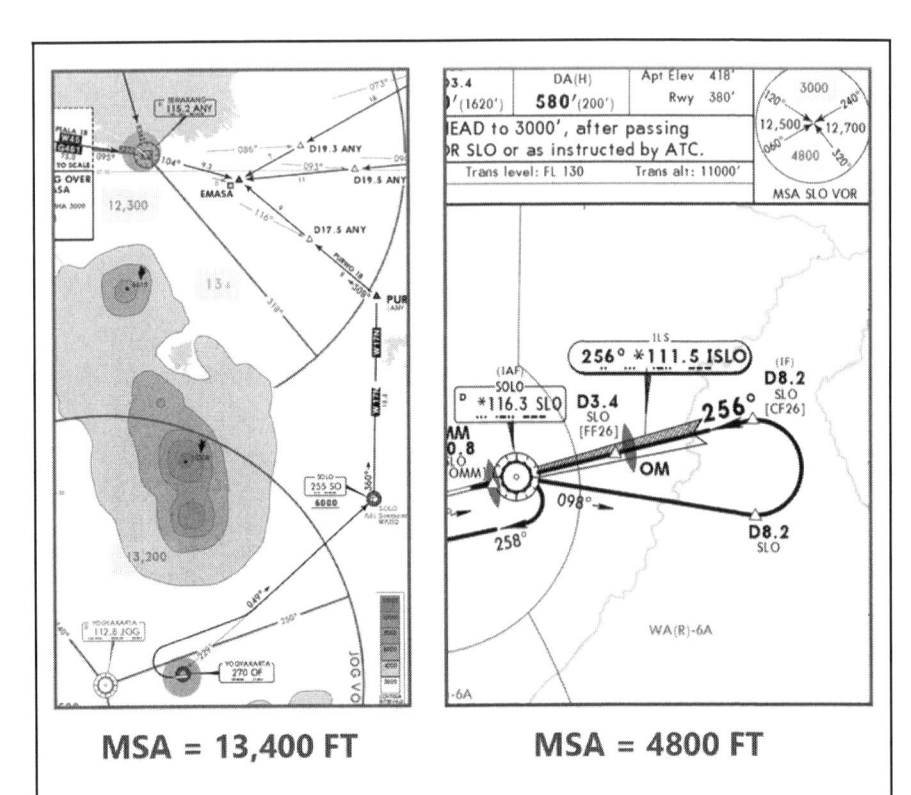

MSA = 13,400 FT **MSA = 4800 FT**

Above Left: According to these charts, a flight from Yogyakarta to Semarang must fly at a minimum of 13,400 feet to remain clear of terrain; far higher than an unpressurised Caravan can legally fly without oxygen masks.

Above Right: We need to think outside of the box. By finding another airport nearby our departure and arrival airports, we can find a much lower MSA of 4800 feet. Our flight is now legal.

The weather at both Yogyakarta and Semarang was IFR, with the cloud base a couple of hundred feet above the minimums. The examiner asked me how much fuel I wanted to take, and to justify that amount. I asked for 950 lbs of fuel. This included 200 lbs of trip fuel, another 200 lbs of alternate fuel (to get us back to our destination), 150 lbs (about 30 minutes) to hold for bad weather, and the standard 400 lb reserve.

Above: The cockpit from the Caravan simulator. For some bizarre reason, this was configured with analogue instruments, despite most of the Caravans in Susi Air having G1000 displays.

I was to sit in the left seat for the first time. I had a Training Associate sitting in the right seat. The layout of the cockpit was completely different to most of the other Caravans in Susi Air, which made my instrument scan a bit more challenging. The flight itself was fairly straight forward though; there were no emergencies or abnormal situations. This was fair, given that the change in seat and instrument configuration provided a very high workload. However there was a thunderstorm overhead Semarang by the time that we arrived, which meant that we needed to hold. I asked the TA to check the weather for Solo and Yogyakarta. The weather was good at both locations and Solo was right next to us. We had plenty of fuel to hold.

Satisfied that I had checked the weather for my alternates, the examiner then cleared the storm. I flew two approaches into Semarang. It was necessary to go around on the first approach, as the cloud base had dropped to below minimums. I checked our fuel and discussed with the TA if he wanted to try again. We both agreed that we had enough fuel, so I made another approach. This time we were visual with the runway and I could land. I taxied to the apron and shutdown the engine. The examiner then paused the simulator. He then said three words which I will never forget; "Congrats, you've passed".

That was two assessments done. Now I had just one last assessment; the final interview with the Chief Pilot. The interview lasted about 30 minutes, with half of the questions based on the aircraft systems, and the other half being more practical, scenario based questions.

I still remember some of the questions which he asked me:

"What do you do when you're flying in cloud below a very high Grid MORA and have a thunderstorm in front of you?".

I remembered back to my experience flying in the Papua highlands with Simon, when we had the same scenario. "If we can't climb above the Grid MORA, we need to stay on the company track and fly through the thunderstorm", I replied. The Chief Pilot smiled. That was the answer that he wanted to hear.

"When are we allowed to fly IFR on a commercial flight with passengers?"

I remembered back to my flight with Kyle when we were getting radar vectors in Balikpapan. "Legally speaking, we can't plan to fly IFR", I said. The Chief Pilot stared at me. "Go on", he asked. I told him, "However sometimes flying IFR is the safest course of action. Safety always supersedes legality". Again, the Chief Pilot smiled. He seemed happy with my answers so far.

The Chief Pilot then looked at me sternly. "Under what circumstances are you allowed to call Susi and Christian at 3 o'clock in the morning?"

My heart began to race. That news managed to travel pretty damn quickly! The Chief Pilot laughed. I nervously laughed back. Then he shook my hand. "Ok Dan, based on the results of your written exams, simulator and interview, I'm happy to put you down for the next Command Upgrade course", he said. I sighed with relief.

The next Command Upgrade course was in one month's time. I had just one final tour left as a First Officer.

CHAPTER 37

A NICER SIDE TO AHMED

I was to be based in Jakarta for my final tour as an FO. Jakarta had a couple of satellite bases which were used for ad hoc flying contracts. One such contract was in Ketapang, West Kalimantan. I was rostered for a 4 day tour there with none other than...Ahmed, the Deputy Base Manager for Jakarta. I must admit, at first, I had some serious concerns about flying with this guy again. But with only a couple of weeks remaining before I would start my Command Upgrade course, now seemed like a pretty bad time to be rocking the boat. I gritted my teeth and got on with it.

When I met Ahmed at Jakarta Sukarno-Hatta airport for our connecting flight to Kalimantan, he seemed pleasant enough. To be fair, he was usually a friendly, sociable person. However I knew full well that his mood could change very quickly when he was flying. Not only were we going to be flying together for 4 days straight, but we were also going to be living together in the same house, with no other people, in the middle of nowhere. I didn't want us to end up getting into a heated argument about something whilst we were out flying. That would have made things pretty damn awkward for the remainder of the tour.

However I remembered something which I had read in a psychology book a couple of years earlier. It was in regards to how to confront someone who you have a problem with, in a positive way. And this brings me to the final lesson of this book.

LESSON 22: ALWAYS FIND AT LEAST ONE THING WHICH YOU LIKE ABOUT SOMEONE

I had two choices here. I could shut up and pretend to agree with everything that Ahmed did, regardless of how dumb or reckless it was. Alternatively, I could confront him. Given that I was getting upgraded to Captain soon, it was quite tempting to choose the first option. However this would have undermined the very purpose of having two pilots. It would have also come across as being insincere, as Ahmed knew full well that I didn't like his style of flying. This passive-aggressive attitude would not be helpful in the long term, as ultimately we would both secretly resent each other, possibly leading to a larger conflict in the future.

However bluntly confronting him about aspects of his flying wouldn't have been ideal either. He definitely didn't take criticism well, and furthermore, he was my boss. Whilst sitting together as passengers on the flight to West Kalimantan, I told him this:

"Ahmed, you already know that I don't agree with some of the ways you fly the aircraft. I don't like the way that you make home-made GPS approaches when flying through cloud. I don't like the way that you rush me when I'm filling out the weight and balance either. However some of the many things which I do like about you, is that you are hard working and sociable".

Ahmed was taken aback by what I had just said. How was he going to react to his copilot telling him this? He paused, then he smiled. "Wait a moment, I didn't even think you liked me!", he said, "Thanks man I appreciated that!". Everything that I said to Ahmed was 100% true. It was genuine. And how did Ahmed respond with what I had told him? He took extra care to fly the aircraft legally and safely, without rushing me during the turnarounds. Don't get me wrong, he probably still went back to his old ways when he was flying with other FOs. However he made an effort to change his behaviour when he was flying with me. I really appreciated that.

In Ketapang we had one ferry flight without passengers. Ahmed let me sit in the left hand seat for this flight, so that I could practice the engine start. I must admit, he was actually a pretty good instructor. This was just what I needed before my Command Upgrade course. I may not have agreed with everything that Ahmed did, however at the time he still had more Caravan experience than I did. I could still learn a lot from him. We spent the rest of our tour together in Ketapang, on very good terms.

And it was just as well. Unbeknown to me at the time, I would spend a further 3 years flying for Susi Air, eventually becoming an instructor for the Caravan. During this time, I would be working with Ahmed a lot. He spent much of this time as my boss. Although there were times in the future that we would have differences of opinion on certain things, and sometimes quite heated, we would ultimately always work out our differences. This was also just as well from his point of view. In the future, I would one day be <u>his</u> examiner for his Pilot Proficiency Check!

I thought that this chapter about Ahmed would be the perfect way to end this book. However this book is just the first of three parts. I have so far, only scratched the surface of my experience flying at Susi Air. The best adventures were yet to come; medical diversions, near misses, unbelievable holidays, the "Worst Place to be a Pilot" film crew and a new, bat shit crazy Chief Pilot. (My colleagues at Susi Air will know exactly who I'm talking about).

Stay tuned for more.

Above: Swimming with sharks whilst on holiday in Karimunjawa, Java.

Printed in Great Britain
by Amazon